For over forty years *The Revels Plays* have offered the most authoritative editions of Elizabethan and Jacobean plays by authors other than Shakespeare. The *Companion Library* provides a fuller background to the main series by publishing important dramatic and non-dramatic material that will be essential for the serious student of the period.

Three seventeenth-century plays on women and performance
eds Chalmers, Sanders & Tomlinson
'Art made tongue-tied by authority' Clare
Drama of the English Republic, 1649–60 Clare
Three Jacobean witchcraft plays eds Corbin, Sedge
The Stukeley Plays ed. Edelman
Three Renaissance usury plays ed. Kermode
Beyond The Spanish Tragedy: A study of the works of Thomas Kyd Erne
John Ford's political theatre Hopkins
The works of Richard Edwards King
Marlowe and the popular tradition: Innovation in the English drama before 1595 Lunney
Banquets set forth: Banqueting in English Renaissance drama Meads
Thomas Heywood: Three marriage plays ed. Merchant
Three Renaissance travel plays ed. Parr
John Lyly Pincombe
A textual companion to Doctor Faustus Rasmussen
Documents of the Rose Playhouse Rutter
John Lyly: Euphues: The Anatomy of Wit and Euphues and His England ed. Scragg
Richard Brome: Place and politics on the Caroline stag Steggle

John Lyly and early modern authorship

Manchester University Press

THE REVELS PLAYS COMPANION LIBRARY

John Lyly and early modern authorship

ANDY KESSON

Manchester University Press

Published by Manchester University Press
Altrincham Street, Manchester M1 7JA, UK
www.manchesteruniversitypress.co.uk

British Library Cataloguing-in-Publication Data is available

Library of Congress Cataloging-in-Publication Data is available

ISBN 978 1 7849 9369 6 *paperback*

First published by Manchester University Press in hardback 2011

This edition first published 2016

Printed by Lightning Source

Rip up my life, discipher my name, fill thy answer as full of lies as of lines, swel like a toade, hisse like an adder, bite like a dog, & chatter like a monkey, my pen is prepared and my minde; and if yee chaunce to finde any worse words than you brought, let them be put in your dads dictionarie.

John Lyly, *Pap with an Hatchet*

in memory of my parents

CONTENTS

GENERAL EDITORS' PREFACE

Since the late 1950s the series known as The Revels Plays has provided for students of the English Renaissance drama carefully edited texts of the major Elizabethan and Jacobean plays. The series includes some of the best-known drama of the period and has continued to expand, both within its original field and, to a lesser extent, beyond it, to include some important plays from the earlier Tudor and from the Restoration periods. The Revels Plays Companion Library is intended to further this expansion and to allow for new developments.

The aim of the Companion Library is to provide students of the Elizabethan and Jacobean drama with a fuller sense of its background and context. The series includes volumes of a variety of kinds. Small collections of plays, by a single author or concerned with a single theme and edited in accordance with the principles of textual modernisation of The Revels Plays, offer a wider range of drama than the main series can include. Together with editions of masques, pageants and the non-dramatic work of Elizabethan and Jacobean playwrights, these volumes make it possible, within the overall Revels enterprise, to examine the achievements of the major dramatists from a broader perspective. Other volumes provide a fuller context for the plays of the period by offering new collections of documentary evidence on Elizabethan theatrical conditions and on the performance of plays during that period and later. A third aim of the series is to offer modern critical interpretation, in the form of collections of essays or of monographs, of the dramatic achievement of the English Renaissance.

So wide a range of material necessarily precludes the standard format and uniform general editorial control which is possible in the original series of Revels Plays. To a considerable extent, therefore, treatment and approach are determined by the needs and intentions of individual volume editors. Within this rather ampler area, however, we hope that the Companion Library maintains the standards of scholarship that have for so long characterised The Revels Plays, and that it offers a useful enlargement of the work of the series in preserving, illuminating and celebrating the drama of Elizabethan and Jacobean England.

J. R. MULRYNE

SUSAN BROCK

SUSAN CERASANO

ACKNOWLEDGEMENTS

I am grateful to the Arts and Humanities Research Council which sponsored the research for this book at the Shakespeare Institute, University of Birmingham, and then at the University of Kent.

At both the Shakespeare Institute and the University of Kent I benefited from generous support from staff and students. John Jowett, Martin Wiggins and Kate McLuskie all supervised my doctoral work at the Institute at some point, and Catherine Richardson did so following my move to Kent. She is now a colleague and her continued support has been particularly appreciated. I've benefited from particular help from many other academics at these institutions: Cath Alexander, Jaq Bessell and Kate Rumbold at the Shakespeare Institute, Tom Lockwood and Gillian Wright at Birmingham, and Emma Bainbridge, Jennie Batchelor, Stella Bolaki, Barbara Bombi, Alixe Bovey, Peter Brown, Paddy Bullard, Rosanna Cox, Vybarr Cregan-Reid, Helen Gittos, Ken Fincham, Sarah Horgan, Sarah James, Bernhard Klein, Donna Landry, Monica Mattfeld, Ariane Mildenberg, Jan Montefiore, Irene Musumeci, Will Norman, Ryan Perry and Sarah Wood at Kent. I'm grateful to Stanley Wells, Yves Peyré, Agnes Lafont, Janice Valls-Russell, Gillian Austen, Sarah Annes Brown, Laurie Maguire, Katherine Heavey and Neil Rhodes for offering me early opportunities to share my work. I'm grateful to Manchester University Press for their support in publishing this book, and to my anonymous first reader for a strident response to the work which saved me from some very embarrassing errors. Though I have not adopted all the changes proposed, I was grateful for the opportunity to rethink and rearticulate my ideas. My second reader revealed herself to be Emma Smith, whose encouragement of my work here and elsewhere has been invaluable.

Leah Scragg taught me Shakespeare at Manchester University, and then introduced me to a funny writer with a flowery name. This book is in many ways her fault and I am grateful to her and Don for many years of support and friendship. She has done more than anyone to keep Lylian criticism alive in recent years, and I hope she will not be too horrified by my own contribution to the field.

Thanks also to the many actors, directors and theatre companies who have been part of this project: David Bellwood and Release the Hounds; Claire Bridge, James Wallace and the Globe Read Not Dead team; Tom Littler and Primavera Production; Perry Mills and the King Edward Grammar School boys; Stephen Purcell and the

Pantaloons; Brett Santry of the American Shakespeare Center's Blackfriars Playhouse; and the Shakespeare Institute Players, and especially Kelley Costigan, Cait Fannin, Brian Willis and Barbara Santana. The actors Tom Frankland, Martin Hodgson, Frances Marshall, David Oakes and Rebecca Todd shared many ideas with me after performing Lyly, as did the musicians Mat Martin and Kirsty McGee.

Thanks to the slightly horrifying number of friends kind enough to read and comment on parts of this book (and apologies to anyone I've left out): Philip Bird, Christie Carson, Juan F. Cerdá, Elle Collins, Denise Creamer and Tom and Beth Gill, Florence Daniels, Farah Karim-Cooper, Felicity Dunworth, Jeannie Farr, Matthew Frost, Farah Karim-Cooper, Peter Kirwan, Cecilia Lindskog, Emily Linneman, Michelle Morton, Sylvia del Nevo, Emily Oliver, Pete Orford, Kerry-Sue Peplow, Eoin Price, Stephen Purcell, Derek Ryan, Kate de Rycker, Peter J. Smith, Clare Smout, Erin Sullivan, Mark Taylor, Wendy Trevor, Greg Walker and Ben Worthy. Terry Smith first convinced me how exciting early modern performance and scholarship could be: though I can't promise he'll recognise much of himself in this book, I doubt I'd have written it without him. Many of my students have helped me think through my work in the seminar room.

A number of scholars were willing to offer advice and information at times of need: thanks to Guyda Armstrong, Petr Barta, Juliet Fleming, Eugene Giddens, Andrew Hadfield, Zachary Lesser, Robert Maslen, Ken Pickering, Chloe Porter, Barbara Ravelhofer, Will Sharpe, Patrick Spottiswoode, Gary Taylor and Katharine Wilson. Lucy Munro and Marion O' Connor helped me turn my research into a book, and Sarah Dustagheer read the whole thing at an early stage and has been an important part of this project.

My family have been incredibly supportive whilst I worked on this project. Indeed the day before I sent the final typescript for this book to the publisher, my grandfather Peter Thompson handed me a copy of Frederick Wood's *Current English Usage* (I imagine I'm not the only English lecturer who gets such gifts from relatives). It fell open on a page that provides additional evidence for an argument made in Chapter 5 of this book: a wonderful coincidence! Thanks and love to my sister, Denise Riggs, to Peter and Kate Thompson, Rosemary Graham, to Adrian, Phoebe and Harris Riggs, and to my new family the Tuckers, Ali, Lennie, Val and Vinnie. Jimmy Tucker has shared the intellectual and emotional weight of this project, and I'm thrilled he's waited around for me to finish it.

When I submitted the draft typescript to the publisher, I dedicated the book to the memory of my father, Rod Kesson. However, my mother Monica passed away as this book was in its final stages, and so I now dedicate it to the memory of two remarkable people. The dedication at the front of the book may make a little less sense now, but it represents even more love. My parents would have been pleased to have an excuse not to read the book, but they would be equally pleased that I have finally finished it. But I would like also to mention a remarkable friend, Lizz Ketterer. Lizz did read the whole thing and was my most helpful and hilarious reader. All of their support, humour and kindness are much missed.

INTRODUCTION: OUR LYLY?

At the start of Lyly's second work, *Euphues and His England*, the titular character Euphues tries to tell his friend a story as they sail to England. Unfortunately the friend cannot hear him, because he has spent the journey being sick over the side of the boat, and is now 'more ready to tell what wood the ship was made of than to answer to Euphues' discourse'.[1] Eventually he does manage to make a reply, with words likely to worry anybody who has ever tried to tell a story:

> In faith, Euphues, thou hast told a long tale. The beginning I have forgotten, the middle I understand not, and the end hangeth not together. (182)

Lyly's readers must have been inclined to agree. By this point in the first edition Euphues has indeed told a long tale, speaking for 25 of the book's first 27 pages, beginning with one story, moving into another at its middle and ending with a Rough Guide to Elizabethan England. Euphues bases this guide on Caesar's account of his invasion of Britain, describing contemporary English people (of the sort likely to be reading Lyly's book) as savages covered in woad, 'terrible to behold', who, Euphues adds, 'shave all parts of their body' (182). Presumably only the most retro, gothic and depilatory amongst Lyly's readers would have read this description without amusement mixed with distrust for Euphues as a storytelling authority figure.

Lyly's second book therefore begins with someone failing, at great length, to tell a story, and Euphues' friend confirms for us that this is the author's intent. It begins with a description of England which is sixteen hundred years out of date, and a lecture delivered to a listener, or a supposed listener, who is being sick over the side of the boat. Lyly's text trained early readers to recognise his work as playful, challenging and fun, and indeed we shall see contemporaries repeatedly praise him for his wittiness or, in one case, criticise him for his trickiness. Such terms appear to describe the same rhetorical effects from differing points of view and are therefore useful signposts for understanding his work. This is important to stress from the outset because Lyly, if he is read at all now, tends to be read as a self-important, serious and straightforward writer, but the start of this second work undermines all those assumptions. The apparent self-consciousness of Lyly's opening to *Euphues and His England* is confirmed from within the text by the complaint that Euphues' story was forgettable, incomprehensible and inconclusive: Lyly opens his story by warning his readers to suspect and interrogate stories. It is, after all, a good principle in oratory, and incumbent on any orator in the sixteenth century or in ours to make sure that the listener can hear you, that they can understand you and that they are not vomiting into the sea.

Early modern Lyly

Lyly's contemporaries were in no doubt as to his accomplishments as an orator. It was in precisely those terms that he was praised in the middle of his writing career as the foremost early modern author. William Webbe admitted that by 1586 the English had failed to create poetry to compete with Homer or Virgil, but, he claimed, they had equalled classical models in their prose. He therefore praised 'the great good grace and sweete vayne, which Eloquence hath attained in our speeche, because it hath had the helpe of such rare and singuler wits'. Amongst these wits 'there is none that will gainsay, but Master *John Lilly* hath deserved moste high commendations'. By 1586, only two prose fictions and two plays by Lyly were available to the book-reading public, but Webbe already felt able to put him forward as the rhetorical exemplar not only of his generation but in the history of the English language. He assumed his readers would be absorbed in, and not just familiar with, Lyly's 'workes':

> surely in respecte of his singuler eloquence and brave composition of apt words and sentences, let the learned examine and make tryall thereof thorough all the partes of Rethoricke, in fitte phrases, in pithy sentences, in gallant tropes, in flowing speeche, in plaine sence, and surely in my judgment, I thinke he wyll yeelde him that verdict, which *Quintilian* giveth of bothe the best Orators *Demosthenes* and *Tully*, that from the one, nothing may be taken away, to the other, nothing may be added.[2]

Ten years later, in 1596, Thomas Lodge drew up a list of contemporary 'Divine wits, for many things as sufficient as all antiquity', and headed it with Lyly: '*Lilly*, the famous for facility in discourse: *Spencer*, best read in ancient Poetry: *Daniel*, choise in word, and invention: *Draiton*, diligent and formall: *Th*[omas] *Nash, true English Aretine*.'[3] Francis Meres included Lyly in a similar list in 1598, where he appears in front of Lodge, Gascoigne, Greene and Shakespeare. Lyly is one of only two writers given further description, 'eloquent and witty', stressing his oratory and his ability to surprise.[4] A generation later, when Shakespeare's plays were published in 1623, Ben Jonson sought to praise Shakespeare by comparing him to the two great English comic writers, Chaucer and

Lyly. Jonson's reference to 'our *Lily*', Leah Scragg points out, indicates either 'a particular affection for the work of the older dramatist' amongst Jonson and Shakespeare, 'or a nationalistic pride in his achievement'.[5] Almost certainly, Jonson's pronoun incorporates both possibilities and, when he praises Shakespeare for outshining Lyly, he posits the earlier writer as the benchmark of literary greatness. Finally, in 1632, Edward Blount published six of Lyly's plays, naming the writer, on the title page, 'the onely Rare Poet of that Time, The Witie, Comicall, Facetiously-Quicke and unparalelld'.[6]

Throughout these contemporary references to Lyly is a sense of someone innovative, incomparable and outstanding. This is evident in Webbe's language of the 'most high' and 'best', but it is present too in less immediately obvious language, such as Lodge's and Blount's use of the word 'the'. Here the definite article is being used in the same way as it is in the phrase 'Alexander the Great', to denote superlative excellence.[7] Thus '*Lilly*, the famous for facility in discourse' means that Lyly is the most famous in his generation or nation, just as 'the onely Rare Poet of that Time' marks the writer out as not only the outstanding but also the definitive early modern writer. Lyly is, for Webbe, a perfect writer, whilst for Jonson (and for Jonson's Shakespeare) he represents a literary litmus test, the contemporary to outshine. Many of these writers emphasise Lyly's eloquence and wit, and Blount puts these qualities forward as 'unparalelld' by other figures of the time. Lyly's presence in literary lists, and especially at the head of such lists, is significant too. Emma Smith has recently shown the way early modern writers list their contemporaries in groups in which 'Shakespeare is prominent but still not pre-eminent'. Such lists 'reinstate Shakespeare among other playwrights without difficulty', and Smith suggests that 'we might usefully import some of that indifference to our own critical methodologies'.[8] But in Lyly's case, early modern witnesses are not indifferent and Lyly is, very often, prominent and pre-eminent. There is a sense here that Lyly happened to early modern culture, and early modern writers were still trying to understand what this happening might mean.

It is difficult to overstate Lyly's impact on early modern culture, but this book will do its very best. As the quotations above suggest, Lyly became the most famous Elizabethan writer in his own time, famous for his rearticulation of the structure of the English prose sentence, for his ability to delight in storytelling in order to astonish readers and audiences and for his ability to question and defamiliarise the process of telling a story. Lyly's characters became famous too, particularly his character Euphues, who was far more famous than Hamlet, Tamburlaine or the Faerie Queene in the early modern period and gave the English language a new word, euphuism. Lyly's prose fiction was the best-selling and most widely read literary work of the period. Ian Green suggests that we use a quantitative methodology to assess whether or not a text is a best-seller, based on whether it is printed at least five times in thirty years, a figure 'low enough to include steady sellers as well as best-sellers, but high enough to eliminate those works which do not appear to have caught the public imagination sufficiently to warrant much more than a couple of editions'.[9] Lyly's work meets this criterion several times over, outselling any contemporary literary work, despite the slippery and anachronistic nature of the term 'literary' itself.[10]

His plays seem to have been the most famous theatrical events of the 1580s, just as Nashe, Kyd, Marlowe and Shakespeare began their writing careers, and they now represent the only body of plays written by a single author surviving from the 1580s, that crucial decade for early commercial drama in permanent playhouses. This is no accident, but is due to the fact that Lyly was the first Elizabethan to see a series of his plays go into print, and the first writer to see his plays reprinted. His first play, *Campaspe*, went into three editions in its first year, 1584, and in the same year *Sapho and Phao*, his second play, went into two editions; it would be another thirteen years before another play, and another playwright, came close to equalling this achievement, with Ben Jonson's *Every Man Out of His Humour*. Helen Ostovich describes the three editions of Jonson's play in 1597 as 'a wild success by play-publication standards', but it was a success that Lyly had already achieved in a less established market.[11] Lyly's first two plays were printed in five total editions in 1584, a record which no other early modern writer appears to have equalled with their first dramatic publications. Lyly reorganised the prose sentence, found a new voice for subversive irony and showed his contemporaries how to rewrite the rules for dramatic composition. He was, above all, a brilliant writer, and, though his brilliance has been undervalued in the last four hundred years, recent performances at the Globe and elsewhere have rediscovered an extraordinary and unparalleled playwright. Thus it is that Blount could promise his readership that '*when Old* John Lilly, *is merry with thee in thy Chamber, Thou shalt say, Few (or None) of our Poets now are such witty Companions*' (*Six Court Comedies*, B2).

Later Lyly

But following Blount, future generations had few chances to be merry with Lyly, in or out of their chambers. Lyly had at least one contemporary detractor, Gabriel Harvey, who claimed to be speaking for many more when he warned in 1589 that 'The finest wittes preferre the loosest period in M. [Roger] Ascham, or Sir Philip Sidney, before the tricksiest page in Euphues'.[12] Harvey's complaint shows that Lyly's famous wittiness was not universally celebrated. Lyly's work remained in print until the late 1630s, three decades after his death, but after the wars of the 1640s an entire century passed in which his work was unavailable in English. Except for a few references amongst antiquarians, he seems to have been forgotten. Unfortunately for Lyly, his work was then rediscovered in the 1740s at the very time that Shakespeare was being claimed, on stage, in books and in festivals, as a national champion. Michael Dobson shows that this had the effect of giving Shakespeare's plays 'the status of canonical texts, and, concurrently, of canonizing Shakespeare himself as the paradigmatic figure of literary authority (making him into "the bard", a "hero")'. As part of the effort to make Shakespeare seem both singular and exemplary, his achievement had to be distinguished from his contemporaries' and they had to be denigrated, and in the eighteenth century Lyly is repeatedly described as an infection or disease for which Shakespeare was the cure. As the final chapter of this book shows, this process had disastrous consequences for the way Lyly came to be understood, and as a result he has since been either ignored or vilified by a majority of readers. Dobson has demonstrated the 'specifically Enlightenment origins and interests' lying behind Shakespeare's current ubiquity, and we should be equally suspicious of the Enlightenment origins of Lyly's current cultural invisibility. James Shapiro warns us that eighteenth-century 'anachronisms underscore how irrevocably the nature of authorship had changed since Elizabethan times (though they have changed comparatively little since then, so that we stand much closer to [eighteenth-century] contemporaries than they do to Shakespeare's'.[13]

Despite his centrality to early modern literary culture, then, Lyly is now a largely forgotten figure, confined to the periphery of the canon. Even Stanley Wells, a major advocate for Shakespeare's contemporaries, describes early modern drama as 'poetic and rhetorical because this was the current theatrical mode, emerging from a period when all drama had been written in verse', defining this period as 'lasting for a comparatively short time, from the late 1580s to, I suppose, the 1620s'.[14] This summary of the period excludes Lyly on two counts, firstly because the majority of Lyly's plays (seven out of eight) are written in prose, not verse, and secondly because his plays were written in the early and late 1580s, awkwardly scattered either side of Wells's first terminal point.

The same problem occurs in the dates given in the 1997 Oxford History of English Literature's *English Drama 1586–1642: The Age of Shakespeare*. This is perhaps surprising, since the book was written by G. K. Hunter, the foremost Lyly scholar of the last century, and yet its title reminds us of the way Shakespeare has dominated this period whilst it actively excludes half of Lyly's writing career from that period, demonstrating once again Lyly's problematic relationship with the way we remember early modernity. Lyly obeys neither Hunter's historical division nor Wells's aesthetic definition, and by escaping or eluding these definitions of the period he is also eclipsed or obscured by them. It is easy, of course, for a specialist study to criticise writing projects with a wider remit, and, if we continue to regard Lyly as a minor figure, then these problems might seem pedantic and unhelpful. But if the period is seen from Blount's point of view, with Lyly as its major figure, his problematic position within summaries of the period begins to make these summaries themselves problematic. In other words, these summaries do not reflect oversight on the part of individual editors and authors. As important contributions to the field, they demonstrate, in their cumulative effect, a wider Lyly lacuna within critical discourse. The way we have come to remember and represent the early modern period excludes a writer who felt central and revolutionary to contemporaries.

If scholars have not been encouraged to consider Lyly's importance to early modern literary culture, even being trained to edit Lyly out of the period, then it is no surprise that the experience of studying his work at university has not always been a happy one. Wells has joked that Lyly's prose fiction might be set as a punishment to misbehaving undergraduates, and two references to Lyly's standing on university courses suggest that such a punishment might be highly effective.[15] In a programme note to his school production of Lyly's *Endymion* in 2009, the teacher and director Perry Mills described his experience at university of 'wrestling with a little of [Lyly's non-dramatic] prose (before skipping onto T. W. Craik's *Minor Elizabethan Tragedies* and the *Henry VI* plays [...])'.[16] This is a particularly important example of the way that the academic conception of Lyly's work can actively inhibit and discourage engagement with it, because Mills found that directing *Endymion* for the theatre transformed his understanding of the writer. This is a discovery that has recently been shared by a number of actors, directors and audiences following an unprecedented run of university productions and theatre-based staged readings of Lyly's work in the UK, Australia and the US. But Mills's memory of undergraduate study suggests that modern encounters with Lyly tend towards pedagogical rites-of-passage, part of the teleological build-up to Shakespeare. Mills also suggests that his required reading was Lyly's first work, surely the least attractive for Lyly's modern readers. *Euphues: The Anatomy of Wit* was successful in its own time precisely because it challenged early modern readers: asking a student to read it as an introduction to Lyly or to Shakespeare is the equivalent of recommending James Joyce's *Ulysses* as an introduction to the European novel.

The other evidence for Lyly's role at current universities also demonstrates Shakespeare's authoritative influence over undergraduates, with rather more explosive results. In 2005 a disgruntled New York undergraduate wrote a response to her weekly reading on her blog, 'the twee life of me', and told her internet readership,

> if someone suggests you read Lyly's proto-novel *Euphues*, run like the motherfucking wind. If someone compares *Euphues* to Shakespeare, slap that bitch. And if you do have to read *Euphues*, try like hell to purge it from your memory.[17]

Here again Lyly's first work fails to recommend itself to a student, and once again there is evidence that Lyly has been taught, as with Mills, as a prelude to Shakespeare. In this case he is also a prelude to the novel, as though he is being used to mark out the periphery of two defining parts of the literary canon. As a consequence, this student's reading experience is in direct contrast to the one Blount promised to his readers, who were assured they would want to 'thanke mee, that brings him to thy Acquaintance' (A5v–A6). Where Blount wrote of Lyly's merriness, this student advocates violence to anyone who compares Lyly to Shakespeare. The fact that both Blount and blogger are writing light-heartedly does not affect the evidence they provide of a profound discursive shift in Lyly's position within the canon, a shift in the way readers relate to what they read. Both Jonson and the blogger use Lyly to praise Shakespeare, but where the early modern comparison of the two writers could be mutually celebratory, for a modern reader the comparison was to Lyly's detriment.

One more piece of evidence points to the way that Lyly has come to be read. In the Shakespeare Institute Library copy of F. W.

Fairholt's edition of *The Dramatic Works of John Lilly* (1858), a reader has written on the first page of *Endymion* a note entitled 'For Shakespeare'.[18] Before beginning to read Lyly, then, the reader was already thinking about Shakespeare: Lyly was simply a kind of contextualisation, and was being read through a Shakespearean prism. As the reader went through the play, he or she recorded under this heading items of Shakespearean interest: Lyly's *miles gloriosus* Sir Tophas, for example, is 'a faint adumbration of Falstaff & Holofernes'. Lyly's *Endymion*, a play that transformed Mills's impression of Lylian authorship, was here being read 'For Shakespeare'.

This method of reading the play did not endear the author to the reader, and on the final page of *Endymion* is written the firm and exasperated rejection, 'Is it possible to conceive anything more leaden & somniferous than this wretched drama?' This reading of the play, beginning with Shakespeare and ending with disgust, offers further evidence for the detrimental effect of the Shakespearean prism upon ways of reading Lyly. Mills suggests that the way round this interpretative impasse lies in the rehearsal room and on stage, but Lyly has had relatively few encounters with theatre practitioners since the 1580s. The Royal National Theatre's executive director Genista McIntosh has explained that Shakespeare's cultural prestige actively militates against the successful marketing of his contemporaries' work to modern theatregoers.[19] Lyly's reception, like many of his contemporaries', has become displaced by and dependent upon Shakespeare's.

And yet Jonson and Blount suggest that we think differently about Lyly and early modern authorship. In addition to his Lyly volume, Blount was the major financier of the Shakespeare folio, in which Jonson made his tribute to Shakespeare using Lyly. Over a long career, Blount had been involved in the publication of all the major works of Edmund Spenser and Philip Sidney, and had published works by Christopher Marlowe, Thomas Hobbes, George Chapman, Jonson and Samuel Daniel and the first English translations of Montaigne and Cervantes. Gary Taylor has emphasised his 'profound impact on English cultural life': 'He had an unparalleled gift for recognizing new works that would eventually become classics: he was more consistently successful in anticipating the cultural consensus of the future than [...] any other early modern critic'.[20] Blount was the lead publisher behind the Shakespeare First Folio, providing the major funds for the project that preserved in print what would go on to become the central texts of English literature. Blount is responsible for gathering Shakespeare's work together, and his compilation of Shakespeare plays includes the only print witnesses to half of Shakespeare's work. This book argues that Lyly helped to create the market for printed plays. Since almost nothing of Shakespeare's works survive in manuscript, it is no exaggeration to say that if his work had not been printed then Shakespeare would now be a marginal, if not completely forgotten literary figure: an unfamiliar version of the *Henry IV* plays, a single speech from *Titus Andronicus* and a series of revisions for a play called *Sir Thomas More* survive to record Shakespeare's work in manuscript.[21] Without printed versions of his plays, Shakespeare would be remembered now as an actor who had a minor part in one of Ben Jonson's comedies.

But it may come as a surprise to modern readers that, despite his detailed knowledge and love for what are now the most popular early modern works, Blount considered a very different writer to represent the foremost contemporary who ought to become a classic. In 1632, nine years after its first publication, the Shakespeare play collection was republished, but Blount did not involve himself in this venture. Instead, and as his final professional project, Blount committed himself to collecting together and publishing six Lyly plays. In the Shakespeare folio, Jonson had claimed that Shakespeare had improved on Lyly's standard, providing evidence that Lyly represented a model of excellence some time after his death, but for Blount, the publisher of Marlowe, Jonson and Shakespeare, the unparalleled writer of the age was Lyly himself.

The front matter of Blount's publication presents his book as an intervention in Lyly's dwindling fame. The only rare poet of the Elizabethan period had apparently become a forgotten figure in the reign of Charles I. This is a familiar fate for writers of the period; despite its later fame even the Shakespeare First Folio appears to have been a financial disaster for its publishers, and this fate accords with other evidence that Shakespeare's cultural visibility diminished soon after his death.[22] The same process affected Lyly's fame in the Caroline period. 'Light Ayres are now in fashion', Blount tells his readers, and Lyly's works lie 'like dead Lawrels in a Churchyard': 'A sinne it were to suffer these Rare Monuments of wit, to lye covered in Dust, and a shame, such conceipted Comedies, should be Acted by none but wormes' (A3v–A5v). As his final publication, Blount put forward a writer who was the exceptional and incomparable author of his time, the creator of literature that was both hilarious and unpredictable, whose neglect in the Caroline period was a cultural sin and a literary shame. '*Oblivion*', Blount promised, 'shall not so trample on a sonne of the *Muses*; And such a sonne, as they called their Darling' (A5v). But, as we have seen, Oblivion has been trampling ever since.

The current book proposes to consider Lyly from Blount's point of view, using evidence for his unparalleled success and influence to rethink his role as the major literary figure of his age. In doing so it opposes itself to a conventional critical view of Lyly that sees him as hopelessly irrelevant, pretentious and effete. In this respect, Lyly's most influential critic has been his critic in both senses of the word. G. K. Hunter's *John Lyly: The Humanist as Courtier* was published in 1962, and no other book printed in that decade exerts such an influence over contemporary debate of the early modern period. Jennifer Richards noted its continued influence as recently as 2003 and Christopher Warley suggested in 2005 that, 'if one were to look [. . .] for a date marking the beginning of New Historicism's account of Renaissance England, one could do worse than 1961 [*sic*] – the date G. K. Hunter's *John Lyly* was published'. Warley then finds that 'Hunter's voice is audible' in much future work on court literature.[23]

Hunter's book was indeed tremendously liberating in its take on the Renaissance, which Hunter saw as a politicised and contested cultural event. With its decisive and influential attack on Whiggish concepts of historical progress and its insistence on the social construction of literary conventions, Hunter's book introduced methodologies and ideological standpoints that inspired new historicism some twenty years before that term was coined. The book's central construction of Lyly as a humanist who was also a courtier was deeply problematic, but, because most of its readers were more interested in his depiction of the period than in his avowed central subject, Hunter's vision of Lyly has never been effectively challenged.

Hunter's influence over subsequent Lylian scholarship is easy to prove. His resonant subtitle reverberates through criticism of the period, whether it specifically concerns Lyly or mentions his work with reference to another topic. Only Greenblatt's *Renaissance Self-Fashioning* has entered critical discourse in a comparable manner, but whereas Greenblatt's phrase is used with self-conscious ideological intent, Hunter's phrase seems to subconsciously haunt discussions of Lyly's work, restricting their critical scope. Carter Daniel makes his debt to Hunter explicit in his modern-spelling collection of Lyly's plays, the only such collection of his work, which opens with the claim that '[t]o the end he was, in G. K. Hunter's phrase, a humanist turned courtier [. . .] striving to put his learning to use in the service of the queen'.[24] Made at the height of new historicist and cultural materialist readings of the period, such a claim demolishes Lyly's claim to the attention of any reader interested in the political significance of literature, inscribing Lyly's work and Daniel's edition within the sycophantic relationship of a writer in service to his monarch. The Revels Plays series has made Lyly's work newly available to readers in accessible, clear editions, but the earlier editions, by David Bevington and Hunter himself, are strongly influenced by Hunter's paradigm. Thus Bevington cites his fellow editor Hunter to claim Lyly's work 'as a compliment to Queen Elizabeth', once again enclosing Lyly's often dissident and disruptive work within the reassuringly all-encompassing context of monarchical authority.[25] Hunter and Bevington's editions include those of Lyly's most famous plays, *Endymion* and *Gallathea*, and readers are being persuaded in these recent editions that Lyly's quintessential conservatism is self-evident, that any subversion is already contained by its courtly context and that he is a writer who writes only to flatter and pay tribute.

The brilliance of Hunter's book on the subject of the Renaissance means that this view of Lyly extends well beyond the rather diminutive field of Lylian criticism, so that in her study of Elizabethan literature and the Virgin Queen Philippa Berry reminds scholars that 'G. K. Hunter suggested that Lyly was a humanist turned courtier, forced to subordinate his humanist ideals of moral instruction to a courtly aesthetic'.[26] An even wider readership is introduced to Hunter's Lyly in the recent RSC edition of Shakespeare's *Works*, where we encounter a Lyly who

> flattered the queen while at the same time appealing to the classical learning of the social elite and exploiting the aura of flirtation and femininity that was inevitable in a court where ambitious males vied for Her Majesty's attention. In Lyly's hands, courtship was inseparable from courtiership[.][27]

In the most recent scholarly publications, the modern reader is encouraged to encounter Hunter's 1960s Lyly via that particularly and peculiarly authoritative slogan, *The Humanist as Courtier*, a man whose work was intended for and limited by the figure of the queen.

Now that it is fifty years old, however, it is time to consider whether this formula adequately describes Lyly's work or defines his biography in the way scholars assume. In an age in which learned references and aristocratic patronage were the preconditions of literary publication, it is difficult to see how any writer could escape humanist influence and courtly ambition. The phrase 'Humanist as courtier', in other words, does not capture anything unique about Lyly, and it has severely constricted our understanding of his work. It also seems to radically undervalue Lyly's role as a popular writer with an unparalleled reach beyond the court, and to overestimate the obedience and submission of a man who spent much of his career responding to the offence or misunderstandings that his work provoked.

As this brief survey of current scholarship testifies, one effect of Hunter's book was to insist on Lyly's work as politically as well as aesthetically impotent. His work is seen to be circumscribed by its courtly provenance, and this reputation as a court writer has been considerably overstated, rooted as it is in the title of Blount's 1632 *Six Court Comedies* rather than the wide and popular readership projected in Lyly's paratextual material. This view of Lyly as a quiescent, gentle sort of writer is in direct tension with the fact that Lyly repeatedly calls attention to the failings of authority figures in his work, repeatedly confronts censorship and the abuse of power and spent much of his career in apparent disfavour at court. He is a writer fascinated by monsters, necromancy and transgression, but appears in Park Honan's biography of Shakespeare as a 'dainty', 'delicate' and 'short-statured man', the latter detail perhaps suggesting the need to bring him down to size.[28]

Indeed, Lyly's association with Elizabeth has often led his work to be tainted with a curious kind of displaced sexism. For Berry, Lyly was 'more passive and contemplative' and concerned with 'elegance', 'beauty' and 'surface beauty', unlike an earlier generation of writers who are praised for being 'active and assertive' in their 'definitions of masculine courtiership and courtliness'.[29] For a startlingly wide variety of critics, many of whom themselves engage with a sophisticated analysis of phallocentrism, Lyly appears to be denigrated because of his association with a powerful woman, radically compromised by his demeaning role writing for a female monarch: a dainty, short man, fashionable and flirtatious, a sycophantic servant to the queen, passive, elegant and beautiful. Jennifer Richards argues that early modern critics tend to construct courtesy discourse in general as a form of communication that 'disseminate[s] an effete, dissembling courtly rhetoric that performs the subordination of the male aristocrat to a despotic monarch', and this fate has clearly attached to Lyly.[30] As the final chapter of this book makes clear, representations of Lyly's writing and authorship as inappropriately feminine are deeply rooted in late nineteenth-century concerns over manly style and were given an electric vitality by the aftermath of Oscar Wilde's trials and death. If reception history involves the application and interpretation of past literature within the present, the names of the principal figures may well be contributing here to an almost allegorical significance, in which the flowery and girly Lyly is outsized and outclassed by the man who shakes his spear.

If Elizabeth overshadows Lyly for historicist scholars, then it is Shakespeare who occludes his work for many other readers. Hunter's book once again offers the most influential paradigm for thinking about Lyly and Shakespeare, and his book can be read as an attempt to reduce, or at least contain, Lyly's brilliance and influence in order to make way for the coming Master. Lyly's displacement by Shakespeare is written into the structure of Hunter's book, which concludes with two chapters called 'The victim of fashion' and 'Lyly and Shakespeare'. Martin Wiggins worries at the start of his book, *Shakespeare and the Drama of His Time*, that the word 'and' opposes 'two bodies of material, the "Shakespearian" and the "non-Shakespearian", which were not distinct until later cultural history made them so'.[31] This effect certainly attaches to Hunter's chapter, in which the apparent neutrality of the title 'Lyly and Shakespeare' operates within a critical discourse that valorises one writer by denigrating another, so that Lyly, 'victimised by fashion', is forced to make way for his superior successor. Hunter's penultimate chapter traces '[t]he brief afterlife that remained to Lyly' after the mid-1580s, which was to endure an 'accumulation of sneers' and to 'accompany the gradual descent of the Elizabethan ideal of elegance'.[32] The current book shows these claims have no empirical foundation, but the evidence against Hunter was available to him as he wrote, and thus exacerbates his project to confine Lyly's importance to the early 1580s. The success of the Hunter paradigm suggests how useful it has been in protecting the idea of Shakespeare's unique, solitary genius.

In the last chapter, Lyly is 'given new life' by Shakespeare, who, in turn, 'grows out of Lyly'.[33] The idiom and cultural assumptions of Hunter's metaphors, which make both writers sound like literary zombies, have patently dated, but their content has not been challenged and continues to be cited: our Lyly is still Hunter's Lyly, helplessly and uniquely victim to fashion and elided from literary history by his greater reincarnation or outgrowth. Hunter is right to note that responses to Lyly's work changed over time, that Lyly's work dated and that Lyly apparently stopped writing new works for the print market. But these processes were not unique to Lyly, and Hunter's reification of individual responses into a single paradigmatic failure, an 'accumulation of sneers', distorted the evidence in a manner that has proved highly attractive to literary critics, theatre historians and early modern scholars ever since.[34] Hunter had access to evidence that Lyly's work continued to be influential until the first English civil war, but instead insisted that this influence was over by the mid-1580s in time to make way for Shakespeare. As the present study shows, Lyly became more popular after Shakespeare's career began, despite Hunter's claims to the contrary, and we now need to rethink the importance of this overlooked and extraordinary writer. In 1623, as we have seen, Jonson praised Shakespeare with reference to Lyly. Blount published Jonson's phrase, 'our *Lily*' and it prefigures his own later claim that 'Our Nation are in his debt for a new English which hee taught them'. It is therefore a mark of profound paradox that a figure so central to Shakespeare and Jonson's authorship in particular and to English culture in general should have become displaced and occluded by the very men who celebrated him as the great writer of their time. This book suggests new ways to think about our Lyly, to recover this great Elizabethan and the impact he made on early modern authorship.

Euphuism

A major stumbling-block for Lyly scholars or prospective Lyly readers has been the idea of his writing style, often described by the unwieldy word 'euphuism'. In the preface to the *Anatomy*, Lyly warned his readers to beware of stylistic ambition: 'It is a world to see how Englishmen desire to hear finer speech than the language will allow, to eat finer bread than is made of wheat, to wear finer cloth than is wrought of wool' (29).

Despite this explicit scepticism about rhetorical power, writers tend to identify Lyly with particular rhetorical tropes, techniques and styles, perhaps above all a particular rhetorical intent or psychological need. Jonas Barish, in the course of showing how Lyly's work identified and questioned opposition and antithesis, located this technical detail within Lyly's personal psychology, making euphuism pathological. Thus antithesis was 'habitual and even obsessive [. . .] in Lyly's thought', and 'parison, far from being merely a superficial device of sound-design, is, one might almost say, an instrument of thought whereby Lyly apprehends the world, and from which he cannot escape'. Michael Pincombe similarly writes of 'Lyly's euphuistic instincts', and Richard Lanham of Lyly's 'Compulsively patterned prose'.[35] A general tendency to confine Lyly's writing to euphuism ignores a number of highly productive problems. Firstly, Lyly's use of the various techniques scholars have herded together as 'euphuism' varies across his writing. The two prefaces to *Euphues: The Anatomy of Wit*, for example, are very different in their stylistic texture, the first making use of classical references which the second avoids. Lyly's authorial choices, therefore, are more interesting and flexible than the term euphuism implies, at least when used to suggest machinated writing, a prose automaton.

Secondly, and for this reason, Lyly's prose escapes attempts to reduce it to a series of formulae. Prose is difficult to define in any case, particularly when being used by somebody considered by his peers to be its most able and dexterous user. Elizabeth Fowler and Roland Greene warn that prose is 'one of the last undefined, untheorized bodies of writing in the early modern European languages', hovering between 'the categories of medium and genre'.[36] Lyly's writing, like his dramaturgy, has been treated as something static and formulaic, but on the contrary it is live as well as lithe, capable of transforming in front of the reader or listener. Indeed, Lyly's contemporary John Hoskyns praised him in *Directions for Speech and Style* precisely for his 'varieties' of ornament, adding that Lyly had demonstrated his even greater authorial variety by becoming less reliant upon these rhetorical patterns: 'But Lyly himself hath outlived this style and breaks well from it'.[37] Towards the start of the *Anatomy*, the narrator writes: 'neither is there anything but that hath his contraries' (43). Lyly's writing enacts this statement, encoding multiple and contradictory meanings into apparently simple statements.

This is not an attempt to deny that Lyly regularly uses the techniques associated with euphuism. Scholars are right to show that Lyly's writing, like much of early modern writing which has been labelled euphuistic, combines a series of rhetorical tropes, composing and organising prose by repeating sounds, syntax and allusions. Sounds are repeated in the form of word repetition, alliteration and rhyme (sometimes called homoeoteleuton, homoeoptoton or similiter cadens when used in prose).[38] In the above quotation, for example, Lyly repeats the word 'finer' across his three sentences, allowing its different meanings to point up the various comparisons being made between rhetoric, food and clothing. Syntax is repeated so that successive clauses echo one another's length (isocolon) or grammatical structure (parison). In 1593, writing in Lyly's wake, Henry Peacham described this technique as 'a figure or forme of speech which maketh the members of an oration to be almost of a just number of sillables'.[39] This technique is also in evidence in the quotation above, where the main verb 'desire' introduces three clauses which are isocolic (each clause contains the same number of words) and parisonal (each clause combines infinitive, comparative and noun). Total repetition is avoided by the first of the three phrases, whose wording, 'than the language will allow' is a variation on the formula of the next two phrases. Finally, writing labelled euphuistic incorporates external sources within its own continuous prose, a form of unacknowledged quotation from one of three sources: (1) mythology or classical history, (2) classical and medieval encyclopaedias of the natural world and (3) popular proverbs. In the quotation above, the opening phrase 'It is a world to see' is an appeal to proverbial knowledge. We can find examples of the other two kinds of source elsewhere in this epistle, which opens with reference to Parrhasius and Helen and moves on to a spotty leopard. These repetitions of sound, syntax and citation characterise much of Lyly's writing and other forms of writing which scholars call euphuism.

It is important to stress that none of these techniques is distinct to Lyly or other so-called 'euphuists'. Walter Ong reminds us that the repetition of sound was a fundamental early modern writing technique: 'Well after printing was developed, auditory processing continued for some time to dominate the visible, printed text.' Likewise, the quotation and paraphrase of learned sources were an endemic part of early modern culture; the pedagogical habit of commonplacing promoted what Ann Moss calls 'variations round a commonplace theme and [...] a fund of quotations, intertextual allusions, or gnomic improvisations'.[40] But Lyly's writing is distinguished by a willingness to use these techniques as an organising principle, and in doing so he taught early modern writers new ways to write prose quickly. Such techniques are strikingly similar to forms of verse composition, and provide content and rhythm to the medium of prose which it otherwise, almost by definition, seems to lack, not in practice but in principle. By developing these rhetorical techniques, Lyly helped to redefine and renegotiate the parameters of the English sentence. For the reasons given above and in Chapter 5, references to 'euphuism' in this book should be taken with very big quotation marks.

Repertory and single-author studies

Though the three parts of this book are broadly chronological, moving from Lyly's early work, his prose fiction, to his later work in the theatre and then on to his reception, the present study is not a biography. Recent scholarship has rightly insisted on the problems associated with studying the early modern period via only one writer, or indeed from the point of view of authorship at all. As Lucy Munro puts it in relation to the period's drama, '[i]t is impossible to locate a historicised study of the creative process purely in the intentions of dramatists', who were 'unable, or in many cases unwilling, to exercise sole authority over their plays'.[41] The turn to repertory studies was in part prompted by Barthes's and Foucault's famous rejection of the concept of the author as a unifying source of authority, whilst Gayatri Chakravorty Spivak's definition of the writer as only 'a reader at the performance of writing' led her to insist that single-author courses at university were 'an insult to world literature'.[42]

The present book blurs distinctions between authors, readers and texts. It does so partly in relation to the theatre because Lyly's plays defined 1580s boy company theatre in their own time and because they now provide our major witness to them, since Lyly's work has survived much better than any other writer in those companies. Lyly's writing career was unusual in a number of respects. Wells has observed that Lyly is the only early modern playwright for whom there is no direct evidence that he wrote in collaboration (though this need not mean that Lyly was any less collaborative than his contemporaries, but rather that his name is the only one associated with his, or the, work).[43] Moreover his modern editors are in agreement that he exercised an unusual degree of control over the rehearsal, performance and publication of his plays. Bevington suggests, for example, that he collaborated with the publisher Thomas Cadman in the 1584 editions of *Campaspe* and *Sapho and Phao*, and Scragg makes a similar suggestion in relation to William Wood's 1601 edition of *Love's Metamorphosis*.[44] Identified in his own time as the leader of his company, the direct recipient of the fee for his court performances and the man who sold his play on to a publisher, Lyly was in a unique position, as G. K. Hunter explains:

> His play text thus had a different status from those of Shakespeare (say) or of any dramatist who sold his text to an acting company. Lyly had sold his play only to himself, since he himself controlled the acting company, and since (therefore) the power to release it to be printed it [*sic*] lay exclusively with him.[45]

Hunter's language of the author's 'status', 'contro[l]' and exclusive 'power' implicitly offers a counterpoint to Munro's proposition that authors lacked 'sole authority over their plays'. Within the collaborative world of early modern theatre, at a time when few single writers took responsibility over an entire script, Lyly had an unusual degree of authority over his text in performance and publication. He approximated and anticipated the 'general and in itself remarkable habit of sole authorship' that John Jowett attributes to Shakespeare (though we should remember that apparent sole authorship may disguise unacknowledged forms of collaboration and beware the critical tendency to laud the one and denigrate the other).[46] Distinctions between an authorial corpus and a company repertory are further minimised by the fact that Lyly's eight surviving plays represent a majority of the ten or eleven surviving scripts written for child companies in the 1580s (the others are Peele's *Arraignment of Paris*, Munday's *Fedele and Fortunio* and, possibly, Marlowe and Nashe's *Dido, Queen of Carthage*).[47] For early modern cultural reasons and because of the partly haphazard survival of playtexts into the modern era, then, Lylian authorship blurs the distinction between repertory and single-author studies.

But such a claim does not contest the validity of repertory studies; it simply demonstrates the function of authorship within repertorial systems. As Jowett puts it, 'the author-centred text and the theatre-centred text [...] might coexist in the self-same document', and at least one surviving manuscript 'blurs the distinction between authorial papers and theatrical manuscript'.[48] This is exactly what Scragg finds in the evidence of the printing of *Love's Metamorphosis* and *Gallathea*: 'Lyly's close involvement in the production of his own plays [...] minimiz[es] the distinction between' authorial and playhouse copy.[49] But the blurring of this distinction demonstrates that even single authors worked within a collaborative theatre, just as collaborative theatre incorporated semi-autonomous work. By tracing the function of one writer's authorship, the present book shows how the marketing force of Lyly's name and the innovative print forms to which it was attached created new ways of writing and new ways to allow writing into the more permanent medium of print. It therefore approaches authorship not as a means to narrow literary focus but to demonstrate the implications of authorship for a range of contemporary writers, publishers and readers. As Terence Hawkes has insisted,

> The notion of a single 'authoritative' text, immediately expressive of the plenitude of its author's mind and meaning, would have been unfamiliar to Shakespeare, involved as he was in the collaborative enterprise of dramatic productions[.][50]

Of all early modern playwrights, Lyly perhaps exercised most authority over his plays, both on stage and in print, but his close involvement with the Earl of Oxford and the queen's court enclosed whatever textual 'authority' he had within a strictly hierarchical and censorious culture. With their emphasis upon the collaborative nature of 'the creative process' and 'the collaborative enterprise of dramatic productions', Munro and Hawkes demonstrate the importance of understanding Lylian authorship as part of a collaborative and stratified society. In repertory studies, as Helen Ostovich, Holger Syme and Andrew Griffin put it, 'the author is displaced by the company' to return us to a time when 'early modern theater-goers did, by and large, go to see a Strange's Men play rather than one by Kyd'.[51] But whilst Kyd's name was not attached to his most successful play, *The Spanish Tragedy*, until after the close of the commercial theatres, we shall see that Lyly's name was identified with his prose fiction, with the character Euphues, with a prose style and with the 1580s boy theatre companies. He may well have been brought into Oxford's boy company precisely because of his name and, as argued in Chapter 4, his name seems to have helped sell the plays in print. The present book therefore argues for a greater flexibility about the place of the writer within theatrical repertories, and indeed stationer portfolios.

Booking the theatres, dramatising the page

A greater attention to Lyly's place in early modern literary culture also asks us to rethink the relationship between the printing press and the theatre. Julie Stone Peters tells us that '[t]he study of the relationship between theatre and printing is [...] not a sideline in the history of communication but the paradigmatic instance of the interaction between text and performance'.[52] Lyly's work and its immediate reception constituted part of this shared history, whilst the dynamic relationship between performance and text helped to create the market for two basic kinds of English literature, namely printed single-story fiction and printed drama. Though the creation of these two markets can by no means be explained purely in Lylian terms, the part he played in their histories was fundamental: his authorship helped to produce the conditions in which a variety of single-story books could be published.

Certainly, a better understanding of Lyly's work will afford early modern scholarship a better understanding of literary and theatrical culture. These two cultures are often polarised and studied independently. English prose fiction began to be published before commercial plays were printed in any great number; prose fiction was subsequently used as source material by commercial playwrights; it is often constructed as a lesser art than commercial theatre. For these reasons, Tudor fiction is often thought to be prior, earlier, even more primitive than Tudor commercial drama. In fact, the two forms may be coeval. The first major story collection, *The Palace of Pleasure*, appeared in 1566, a year before London's first permanent and purpose-built playhouse, the Red Lion, opened. Within a year, two new spaces for storytelling appeared, one bibliographical, the other architectural, and each provided a model for subsequent imitation. Ten years later, a new volume of prose stories appeared, modelling itself on *The Palace of Pleasure* in its very name, calling itself *Petite's Palace of Petite his Pleasure*. That same year the Red Lion was used as a business model when two more playing spaces opened: James Burbage's Theatre in Shoreditch and Richard Farrant's hall in the Blackfriars precinct. It has not previously been recognised that these two markets for theatregoers and book-buyers began in the same years, as the two storytelling media found new ways to organise, promote and provide their stories. Indeed scholars have preferred to stress the differences between these contemporary and co-dependent institutions, yet the period from 1566 to 1576 witnessed new architectural and bibliographical spaces for the telling of stories in the name of commercial entertainment in and around the City of London. Those seeking narratives and stories could suddenly find them in new places: permanent theatre buildings and story-miscellanies. It was John Lyly who moved between these two markets and, by doing so, redefined them, writing the era's best-selling prose fiction before moving to Farrant's new Blackfriars hall playhouse and writing the first plays to be reprinted in the same year as their first editions.

The concurrent creation of these two media demonstrates previously unremarked but profound changes in modes of Elizabethan storytelling entertainment. Mary Ellen Lamb and Valerie Wayne have recently begun to investigate relationships between these two forms of storytelling in their essay collection *Staging Early Modern Romance*, revealing a fecund site for future scholarship to which the present book also contributes.[53] This is important precisely because the two entertainment forms are usually treated as discrete, segregated media, entrenched in a regimented and reiterated hierarchy that subordinates early modern prose fiction to early modern drama. As a result, few critics working in one field have acknowledged or interrogated developments in the other, and Tudor prose fiction and Tudor drama have most often been studied as though they were totally unrelated literary phenomena.

Indeed, the reception history of early modern drama has seen it become an increasingly elite art form, both in critical and in social terms, whilst early modern and much modern fiction has insistently been read and treated as 'low' culture. Lori Humphrey Newcomb persuasively traces this process in *Reading Popular Romance in Early Modern England* by following the critical fortunes of Greene's *Pandosto* and its stage version, *The Winter's Tale*, across four centuries. Steve Mentz and Constance Relihan have both argued that Tudor fiction has been downplayed by scholars who would prefer to locate the start of English prose storytelling in the form of the eighteenth- and even nineteenth-century novel.[54] The marginalisation of Tudor fiction clearly does have the canonical function that Mentz and Relihan describe, of accentuating, by diachronic, historical isolation, later achievements in fiction. But the marginalisation of Tudor fiction has a second canonical function, of accentuating, by synchronic, contemporary isolation, Tudor achievements in drama and poetry. As Barbara Fuchs puts it, the 'strange, ahistorical categorization' of Shakespeare's later plays as romances operates as part of a wider 'neglect of prose romance' and 'uncritically reflects the hierarchies that have long organized this corpus'.[55] Our collective lack of interest in Tudor fiction therefore serves two canonical functions, promoting the 'unique' achievements of Renaissance drama as well as the eighteenth-century novel. This appears to send us back to the New York blogger and her concern to protect Shakespeare and the novel. Despite entrenched critical binaries, early modern theatre and printed storybooks were vitally and vibrantly related.

Certainly the diminutive and segregated field of prose fiction criticism distorts and disrupts our understanding of early modern literary culture, in which markets for stories in books and theatres were created conterminously, competing for consumers' money at the same time as they provided one another with narrative sources. It is therefore to the detriment of early modern studies that these two related forms of literature are studied in segregation. It may be of interest to Shakespeare scholars that Shakespeare adapted Lodge's *Rosalind* in its stage version, *As You Like It*, but it is at least as important to note that the story was of simultaneous interest to a prose fiction writer and a playwright, to note that book readers and audience members alike invested in this story of a transvestite who is, by rights, a future duchess. And whilst *Rosalind* went through nine editions before 1640, *As You Like It* was not printed as a single book until 1734, well over a century after it was written. Cinemagoers generally do not go to the cinema to see a particular scriptwriter's film, and early modern theatregoers may have likewise watched *As You Like It* as a staging of Lodge's *Rosalind*. Indeed, since the title of Lodge's prose fiction was changed from *Rosalind: Euphues Golden Legacy* to, simply, *Euphues Golden Legacy*, audiences may well have thought they were watching a Euphues story or a Lyly play rather than one by Shakespeare. The relationship between the play and the prose fiction underlines the difference between early modern and modern literary culture, and emphasises the mutually supportive culture of early modern theatrical and bibliographical storytelling.

The current book offers a contribution towards a new appreciation of the interrelations of prose fiction and drama, and the relationship both literary forms have with the medium and economics of print itself. It presents Lyly as a writer who played an important, formative part in two new modes of early modern storytelling and their mediation in print. In an era of idiosyncratic writing, Lyly is a distinctive figure. Although we have seen reasons to be wary of drawing conclusions from such attributions, it is nevertheless the case that Lyly is unique in having a canon which appears to be sole-authored, and we can see from references to his work that contemporaries considered his authorship to be unique. Wells has further claimed Lyly as 'the only major dramatist to have composed exclusively for a boys' company'.[56] He is the only playwright to compose the majority of his works in prose. Now that Scragg has demonstrated that all of Lyly's plays may have been written before the dissolution of his later company in 1590, they can be seen to represent the fullest authorial canon to survive from the 1580s, making Lyly, for Paul Whitfield White, 'the one major English playwright for whom we have extant plays extending across the decade of the eighties'. White has called the 1580s a 'perplexing decade for theater historians', the decade in which the new theatre companies moved from a reliance on old touring plays and began to market themselves as purveyors of new plays.[57] By rethinking Lyly's place in early modern writing, then, we can begin to rethink the first generation of playwrights, actors and theatregoers who helped to define the commercial theatres.

Writing to power

In 1988 Stephen Orgel asked, '[A]re we sure we know what constituted a good poem in 1600?'[58] Years later, this continues to constitute a good question. In addition to the problems of reception which beset any attempt to understand historical literature, Shakespeare's ongoing totemic status in modern culture easily and disarmingly warps our perception of early modern culture. The result of these processes is that Lyly is either forgotten or depicted as a conventional and unadventurous writer and an ingratiating royalist: Sandra Clark shows that Beaumont and Fletcher suffered the same fate.[59] But let us end this introduction by turning to the opening of the first work he published, the *Anatomy*:

> Parrhasius, drawing the counterfeit of Helen [. . .] made the attire of her head loose; who, being demanded why he did so, he answered she was loose. Vulcan was painted curiously, yet with a polt foot; Leda cunningly, yet with her black hair. Alexander, having a scar in his cheek held his finger upon it that Apelles might not paint it. Apelles painted him with his finger cleaving to his face. 'Why', quoth Alexander, 'I laid my finger on my scar because I would not have thee see it'. 'Yea', said Apelles, 'and I drew it there because none else should perceive it, for if thy finger had been away either thy scar would have been seen or my art misliked'. Whereby I gather that in all perfect works as well the fault as the face is to be shown. (27)

A traditional analysis of this passage would focus on its euphuism: in other words, its recurrent use of classical paradigms and its balancing and repetition of certain words ('loose') and syntax ('"Why", quoth Alexander', '"Yea", said Apelles'). But since we have already seen Euphues tell a long story which Philautus then calls into question, we might want to ask how Lyly or his narrator arrives here at the insight, 'Whereby I gather'. The notion that perfect works should incorporate the rough with the smooth ('face' here is being used in its Latinate form, *facies* meaning beauty) seems an imperfect summary of the anecdotes that have gone before, and the transitions from Helen's morally suspect beauty to Vulcan's lameness, from Leda's departure from classical conventions of perfection to Alexander's blemish create a matrix of meaning, something non-linear which therefore offers a range of conclusions for the reader to draw.

Above all, Lyly's opening to the *Anatomy* gives us an image of the painter Apelles and the king Alexander in a surprisingly physical and political debate. Alexander attempts to censor his scar 'because I would not have thee see it', asserting the monarch's ability to control his image. But Apelles refuses that right, somehow managing to co-operate with whilst also preventing the act of censorship by catching the king in that act and, yet more provocatively, pointing at the very thing he wishes to hide. Lyly leaves these two men in a state of standoff, requiring the reader to resolve this moment and offering multiple insights in addition to the one explicitly provided. From the first, then, Lyly staged conflict between monarch and artist, power and representation, and, whilst an emphasis on euphuism might encourage us to see how his prose fits together, it is also worthwhile reading Lyly to see how his sentences refuse to fit and refuse to supply resolution. For a writer who often seems to use Apelles as a means to discuss the experience of authorship, this passage encourages us to rethink Hunter's image of the quiescent, complacent court writer. It is Apelles, not Alexander, who gets the last word here, forcing his monarch into a position he did not intend to adopt. In his bibliographical innovations, his stylistic experimentation and his tacitly anarchic representation of monarchy, Lyly was a new creative force in early modern literature. If Middleton is 'our other Shakespeare', as Taylor has recently claimed, then Lyly may be our other Middleton.[60]

In order to understand the extent of Lyly's importance for early modern authorship, this book is divided into three parts, on prose fiction, drama and reception. The first two parts study Lyly's impact on early modern culture, focusing on prose fiction and drama respectively: in each part, the first chapter assesses Lyly's originality and the second chapter assesses the impact of that authorship upon the print market for each of those literary forms. The first two parts of this book therefore permit a clear demonstration of how Lyly's work was innovative and how it was received and commodified by his contemporaries. Since the importance of Lyly's authorship for early modern culture has not been extensively recognised within criticism of the period, however, the third part of the book examines Lyly's reception history up to the present day, focusing in particular on nineteenth-century uses of the word euphuism as part of a debate over appropriate literary male style. As we have already seen, this debate went on to colour and distort critical estimations of Lyly's work in the twentieth century and beyond. The first two parts of the book, then, demonstrate Lyly's importance, and the final part explains how that importance came to be forgotten.

Garrett Sullivan suggests that examining 'the difference between texts produced by a writer located outside an established literary tradition and one who is planted squarely inside it' may permit 'the excavation of lost epistemologies'.[61] This book does not so much examine the differences between the absolutely canonical and the absolutely non-canonical as trace the difficult, often fragmented process of establishing that which lies between them, the lily border of the canon. Thus the emphasis upon Lyly's work alongside the production and reception of other prose fiction (Part I) and plays (Part II) enables a new understanding of the ways different kinds of text and different kinds of textual authorship could be received, commodified and celebrated in the early modern period. The third part then examines how Lyly came to be excluded from the early modern canon.

Introducing a recent book on Middleton, Swapan Chakravorty notes the continuing currency of Margot Heinemann's strikingly honest and rather sad confession that when it comes to Middleton, 'we are still none too sure how to take him'.[62] Heinemann's phrase registers the displacing friction that can occur when a critic, positioned and surrounded by prevailing critical discourses to read a writer in a certain way, discovers that the writer will not obey the paradigm. That, of course, is just one of the reasons to reconsider writers confined to the borders of the canon. By examining the period in which Lyly helped to define contemporary literature against a reception process that has seen him confined to the edges of literary history, this book offers the opportunity to appraise the early modern period afresh. Considering Lyly is just one way in which we can begin to reconsider Shakespeare's period and the historical processes in which that period became defined as Shakespeare's. Recent performances and staged readings of Lyly's plays have astonished and amazed those accustomed to assume that Shakespeare is the ultimate arbiter of literary and dramatic greatness in this period, and at the Globe Lyly remains the only writer whose work has made audiences laugh *and* cry during a staged reading. In Lyly's second play the young boy Phao asks the wise woman Sibylla, 'What shall become of me?', and receives the answer, 'Go dare' (II.iv.143–4). This combination of two imperative verbs is an antidote to Lyly's reputation as a fussy, fusty sort of writer, and this book aims to help its readers go dare in their own responses to Lyly's writing.

Notes

1 John Lyly, *'Euphues: The Anatomy of Wit' and 'Euphues and His England'*, ed. Leah Scragg (Manchester: Manchester University Press, 2003), 182. All references to Lyly's work, unless otherwise stated, are taken from the Revels Plays editions.

2 William Webbe, *A Discourse of English Poetrie* (London: Robert Wallet,

1586), E1v. Throughout the book u/v and i/j have been modernised in quotations.

3 Thomas Lodge, *Wits Miserie, and the worlds madness* (London: Cuthbert Burby, 1596), 57.

4 Francis Meres, *Palladis Tamia* (London: Cuthbert Burby, 1598), 627.

5 Leah Scragg, *The Metamorphosis of 'Gallathea': A Study in Creative Adaptation* (Washington, DC: University Press of America, 1982), 128.

6 John Lyly, *Sixe court comedies* (London: by William Stansby for Edward Blount, 1632), title page.

7 N. F. Blake, *A Grammar of Shakespeare's Language* (Basingstoke: Palgrave Macmillan, 2002), 75.

8 Emma Smith, 'Shakespeare and early modern tragedy', in Emma Smith and Garrett A. Sullivan Jr (eds), *The Cambridge Companion to English Renaissance Tragedy* (Cambridge: Cambridge University Press, 2010), 133 and 147.

9 Ian Green, *Print and Protestantism in Early Modern England* (Oxford: Oxford University Press, 2000), 173.

10 For a much wider engagement with these issues, see Andy Kesson and Emma Smith (eds), *The Elizabethan Top Ten: Defining Print Popularity in Early Modern England* (Aldershot: Ashgate, 2013).

11 Ben Jonson, *Every Man Out of His Humour*, ed. Helen Ostovich (Manchester: Manchester University Press, 2001), 3.

12 *The Works of Gabriel Harvey*, ed. Alexander B. Grosart, 3 vols (1884; New York: AMS Press, 1966), II, 218.

13 Michael Dobson, *The Making of the National Poet: Shakespeare, Adaptation, and Authority, 1660–1769* (Oxford: Clarendon Press, 1992), 1 and 3; James Shapiro, *Contested Will: Who Wrote Shakespeare?* (London: Faber and Faber, 2010), 36–7.

14 Stanley Wells, 'To read a play: the problem of editorial intervention', in Hanna Scolnicov and Peter Holland (eds), *Reading Plays: Interpretation and Reception* (Cambridge: Cambridge University Press, 1991), 31.

15 Stanley Wells, *Shakespeare and Co.: Christopher Marlowe, Thomas Dekker, Ben Jonson, Thomas Middleton, John Fletcher and the Other Players in His Story* (London: Allen Lane, 2006), 64.

16 Perry Mills, 'Directing Lyly', programme note for the King Edward VI School, Stratford-upon-Avon production of Lyly's *Endymion*, Shakespeare's Globe, 08.02.09.

17 wind-up-bird, www.metwee.blogspot.com (accessed 12.06.07).

18 This and all related quotations are from the manuscript annotation in the Shakespeare Institute Library copy of *The Dramatic Works of John Lilly, (The Euphuist.), With Notes and Some Account of His Life and Writings*, ed. F. W. Fairholt, 2 vols (1858; London: Reeves & Turner, 1892), 5 and 85.

19 Genista McIntosh, 'Interlude II: Casting and marketing Jonson', in Richard Cave, Elizabeth Schafer and Brian Woolland (eds), *Ben Jonson and Theatre: Performance, Practice and Theory* (London: Routledge, 1999), 146.

20 Gary Taylor, 'Blount, Edward', *Oxford Dictionary of National Biography* (Oxford: Oxford University Press, 2004) (www.oxforddnb.com, accessed 23.10.12).

21 On *Henry IV* and *Sir Thomas More*, see John Jowett, *Shakespeare and*

Text (Oxford: Oxford University Press, 2007), 190, and, for a sceptical take on the *Titus Andronicus* speech, Brian Vickers, *Shakespeare, Co-Author: A Historical Study of Five Collaborative Plays* (Oxford: Oxford University Press, 2002), 149–50.

22 Gary Taylor, 'Making meaning marketing Shakespeare 1623', in Peter Holland and Stephen Orgel (eds), *From Performance to Print in Shakespeare's England* (Basingstoke: Palgrave Macmillan, 2006), 61.

23 Jennifer Richards, *Rhetoric and Courtliness in Early Modern Literature* (Cambridge: Cambridge University Press, 2003), 66; Christopher Warley, *Sonnet Sequences and Social Distinction in Renaissance England* (Cambridge: Cambridge University Press, 2005), 40.

24 *The Plays of John Lyly*, ed. Carter A. Daniel (London: Associated University Presses, 1988), 20.

25 John Lyly, *'Campaspe' and 'Sappho and Phao'*, ed. G. K. Hunter and David Bevington (1991; Manchester: Manchester University Press, 1999), 164.

26 Philippa Berry, *Of Chastity and Power: Elizabethan Literature and the Unmarried Queen* (London: Routledge, 1989), 112.

27 William Shakespeare, *Complete Works*, ed. Jonathan Bate and Eric Rasmussen (Basingstoke: Macmillan, 2007), 15.

28 Park Honan, *Shakespeare: A Life* (Oxford: Oxford University Press, 1998), 112–13.

29 Berry, *Of Chastity and Power*, 6 and 112.

30 Richards, *Rhetoric and Courtliness*, 2.

31 Martin Wiggins, *Shakespeare and the Drama of His Time* (Oxford: Oxford University Press, 2000), 5.

32 G. K. Hunter, *John Lyly: The Humanist as Courtier* (London: Routledge and Kegan Paul, 1962), 283 and 285.

33 Hunter, *Humanist as Courtier*, 297 and 235.

34 Alistair Fox, 'The complaint of poetry for the death of liberality: the decline of literary patronage in the 1590s', in John Guy (ed.), *The Reign of Elizabeth I: Court and Culture in the Last Decade* (Cambridge: Cambridge University Press, 1995), esp. 241.

35 Jonas Barish, 'The prose style of John Lyly', *English Literary History* 23:1 (March 1956), 14–35 (25 and 16); Michael Pincombe, *The Plays of John Lyly: Eros and Eliza* (Manchester: Manchester University Press, 1996), 142; Richard A. Lanham, *Analyzing Prose*, 2nd ed. (1983; London: Continuum, 2003), 130.

36 Elizabeth Fowler and Roland Greene (eds), *The Project of Prose in Early Modern Europe and the New World* (Cambridge: Cambridge University Press, 1997), 5.

37 John Hoskyns, *Directions for Speech and Style*, ed. H. H. Hudson (Princeton: Princeton University Press, 1935), 16.

38 Russ McDonald, 'Compar or parison: measure for measure', in Sylvia Adamson, Gavin Alexander and Katrin Ettenhuber (eds), *Renaissance Figures of Speech* (Cambridge: Cambridge University Press, 2007), 44.

39 Henry Peacham, *The Garden of Eloquence (1593)*, [2nd and enlarged edition of *The Garden of Eloquence* (1577)], with an introduction by William G. Crane (Gainesville, FL: Scholars' Facsimiles and Reprints, 1954), 58.

40 Walter J. Ong, *Orality & Literacy: The Technologizing of the Word*

(London: Routledge, 1982), 120 (cf. Adam Fox, *Oral and Literate Culture in England 1500–1700* (Oxford: Oxford University Press, 2000), 131); Ann Moss, *Printed Commonplace-Books and the Structuring of Renaissance Thought* (Oxford: Clarendon Press, 1996), 211.

41 Lucy Munro, 'Early modern drama and the repertory approach', *Research Opportunities in Renaissance Drama* 42 (2003), 1–33 (27–8).

42 Roland Barthes, 'The death of the author' (1967), in *Image Music Text*, ed. and tr. Stephen Heath (London: Fontana Press, 1977); Michel Foucault, 'What is an author?' (1969), tr. Josué V. Harari, originally published in Harari (ed.), *Textual Strategies: Perspectives in Post-Structuralist Criticism* (1980), rev. and rpt in *The Foucault Reader: An Introduction to Foucault's Thought*, ed. Paul Rabinow (1984; London: Penguin Books, 1986); Gayatri Chakravorty Spivak, *Outside in the Teaching Machine* (London: Routledge, 1993), 218 and 276.

43 Wells, *Shakespeare and Co.*, 250. For the view that Kyd shares this distinction, see Jowett, *Shakespeare and Text*, 23.

44 Hunter and Bevington, *Campaspe: Sappho and Phao*, 141; John Lyly, *Love's Metamorphosis*, ed. Leah Scragg (Manchester: Manchester University Press, 2008), 2.

45 Hunter and Bevington, *Campaspe: Sappho and Phao*, 2–3.

46 Jowett, *Shakespeare and Text*, 17.

47 On *Dido*, see Martin Wiggins, 'When did Marlowe write *Dido, Queen of Carthage*?', *Review of English Studies* 59:241 (September 2008), 521–41.

48 Jowett, *Shakespeare and Text*, 28 and 29.

49 Scragg, *Love's Metamorphosis*, 2.

50 Terence Hawkes, *That Shakespeherian Rag: Essays on a Critical Process* (London: Methuen, 1986), 75.

51 Helen Ostovich, Holger Schott Syme and Andrew Griffin (eds), *Locating the Queen's Men, 1583–1603: Material Practices and Conditions of Playing* (Farnham: Ashgate, 2009), 2–3.

52 Julie Stone Peters, *Theatre of the Book, 1480–1880: Print, Text, and Performance in Europe* (Oxford: Oxford University Press, 2000), 2.

53 Mary Ellen Lamb and Valerie Wayne (eds), *Staging Early Modern Romance: Prose Fiction, Dramatic Romance and Shakespeare* (London: Routledge, 2009).

54 Lori Humphrey Newcomb, *Reading Popular Romance in Early Modern England* (New York: Columbia University Press, 2002); Steve Mentz, *Romance for Sale in Early Modern England: The Rise of Prose Fiction* (Aldershot: Ashgate, 2006), 9; Constance C. Relihan (ed.), *Framing Elizabethan Fictions: Contemporary Approaches to Early Modern Narrative Prose* (Kent, OH: Kent State University Press, 1996), 4.

55 Barbara Fuchs, *Romance* (New York: Routledge, 2004), 96–7.

56 Wells, *Shakespeare and Co.*, 250 and 64–5.

57 Leah Scragg, 'The victim of fashion? Rereading the biography of John Lyly', *Medieval and Renaissance Drama in England* 19 (2006), 210–26, esp. 210–12; Paul Whitfield White, 'Playing companies and the drama of the 1580s: a new direction for Elizabethan theatre history?', *Shakespeare Studies* 28 (2000), 265–84 (265 and 277).

58 Orgel, *The Authentic Shakespeare*, 232.

59 Sandra Clark, *The Plays of Beaumont and Fletcher: Sexual Themes and*

Dramatic Representation (London: Harvester Wheatsheaf, 1994).

60 Gary Taylor, 'Thomas Middleton', at http://oup.com (accessed 26.06.08).

61 Garrett A. Sullivan Jr, *The Drama of Landscape: Land, Property and Social Relations on the Early Modern Stage* (Stanford: Stanford University Press, 1998), 231.

62 Margot Heinemann, *Puritanism & Theatre: Thomas Middleton and Opposition Drama under the Early Stuarts* (Cambridge: Cambridge University Press, 1982), 1; Swapan Chakravorty, *Society and Politics in the Plays of Thomas Middleton* (Oxford: Clarendon Press, 1996), 2.

PART I

Lyly and prose fiction

CHAPTER 1

Buy the book: imaginative stories in the book market (1566–78)

Lyly's first work was called *Euphues: The Anatomy of Wit*, and G. K. Hunter has proposed the central word of the title as 'a clear indication of his method of work' in all of Lyly's writing:

> His aim is to 'anatomise' or open up an area of life by exploring its divergent inter-related elements [. . .]. What is interesting here is the extent to which anatomy has led to circularity [. . .]. This use of plot to defeat the progressivist assumptions of plot seems even stranger in drama than in a proto-novel of the type of *Euphues*.[1]

Hunter's Lyly is a storyteller with little interest in stories, a man with no sense 'of cause and effect': 'Everywhere in Lyly emotions are brought to our attention as matters to be discussed rather than acted upon.' Peter Saccio, one of Lyly's greatest critics, similarly draws on this idea when he states that 'one will not find any kind of plot at all in *Campaspe*'.[2] Lyly himself likes to claim that the stories in his work are meaningless: the prologue to *Endymion* warns that the play is 'superfluous for the matter', and forbids the audience 'to dispute of' the story 'because it was a fiction' (78), and he assumes a personal voice at the end of *Euphues and His England* to tell his female readers that 'I, gentlewomen, am indifferent' (354). Though this word means something like 'neutral' or 'impartial' rather than 'uninterested', this indifference seems an unexpected stance from a writer who has just produced two stories about Euphues, and Lyly's request in *Endymion* that 'none will apply pastimes' (78) underlines the fact that the play's story has diverse significations.

Anatomies and storytelling

There is much to recommend Hunter's emphasis on the word anatomy. Lyly introduces himself in the *Anatomy of Wit* as 'a fool [that] hath intruded himself to discourse of wit' (29). If the last word of this phrase is an obvious reference to the book's title, the representation of his authorship as a form of discursive intrusion continues the image of his work as an anatomisation. In the same epistle the author describes himself as 'The surgeon that maketh the anatomy' and 'the butcher [who] cut[s] the anatomy of a man' (28). These references to the writer and his writing as something penetrative and intrusive confirm Hunter's claim that anatomy is an important term with which to understand Lylian authorship, and Lyly was the first writer to use the term in a literary sense during what Devon Hodges calls a 'culture of dissection' when, 'with violent determination', as Jonathan Sawday puts it, 'writers of anatomies used their pens as scalpels to cut through appearances and reveal the mute truth of objects'.[3] Lyly's discursive intrusion, his role as anatomist, therefore serves as an image of his disinterested or distant relationship to his material. It also suggests the examination of a static body rather than the linear detailing of a moving narrative, and indeed scholars have suggested that Lyly's writings, and especially his plays, have a peculiarly static energy.[4]

There may be other ways to think about Lyly's discursive intrusion into Tudor storytelling culture, however, and to move beyond this emphasis on static dialogue. Evidence in his plays and prose fiction suggests a greater engagement with plot and its emotive possibilities than Hunter suggests. In three of his first four plays, Lyly staged a tableau in which one character tells a story to another, pausing the present tense of the drama in order to describe the history of the fictive world. In each case, Lyly provides a listener who is moved by and invested in the story. In his second play, *Sapho and Phao*, the boy Phao tells the prophetess Sibylla that he 'cannot love', and she tells him a biographical story in the 'hope [it] shall be as a straight thread to lead you out of those crooked conceits and place you in the plain path of love' (II.i.36, 39–41). Despite the clear intentions of the storyteller, her listener undergoes a range of emotions and arrives at the opposite conclusion to that which she intends. Phao is captivated ('I pray, tell on'), inquisitive ('Was not the god angry to see you unkind?') and is 'driven by your counsel into divers conceits', but ultimately refuses the speaker's intentions: 'but to yield to love is the only thing I hate' (II.i.64, 59, 130–2). Here Sibylla's story seems to fail in its purpose, but nonetheless excites an emotional response from a listener who does indeed almost immediately fall in love. In his next two plays, *Gallathea* and *Endymion*, Lyly once again showed his audiences characters moved and excited by a story. In *Gallathea*, Tityrus explains to his daughter the history of her home and the danger she is in, causing her to experience 'terror' and 'horror' (I.i.55–7). In *Endymion*, Eumenides' curiosity to hear the old man Geron's life story 'hath so melted my mind that I wish to hang at your mouth's end', and he begins and ends the scene by asking Geron to explain who he is (III.iv.2).

In all three cases, stories are not circular. Eumenides is excited in advance by the prospect of a story; Gallathea reacts to a story as it is told; Phao responds to the story at its conclusion. All three gain knowledge and suffer emotionally through the process of storytelling. These scenes demonstrate a writer who is very much invested in storytelling. They also suggest a dramatist skilful in staging the storytelling moment, for Lyly uses these stories to colour and clarify the world of the play: in other words, stories are not only part of the fictional world but help to establish and define it. Thus Geron promises an explanation as he and Eumenides leave the stage together, so that Lyly uses a character's backstory to construct the offstage fictional world of *Endymion*: 'That shall be as we walk, and I doubt not but the strangeness of my tale will take away the tediousness of our journey' (III.iv.204–6). In *Sapho and Phao*, Sibylla prepares the audience for the ideological implications of the love interest of the main plot by describing her failed relationship with a god. As she discovers, the effect of stories upon a listener can confound the storyteller's intention.

Perhaps the most radical use of storytelling is at the start of *Gallathea*. As Leah Scragg has shown, father and daughter seek refuge under a tree, but the father's story transforms the tree from a place of safety to the site of sacrifice. Scragg shows that 'the story the speaker unfolds involves a series of transmutations', a characteristic of Lyly's writing Scragg has done much to emphasise: this demonstrates the vital place of story at the heart of Lyly's writing style.[5] Narrative doesn't just move in itself, it transforms the meaning of the narrator, the listener and their world, and in so doing it radically alters the audience's access to the stage fiction. As these three examples show, Lyly was perfectly capable of appreciating – and manipulating – the emotive and unexpected effects of storytelling.

Lyly's prose fiction also attests to the author's imaginative investment in his stories, not least because Lyly's paratextual comments on his work show us the ways he expected and then rejected future narrative developments.[6] The *Anatomy* closes with a promise of a 'second part', a sequel. In the first edition of the book (December 1578) Lyly explained that 'I left [Euphues] ready to cross the seas to England' (150). Within months of the first edition, Lyly was projecting the storyline of his forthcoming sequel in a new letter to 'THE

GENTLEMEN SCHOLARS OF OXFORD' that was appended to reprints of the first work from 1579 onwards: 'Euphues at his arrival (I am assured) will view Oxford' (151). But when the sequel, *Euphues and His England*, appeared in 1580, it recorded no such visit. Over two years, Lyly had imagined, sketched out and then rejected at least one narrative scenario for Euphues. There seem to be two possibilities here: either these changes represent Lyly's own investment in and uncertainty over his story or they demonstrate his desire and ability to tantalise readers with false promises and possible outcomes. Such problems over narrative choice show Lyly engaging with stories and storytelling, commenting on the process of representation in a manner comparable to some of the more self-conscious choruses of Shakespeare and Peele. The chorus to *Henry V* asks the audience to 'excuse' the 'due course of things, / Which cannot in their huge and proper life / Be here presented'. Peele's chorus to *David and Bersabe* reflects, towards the end of the play, on how 'this storie lends us other store': that is, the source material offers the theatre company further narrative options.[7] Lyly is equally open in sharing with his readers the narrative choices he makes, though, unlike Shakespeare or Peele, his 'storie' or 'huge and proper life' appears to be self-generated rather than based on historical or Biblical sources.

Moreover, in the narrative Lyly eventually did create, his characters are regularly placed in the position of auditors to other peoples' stories. Philautus's excited and self-interested response to Fidus's biographical story is a key example of Lyly's representation of the effect of storytelling upon a listener: 'But he, so eager of an end, as one leaping over a stile before he come to it, desired few parentheses, or digressions, or glosses, but the text, where he himself was coting in the margent' (199).

Breaking into Fidus's story, the narrator sets out Philautus's impatience with what he views as digressions from the main 'text'; but he also makes clear that Philautus himself is creating digressions of his own. This passage makes demands on the imaginative powers of the reader, since the word 'he' in the narrative is left unglossed, and a reader is forced to deduce whether it refers to the storyteller, to Fidus or to either of his male listeners, Euphues or Philautus. A footnote in Scragg's edition gives the only sensible interpretation, explaining that 'he' refers to Philautus (199, n.7), but the important point is that Lyly's text requires readers to make this deduction for themselves: to gloss the text. This is then a passage describing a listener impatient of marginal glosses, but who is himself 'coting in the margent'; it is a passage which places its readers or listeners in the margins themselves, forcing a readerly gloss of an unattached and initially ambiguous pronoun.

This complex image of storytelling represents an engaged and active listener anxious to edit what he hears of other people in order to apply it to himself. Lyly's readers may well have used his work in the same way. Despite his reputation for circular, unemotional or distanced storytelling, Lyly developed narratives that excite and terrify his characters, defy authorial expectations and trouble those of their readers. As an imaginative author revising the *Euphues and His England* narrative, Lyly showed himself to be as engaged in the problems of linear story composition as any of his characters. There are, then, 'cause and effect' and emotional progression in Lyly's stories. Contrary to Hunter, Lyly's role as anatomist did not preclude an interest in the emotive and fictive effects of narration.

The storytelling market

This chapter assesses Lyly's discursive intrusion from another perspective: the emerging market for print narrative into which Lyly's *Anatomy* literally intruded. Lyly's role within this storytelling market was so incisive that it produced a series of imitations that re-imagined his work, style and character and thereby transformed the ways in which stories could be told in books. A series of storytelling models were available to Lyly, in the form of William Painter's multi-volume *Palace of Pleasure* (1566–67), Geoffrey Fenton's *Certaine Tragicall Discourses* (1567), William Baldwin's *Beware the Cat* (written in the early 1550s but published in 1570), George Gascoigne's 'Adventures of Master F.J.' (included in *A Hundreth Sundrie Flowres*, 1573) and George Pettie's *Petite Palace of Pettie his Pleasure* (1576). All these works offered an emergent and ongoing narrative tradition which Lyly both continued and changed. They provided models for Lyly's later innovations, in their titles, styles, narrators, characters and in the way they engaged with an emerging but more established literary model in the book market, the poetry miscellany.

The importance of Lyly's innovation will become clear in Chapter 2, which discusses the unprecedented effect of Lyly's work on his contemporaries. Numerous critics have observed Lyly's immediate impact on the print market, but few have considered why and how his work made such an impact. Even the best recent work on the prose fiction market relies upon the old assumption that Lyly's success can be explained in relation to the character Euphues. Thus

Steve Mentz observes that 'The widespread use of the name Euphues in the titles of later books represents publishers cashing in on Lyly's market success, but it also seems that writers understood that he was a valuable model.'[8] Or, as Katharine Wilson puts it, 'Lyly's quick-witted persona "Euphues" became a celebrity, a phenomenon in print on his first appearance in 1578, his name evoking an instantly recognizable author, narrative, and style.'[9] Both these writers are right to emphasise Lyly's immediate importance, but neither seeks to explain it. It is therefore still unclear what new 'model' Lyly offered to his contemporaries, or what made him 'instantly recognizable' in narrative and style.

Lylian scholars, on the other hand, answer both questions with reference to the prose style we have come to call euphuism. Scragg describes Lyly's prose stories as 'the literary sensation of the age', quoting Blount's 1632 reference to the 'new language' euphuism in order to explain Lyly's impact.[10] Blount does indeed represent important evidence, and was a (very) young man when Lyly's work was first published, but his description of Lyly's impact was written fifty years after the effect it attempts to record. Hunter similarly quotes Blount to explain why '*Euphues* was a success without parallel in its age', whilst, for Leah Guenther, the 'initial colossal triumph' of Lyly's work can be explained by its establishment of 'a linguistic fad'.[11] Both Lylian and prose fiction scholars explain Lyly's immediate success in terms of his style or his character. The problem with these accounts is that the *Anatomy* title page makes no reference to the work's style, and it is therefore hard to see that it could have had what critics seem to be claiming as a marketing effect. The word *Euphues* clearly came to have such an effect (hence the word 'euphuism'), but it cannot have done so in the late 1570s, when the *Anatomy* first started selling out.

In order for a style or a character to become influential, it presumably has to be read and consumed in the first place, and so neither style nor character can adequately explain Lyly's initial success which depended on an unprecedented number and range of bookshop customers choosing this new edition in December 1578 and early 1579. This success was evidently substantial, since Lyly's publisher issued a series of reprints within the first twelve months of the appearance of his first book. Something, in other words, persuaded bookshop customers to seek out, buy and read the book in unexpected quantities, and since the publication of the *Anatomy* precedes the coining of the word *euphuism* by fourteen years, and since the book's title page makes no reference to its style, whatever attractions euphuism later held for Elizabethan readers cannot be used to explain their initial interest in Lyly's book.

Just as importantly, euphuism cannot adequately explain Lyly's later unique and unparalleled reception. This is a vital point because scholars have equated Lyly and euphuism in ways which distort our understanding of both. For euphuism was, by all accounts, an emulated style, one that became copied and commodified, but from the 1580s up to the 1630s, when Lyly's two prose fictions continued to be reprinted, none of the books that reworked Lyly's style was reissued in comparable numbers of reprints. Euphuism, therefore, cannot be used to explain the success of one author alone. By the very nature of its influence – to say nothing of the way it is structured around quotation from other kinds of writing, both canonical and proverbial – euphuism is a multi-authored mode, rather than the peculiar provenance of Lyly himself. Euphuism exceeds Lyly's authorship, in the sense that other writers were euphuistic, but Lyly's authorship also exceeded euphuism, and the style cannot be used to explain the writer's immediate impact on the prose fiction market.

With her focus on Lyly's 'author[ship], narrative, and style', Wilson offers a way out of this impasse. Something else about these books – their authorial and narrative stance – made them attractive to book buyers. Paul Salzman has also suggested ways to think past euphuism, for although in an earlier study he situated Lyly's 'unparalleled success' in terms of his 'flamboyant style [. . .] which attracted the attention of his contemporaries', he also noted that 'Lyly's fiction continued to be popular after his style became outmoded', thus demonstrating the independence of success from style.[12] As the next chapter demonstrates, the 'outmoded Lyly' is a critical construct in need of revision, but at least Salzman acknowledged here that Lyly's success was not dependent on the popularity of his style.

In a recent article, moreover, Salzman anticipates the argument made here by identifying the unique bibliographical structure which made Lyly's first book stand out, though Salzman does not argue for the importance of this innovation. His claim that Lyly's 'fiction points to a new direction in form' needs to be related to Lyly's immediate impact on the print market, which Lylian and prose fiction scholars otherwise relate to his euphuistic style.[13] As this chapter demonstrates, the four main words on Lyly's first title page implied a radical revision of the meaning of prose stories within the book market. *Euphues: The Anatomy of Wit* makes different kinds of promises to bookshop customers from *The Palace of Pleasure* or *A*

Hundreth Sundrie Flowres, promising a single story about a person and an investigation of the conceptual term 'wit'.

By considering the development of the prose fiction market from the point of view of a writer who also wrote plays, this chapter begins a conversation about different kinds of early modern storytelling. Tudor prose fiction has rarely been considered part of the history of novelistic writing. Those early scholars who did concern themselves with Tudor fiction tended to stress its exclusion from the canon, usually with some satisfaction. Thus Ernest Baker warned his readers that it was largely written 'for those of little education and less fastidiousness', and that 'not one has stood its ground as a classic'. William Lyon Phelps told his readers, in the teleologically named *Advance of the English Novel*, 'I certainly would not read, nor advise anyone to read *Euphues*, *Arcadia*, *Rosalind*, *Jack Wilton*, or *Oroonoko*, for their intrinsic value'.[14] Many critics have now demonstrated the inadequacy of these earlier accounts, but revisionist approaches to Tudor fiction have rarely challenged its displacement from the canon by, for example, considering fiction's relationship to the contemporary theatre market, a relationship that was vital for authors, actors, audiences, readers and publishers alike.

This is, then, an unrealised research area, in which early modern literary producers and consumers and modern scholars are engaged in new ways to produce, experience and represent literature. It is therefore important to follow the porous boundaries between print and dramatic modes of storytelling, for it is between these modes that a public authorship we now categorise as early modern emerged. Through the sixteenth century, as Alexandra Halasz and Joad Raymond have shown, the book market speculated on different forms of print and different ways to market it, so that by the 1580s writers were able to think newly about writing for profit.[15] This chapter shows Lyly's innovative position within this speculative market. The 'fool [who] intruded himself to discourse of wit' also transformed the discursive and market representation of prose stories in books. Salzman's realisation that Lyly revised the bibliographical form of Tudor storytelling needs to be read in conjunction with Lyly's narrative and stylistic strategies in order to explain the impact his authorship would have on the print market in the following decades.

Palaces, adventures and anatomies: naming Elizabethan fiction

As Mary Scott long ago observed, medieval England did not embrace the prose short story popular elsewhere in Europe.[16] The identification of literary genre being a fine and fickle art, scholars have disagreed over both the terminology and the timing of the emergence of native prose fiction or novels in English. William Baldwin's *Beware the Cat*, written in 1553, was claimed as the first English novel by William Ringler, who described it as 'the first original English work of prose fiction of more than short-story length'.[17] Whatever the merits of Baldwin's claims as a novelist, his impact on the print market was delayed by seventeen years, for the death of Edward and the succession of his sister Mary made the print publication of the anti-Catholic satire impossible. Eventually published in 1570, Baldwin's story was effectively prevented from beginning the tradition of prose fiction in print.[18] This awkward transition of *Beware the Cat* into print provides ample demonstration that the rise of a market in prose fiction was tied to wider political events, in this case the religious status of the incumbent monarch.

For this reason, it is more helpful to consider George Painter's first volume of *The Palace of Pleasure* (1566) as the first English story miscellany in prose, especially if we wish to privilege the ways book-buyers might have perceived the market. The publication of such an innovative and expensive book some years into Elizabeth's reign is itself significant. As James Raven explains, the Edwardian reign had supported and nurtured print dissemination, creating 'a watershed for English publishing' that was then overturned by 'the haemorrhaging by hasty exile of recently established printing expertise' in Mary's reign. It was only after a number of years of Elizabethan rule that an increased demand for books printed in England and in English 'supported the opening of shops more permanent than stall-board and shed lock-ups'.[19] This new literary genre is a product of these developments. Painter shows signs of acknowledging his own project as an unusual form of composition, and Robert Maslen suggests that Painter's repeated description of the stories he tells as 'straung' has 'connotations of both "innovative" and "foreign"'.[20] Painter's narration apparently felt strange even to the man narrating it.

The Palace of Pleasure was published by Richard Tottell and William Jones in 1566. Raven describes all collaborative publications as 'an evident form of risk limitation', a useful way to understand the decision to collaborate on the first large collection of prose stories.[21]

Since the following year saw not only a second volume of the *Palace* but a similar story miscellany written by Fenton and published by Thomas Marshe, the new availability of prose storybooks seems to have demonstrated a potential market. Marshe published later editions of the *Palace*, apparently specialising in the prose story miscellany, and one of the printers involved in the *Palace*, Henry Bynneman, went on to publish Gascoigne's literary miscellany, *Hundreth Sundrie Flowres*. This is an especially small printing community working together on a new bibliographical form. The Painter and Fenton story-collections are very different, but their similar bibliographical form is of interest here: they show how the new market for prose fiction was defined by the form of the story miscellany.

Tottell's role in the publication of the first prose story miscellany demonstrates that the book form was strongly related to the recently created market for printed poetry miscellanies that Tottell himself had innovated. Despite recent warnings against too rigid a separation between author, printer and publisher, from the wider perspective of the print market it is helpful to privilege the specific agency of the publisher as the person making financial decisions that would determine the shape and structure of the literary product.[22] The publisher of a first edition is especially important as the person or persons responsible for selecting a particular manuscript composition: publishers were therefore, if not always the first reader to come to a text after the writer, then certainly the reader responsible for making a text available to print readers, determining the movement, definition and availability of new kinds of literature.

Tottell is vital in this regard since he had published 'the first printed anthology of English poetry' in 1557, ten years before he co-published the first printed anthology of English prose fiction. *Songes and Sonettes*, now more usually known as *Tottell's Miscellany*, had been published eleven times by Tottell's death in 1593.[23] As Felix Schelling long ago claimed, Tottell's miscellany served as an obvious model for Gascoigne's *Hundreth Sundrie Flowres*, but his prose story miscellany, the *Palace*, was just as important for Gascoigne's 'Adventures'.[24] Moreover, Tottell's poetry miscellany provided the obvious model for his later prose miscellany. Between them, Tottell's poetry and story miscellanies provided terms in which publishers could situate later literary publications.

These terms were explicitly nationalistic. Tottell's epistle to the poetry-miscellany reader articulates a need to compare the 'workes of divers Latines, Italians, and other' to more contemporary works in 'our tong', an idea repeated throughout the preface, which praises 'the honor of the english tong' and 'several graces in sondry good Englishe writers' (1). This comparison clearly emerges out of an attempt to legitimate poetry miscellanies through a nationalistic reading of classical culture, at a time when 'England's self-image in the earlier sixteenth century as a sovereign realm' was ironically founded upon foreign images of authority.[25] Tottell's interest in the reader's 'profit and pleasure' and the writer's 'statelinesse of stile' (1) anticipates his later prose fiction publication, with its dual emphases on the *Pleasure* to be found in the *Palace*. The immediate reprints of Tottell's poetic miscellany offered an obvious context for bookshop customers who considered buying the first prose story miscellanies. These innovations may have particularly struck Lyly's later publisher, Gabriel Cawood, since his father, John Cawood, had collaborated with Tottell in 1557 to publish the first English edition of Thomas More's writings.[26] Tottell's role in Painter's *Palace* demonstrates how formative the poetic miscellany was as a model for the beginning of English prose fiction in print.

An apparent revision of Painter's working title reveals that the eventual name of the book was the result of careful rethinking. Painter's volume of stories was originally recorded in the Stationers' Register in 1562, four years before its publication, under the title 'The Citye of Cyvelitie'.[27] The published title, *The Palace of Pleasure*, changes the words whilst preserving their alliteration and the relationship between a physical, architectural word against a metaphysical, more abstract term. But these continuities in the rhetorical and conceptual relationship of each word in the title are accompanied by a change in emphasis from the city's communal urbanity to the palace's royal exclusivity, and from civility's moral implications of municipality and social order to the aesthetic, subjective and hedonistic experience of pleasure.[28] As Maslen shows, it also 'suggests that [Painter's] collection combines luxury and ornament with an official function, sanctioned by the ruling classes'.[29]

Following Painter, prose fiction became increasingly identified with pleasure, so that Lyly's *Anatomy* was recommended to book-buyers as 'Very pleasant for all Gentle-men to reade' (title page). These marketing formulae became identified with the literary genre of prose fiction itself. In Richard Brome's *A Mad Couple Well Matched*, performed some time after 1635 and published in 1653, a nurse's reference to a medicine that is 'delectable to the younger sort, and profitable to the old' causes the man she tends to suggest that the medicine is 'One of Robert Greenes workes'.[30] A marketing tag had acquired generic meaning, and, as Lyly's title page shows, Painter's title gave prose fiction an association with pleasure that it never lost, at least in marketing terms.

Whilst the prose fiction genre became associated with pleasure, it is the other word in Painter's new title that informed or reflected the composition and presentation of his writing and the selection of source material for translation. In his prefatory material and within the stories themselves, the palace metaphor serves to flatter Painter's patron, his readers and himself. Thus he defines his translated stories as 'the lives, gestes, conquestes, and highe enterprises of great Princes, wherein also be not forgotten the cruell actes and tiranny of some' (I, 5). *The Palace of Pleasure* therefore literally contains the kinds of people a reader might expect to live inside a palace. Although Tottell's poetry miscellany was simply named in terms of its variety (*Songes and Sonettes*), Tottell's Painter publication managed to emphasise variety in a way that also determined the social ambition and narrative focus of the miscellany.

The title also makes obvious claims for the social import of the book's contents. The title's courtly claims are carefully extended by a dedication which describes Painter's patron as a man 'daily resiant in a Palace of renowmed fame, guided by a Queene adorned with most excellent beautie' (I, 6). The epistle to his general readers tells the story of King Alphonsus who fell ill and was given by Quintus Curtius Rufus a collection of stories about Alexander the Great, reassuring the reader that the kinds of stories they are about to read would make suitable reading material for those at the height of the social order. This collection cured the king and he declared 'the exercise and reading of Histories' to be the 'restitutor and recoverie of my health' (I, 13–14). As we have seen, Lyly would reuse the idea of opening his work with reference to Alexander but with much more radical implications for literature, authorship and its relationship to the Crown.

King Alphonsus, Painter explains, represents his general readership, an analogy which would presumably flatter even the most republican of readers. Since Curtius's stories detail the 'gestes and factes of king Alexander', they accord with the contents of Painter's volume, and thus further the analogy by implying that Curtius represents Painter himself, enclosing the author in the courtly milieu he constructs for his readers (I, 13). The *Palace* title, then, incorporates author, patron and readers within an intensely flattering metaphorical social space, and raises this new literary form, a collection of short Italianate stories in English, to the level of a courtly patronage transaction. The rhetoric of the title, prefatory material and main text constructs the book-buyers' decision to pay for a prose storybook as an elite act of patronage. Successfully or not, English print stories were first sold as part of court culture, and offered a way for those outside the court to access and conceptualise that culture.

The title's architectural and aristocratic emphasis continues to function throughout the book. Painter ensures that his readers do not forget the overall metaphor within which each story is bound. He continues the self-conscious self-presentation of his paratexts into the first story, proposing to his readers that 'As the name of Palace doth carie a port of Majestie as propre for princes and greatest estates [...] So, here at our first entrie [in other words, the first story], I thought to staye as it were at the gate of this palace' (I, 15). Thus title is integrated with contents, author is integrated with narrator, and readers are encouraged to keep the title and author in mind as they progress through the narrative. As we have seen, Cawood and Lyly continued this compositional method with Lyly's reference to himself as an anatomist, and at least one of his readers, Harvey, associated Lyly with his character Euphues.[31] The meta-narrative established around the otherwise disparate stories continues to perform a transformative effect upon the reading experience, so that each story repeats the overall statement of the book that the reader's commercial relationship to the publisher and author is in fact characterised by courtly transaction. This means that Painter's title informed his composition, his publisher's marketing terminology and the reader's interpretative choices in a book that began the English prose storytelling tradition in print. The metaphor of the palace also insisted on the volume's copiousness, defining the book as a miscellany.

It was therefore a defining feature of early prose fiction publications that they were sold in terms of their assortment and diversity. Readers were asked to buy stories, not a story. Thus Painter's book was further promoted to its potential readership through its plurality and variety, written and marketed as a collection of short stories. The architectural vastness implied both by Painter's earlier title 'Citye' and in his published title *Palace* encompassed, according to the title page, 'Pleasaunt Histories and excellent Novelles'. The following year Fenton's translations were marketed in terms of their plurality, as 'CERTAINE TRAGICALL DISCOURSES'. Gascoigne's 'Adventures' was also included as part of an anthology of various literary genres, and therefore it too was marketed in print with a title page that in very few words twice mentions its 'sundrie' contents: 'A HUNDRETH SUNDRIE FLOWRES [...] Yelding sundrie sweete savours'. Wendy Wall shows that the book 'opts to reinforce the manuscript collectivity of the project', presenting itself as a multi-authored collection.[32] Leah Knight observes that the term *Flowres* refers to the horticultural etymology of the word 'anthology' ('flower collection'), thereby associating Gascoigne's book with 'a broader culture of collecting in the period'.[33] In all of these books, a miscellany form is marketed using a title page emphasis upon variety and plurality. No bookshop browser had yet been asked to pay money for a single Elizabethan prose story.

Gascoigne began to break this miscellany tradition from within his own miscellany. Yvonne Rodax summarises the prose fiction culture from which Gascoigne departed in narrative terms, describing Painter's stories as tales of 'action, bloodshed and adventure'.[34] Gascoigne and Lyly are far closer to J. Paul Hunter's definition of the novel's emphasis upon 'the daily, the trivial, the common, and immediate', and, if the novel has been defined in terms of its ability to domesticate politics and politicise the home, then Gascoigne's prose fiction offers to narrate a very familiar form of domesticity and Englishness, domesticating narrative itself.[35] George Chapman hoped that his translations of Homer would 'English' the Greek poet; an effect of Gascoigne's story is to 'English' prose narration.[36] After Gascoigne it became possible for an author to invest time and imagination in a familiar, quotidian and fallible man and his illicit sexual desires.

Gascoigne's work is the key transitional work in this respect. The title of Gascoigne's story itself, 'The Adventures of Master F.J.', was not part of the title page, and therefore served no immediate marketing purpose for the work in print. Since it was part of the book's internal rhetoric rather than a more public representation of the book, Gascoigne's innovation in prose story composition, his redefinition of the reader's experience of narrative, had no direct impact on the image of prose fiction in the print market. The story also represents a departure from previous marketing practice, since the plural adventures of F.J. are unified not by a selective, editorial, translating author (on the model of Painter and Fenton) but by the character F.J. himself. Whereas Painter's, Fenton's and Pettie's readers are expected to read the stories purely on the basis of their collection within a miscellany, Gascoigne's readers are asked to invest their time and imagination in the character and adventures of F.J. This had obvious implications for Lyly and Cawood when they came to name their book *Euphues*. This title refers to its central figure, but prospective readers are not to know this: an initial curiosity about the exotic word is channelled by the title page into an interest in the character's single narrative.

If Gascoigne's story is read as a fictional, 'original' and therefore authored story (as opposed to the 'real' story it purports to be), then it also offers a new model for thinking of storytelling as a series of adventures unified as much by the creative mind of the author as by the fictive world of the protagonist. Unlike Painter and Fenton, Gascoigne's work is not a translation, nor does it collect together a series of stories taken from classical and continental sources. The literary form of the 'Adventures' therefore implicitly makes new claims about authorial originality and the narrator's control over a story. It is within Gascoigne's model that Lyly began to write, in the process transforming something that was part of a miscellany structure in Gascoigne's *Flowres* into something that might replace that structure: a single-story book.

Gascoigne's 'Adventures', in other words, marks a departure from the miscellany story collections previously available and a shift from a compositional and promotional rhetoric that emphasised varied *Discourses* and a capacious *Palace* towards a rhetoric that defined the story in terms of a protagonist's episodic, but linear narrative 'Adventures'. In less than ten years, a prose fiction market had emerged and begun to adapt, and the representative and interpretive function of titles and title pages indicates changes to fiction's compositional form and marketing. But despite Gascoigne's promotion of his prose fiction in manuscript and within his printed anthology as 'Adventures', the book as a whole was sold as part of a market for literary miscellanies: *Hundreth Sundrie Flowres*. With Painter, Fenton, Gascoigne and Pettie, prose fiction was still a miscellaneous literary form. Early readers were offered stories to buy only within larger literary collections.

It is this emphasis that Lyly's first publication transforms. An anatomy arguably suggests a body cut up and divided, and therefore defined by its constituent parts, but unlike the potentially disparate contents of a palace or flowerbed, which might be organised by the author figure alone (the architect or the gardener), an anatomy has an original organisation dictated by the unity of the body itself, not by the anatomist. Lyly's title announces itself as new and innovative, his *Anatomy* the first English literary appropriation of the medical term, and appearing in the same year as 'the earliest English-language anatomy textbook'.[37] The full subtitle, *The Anatomy of Wit*, suggests, in Richard Sugg's words, 'an interest in piercing, isolating, defining, and knowing what was otherwise tantalizingly abstract'.[38]

Anatomy also provides a further way in which the histories of printed prose fiction and the public theatres (including indoor playhouses) were interconnected. William Heckscher has pointed to anatomy theatres as 'important chapters in the historical development of the stage', and Lyly's usage shows that they were also part of the development of the prose fiction book.[39]

Within the prose fiction market, the *Anatomy* is the first book to advertise itself in relation to its narrative unity, rather than variety: 'wherin are conteined the delights that Wit followeth in his youth, by the pleasantnesse of love, and the hap-pinesse he reapeth in age, by the perfectnesse of Wisdome'. No previous work could have been summarised in this manner, since no previous book was organised as a single story. For the same reason, Lyly's *Anatomy* is the first of the books discussed that does not contain a contents page: it doesn't need one. Lyly's compositional structure, borrowed from Gascoigne's 'Adventures', revolutionised the bibliographical and marketing strategies of prose fiction. The long fiction story produced a new kind of book, published in Euphues' – and Lyly's – name. Both names would go on to dominate later writers' prose fictions.

This narrative summary demonstrates a number of things. Firstly, it shows a book being sold, for the first time, with reference to its narrative contents. Painter's *Palace* was sold in relation to its narrative form (histories and novels); Gascoigne's book was sold in relation to its generic diversity (sundry flowers); Lyly's book is sold to book buyers constructed as already interested, already invested in the story. Secondly, it demonstrates that this is a book organised around a single story, a story that comprises the whole of the main text of the book. And these two facts show, thirdly, that Cawood and Lyly were aware of the novelty of their enterprise, and used the book's formal innovation to sell it within and beyond the nascent fiction market. Exploiting the current vogue for anatomical spectacle, using the exotic unfamiliarity of the Greek name Euphues, and promoting the book as a dictionary of wit, Lyly and Cawood made appeals well beyond the established fiction market, whilst its description of a single organising story announced its status as a new kind of fiction publication. In effect, Lyly and Cawood exploited the new market for narrative as a form of order which Painter, in particular, had created, and thereby introduced prose stories to a wider potential readership.

When Tottell and Jones published the *Palace*, Bynneman published the 'Adventures' within the *Flowres*, and Cawood published the *Anatomy*, how were these title pages understood?

What did it mean to claim that a prose fiction book was palatial, adventurous, flowery or anatomical? It is not clear, as D. F. McKenzie shows, who determines these titles and who makes these claims, but they had a precise marketing function, presenting the first two books in terms of their miscellany contents and aligning them in relation to aristocratic (*Palace*) and classical (*Flowres*) culture.[40] Cawood's book, on the other hand, played on the interest generated by Gascoigne's story of F.J. to create an entire book organised around Lyly's story of Euphues. Previous critics have explained Lyly's impact on the prose fiction market in terms of its style, but in order to encounter the style readers had first to be persuaded to buy the book. The title's promise of a single story based around a mysteriously named Greek was one way in which Cawood's book was instantly appealing to his customers. It is only with an awareness of the book's title, its various attractions and the way it sets up the book's reception that we can begin to turn to Lyly's famous but often misunderstood prose style.

Narrative and prose style

As we have seen, Painter opened his first story with a reference to 'the name of Palace', the name giving the book its title and conceptual structure. But the metaphor also admits a particular authorial stance towards his subject matter. 'Here at our first entrie', Painter's narrator explained, 'I thought to staye as it were at the gate of this palace' (I, 15). Painter's relatively simple diction frankly admits the central position of the narrator within his narration: the reader is introduced to a storyteller who relates his 'thought[s]' and purposes, foregrounding the mediation of his story.[41]

Painter's narrating figure is inconsistently prominent in his stories, at one time simply relating events, at another interrupting and interpreting them. At the start of the fifth story of the collection, 'Appius Claudius', the reader is told that

> Spurius Posthumius Albus, Aulus Manlius, and P. Sulpitius Camerinus, were sent Ambassadours to Athenes, and commaunded to wryte out the noble Lawes of Solon, and to learne the Institutions, orders, and Lawes of other Greeke cities. (I, 35)

Here direct narrative statements are made without the obviously mediating presence of a storyteller. Painter carefully organises an opening litany of Latinate names as an impressive start to his story, but does not foreground his own authorship within the narration.

Without this presence, the story is often related with only characters' direct and indirect speech interrupting straightforward and apparently objective narrative statements.

But, as we have seen, Painter's preface had quoted King Alphonsus's opinion that 'the exercise and reading of Histories' was the 'restitutor and recoverie of [. . .] health' (I, 13–14). As part of this moral and medicinal writerly project, Painter's narrative voice frequently intervenes within the reader's experience of the stories to point out their moral purpose. Thus although 'Appius Claudius' begins without an overt narrative agent, it concludes with the narrator distancing himself with horror from 'the filthie affection of one noble man' who exposed his home city 'to be a praye to forren nations' (I, 44–5). Such a story is, the narrator declares in the last sentence:

> A goodlie document to men of like calling, to moderate them selves, and their magisterie with good and honest life, thereby to give incouragement of vertue, to their vassalles and inferiours: who for the most parte doe imitate and followe the lives and conversations of their superiours. (I, 45)

A narration which had begun with classical history ends with reference to the present. Painter's increasingly overt narrator insists on the utility of his story (the 'goodlie document') for England's current ruling elite ('men of like calling'). It asserts the nationalistic function of prose fiction by pointing out the ways a country becomes 'a praye to forren nations', providing another link between Tottel's poetry miscellany, with its interest in 'the honor of the english tong', and the same publisher's volume of Painter's stories.

Painter's narrative voice can be equally overt at the start of a story too. Indeed the very next story begins in direct contrast to the objective, historical tone of 'Appius Claudius', when a rather more opinionated and reactionary narrator moralises the tale of 'Candaulus and Gyges' from its first sentence: 'Of all follies wherewith vayne men be affected, the follie of immoderate love is most to be detested' (I, 46). This moral is continued through to the last sentence of the (very short) story, which claims it to be

> A goodly example to declare, that the secrets of Marriage, ought not to be disclosed: but with reverence to be covered, lest God do plague such offences with death or other shame, to manifest to the world, howe dearely hee esteemeth that honourable state. (I, 48)

Anne Lake Prescott tells us that 'Painter [. . .] thinks his tales – his "histories" – are exemplary. Although he does not quite put it like this', but, on the contrary, Painter puts it exactly like this.[42] His narrator once again concludes with reference to the 'goodly example' of his story, switching his focus from national to domestic regulation. In both stories, Painter insists on the social function of his text. In his preface, he had declared the content of his book to be stories that 'maye render good examples, the best to be followed, and the worst to be avoyded' (I, 5). His choice of material and his editorial role as translator reveals a 'didactic goal' which Constance Relihan finds at the heart of early modern prose fiction, but which Gascoigne and Lyly would go on to trouble.[43] Robert Weimann has described how early modern theatre plays across the two medieval conceptual spaces, the locus (a place for fictional dialogue by distant authority figures) and platea (a place for direct and often disruptive audience address).[44] Gascoigne and Lyly similarly play across Painter's two positions of objective storyteller and didactic sermoniser.

Painter's example is thus important because Gascoigne and Lyly both avoid the moralising position of his narrator. Though Painter at times presented himself simply as the editorial curator and translator of his stories, describing the book as a 'provulgation in our native tongue', his narrational voice routinely intervened to point out the social applicability of his story (I, 4). This is a narrating policy that Gascoigne and then Lyly would carefully eschew; and, although both writers occasionally allow their narrators to dwell on the implications of their narratives, this didactic impulse always occurs within an ironic and polymorphous situation. No privileged narrative statements solve the meaning of the narrative for Gascoigne's or Lyly's readers.

Gascoigne's complex reworking of Painter's narrative style is evident in the fact that his narrator is himself a fictional character. G.T. introduces himself at the start of the work as someone in possession of a series of love poems by F.J. which he has 'reduce[d . . .] into some good order' and contextualised by explaining F.J.'s 'history', the 'occasion' upon which the poems were written, an adulterous love affair between F.J. and Elinor.[45] G.T. is thus narrating a story he claims to be true, whilst at the same time highlighting his distance from the facts: the narrative is advanced as a paradoxically accurate and yet imaginative reconstruction of the story behind the poems. In Gascoigne's fiction, the narrator is also a character, and is at his most overt during the story's key sexual scenes, as when F.J. and Elinor meet in a moonlit gallery:

> But why hold I so long discourse in discribing the joyes which (for lacke of like experience) I cannot set out to the ful? Were it not that I knowe to whom I write, I would the more beware what I write. *F.J.* was a man, and

> neither of us are sencelesse, and therfore I shold slaunder him, (over and besides a greater obloquie to the whole genealogie of *Enaeas*) if I should imagine that of tender hart he would forbeare to expresse hir more tender limbes against the hard floore. (168)

Here the narrator addresses a reader he claims to know (part of the conceit that this is a manuscript text intended for only one person), setting up heterosexual eroticism within an explicitly homosocial narrative transaction that celebrates and privileges the masculine sensual experience. This direct reference to a supposed manuscript reader casts the actual reader of the printed text in a peculiar position, an eavesdropper in Maslen's terms.[46] Where Painter's book was couched in courtly language and explicitly defined as strange, whilst reassuring its readers on its moral stance, Gascoigne constructs an intimate manuscript transmission process, casting his book reader as an Inns of Court student: as Gillian Austen puts it, the book 'impersonated a manuscript miscellany', and, in doing so, it casts its reader into an actorly, fictitious role.[47]

Gascoigne engages with Painter's moral universe but does so from an entirely different perspective. Like Painter, Gascoigne depicts stories of extramarital affairs, but the adulterous and 'immoderate love' that Painter described in order that it might be 'detested' is related by G.T. as 'joyes'. Where Painter's narrative voice was condemnatory, G.T. clearly considers sexual conquest as a vital part of F.J.'s masculinity. Both Painter and G.T. assume that their readers will share their very different moral interpretation of the stories, but in Gascoigne the narrator's perspective itself requires interpretation, a fact that has not been noticed by critics who claim G.T. as a moral arbitrator endorsed by Gascoigne himself.[48] The reader is carefully distanced from the actions in the story by G.T.'s indirect sexual language, his confession of his own sexual naivety and the self-conscious way in which he discusses narrative technique ('why hold I so long discourse') and his reader's supposed identity ('I knowe to whom I write'). The key word in the passage is 'imagine': G.T. admits here that he has no idea what happened in the gallery, but is simply relating what his view of F.J. and his assumptions about masculinity make him 'imagine' took place. The entire scene, then, exposes the distance between the narrating figure and the events he describes. Painter advanced his stories as a 'goodlie document' and 'goodly example'; in Gascoigne, the narrator insists that he tells a true story but nevertheless admits that his narration is an act of imagination. By presenting a botched document, Gascoigne refuses his readers goodly examples.

The celebration of adulterous eroticism by a naive and untrustworthy narrator forces the reader to make moral decisions about the story as it is related, whereas in Painter moral decisions were advanced before the story had been told. The most notorious example of this narrative style occurs when Elinor visits the ailing F.J. in his room. The two lovers had begun their sexual relationship with barely covert references to F.J.'s penis. 'Alas servaunt what have I deserved, that you come against me with naked sword as against an open enimie', Elinor had asked exactly two sentences before they first had sex (168). The violence implicit in the lovers' and narrator's erotic language comes to the fore later in the story, when Elinor asks F. J. why he is sickly. F.J. replies that he suspects that he is not Elinor's only adulterous partner, beginning an argument between the two lovers. The repercussions of that argument require the reader to decode complex, violent and inconsistent sexual metaphors:

> The softe pillowes being present at all these whot [*sic*] wordes, put forth themselves as mediatours for a truce betwene these enemies, and desired that (if they would needes fight) it might be in their presence but onely one pusshe of the pike, and so from thenceforth to become friends again for ever. But the Dame denied flatly, alleadging that shee found no cause at all to use such curtesie unto such a recreant, adding further many wordes of great reproche: the which did so enrage *F.J.* as that having now forgotten all former curtesies, he drewe uppon his new professed enimie, and bare hir up with such a violence against the bolster, that before shee could prepare the warde, he thrust hir through both hands, and etc. wher by the Dame swoning for feare, was constreyned (for a time) to abandon hir body to the enemies curtesie. (198)

G.T. apparently anticipated that readers might be concerned by this scene, for he reassures them that Elinor 'founde hir hurt to be nothing daungerous' and imagines that she 'slept quietly the rest of the night' (198). It has been clear to Gascoigne's modern readers, though apparently not to the narrator G.T., that F.J. rapes Elinor. In his edition of the *Flowres*, Pigman suggests that 'G.T., F.J., and, one imagines, Gascoigne share an insouciance about rape only too common in the period'.[49] But this reading appears to presuppose a naivety on Gascoigne's part which is belied by the sophistication of his story, and even though G.T. emphasises his 'lacke of like [sexual] experience', Gascoigne clearly understood the implications of this passage. Indeed his 1575 revision of the story removed the pillows' suggestion that F.J. gave Elinor 'one pusshe of the pike' together with the narrative information that he 'drewe uppon his new professed enimie', pushed her against the bolster and forced himself upon her. Gascoigne and his readers therefore clearly understood this passage in terms of sexual, gendered and abusive power, and G.T.'s failure to comprehend what he describes is part of Gascoigne's narrative technique. The moral certainties written into Painter's storytelling are questioned in Gascoigne's story.

Salzman has called the 1560s and 1570s an 'early period [...] almost entirely devoted to translation and adaptation', and Gascoigne and Lyly are the figures who adapted and transformed this compositional emphasis, writing original stories organised around an original central figure. Salzman has identified the three narrational levels of the 'Adventures': (1) the literary and epistolary texts created by the characters themselves; (2) the actions performed by the characters; and (3) the act of narration.[50] Gascoigne's use of a narrator who is a character in his own right articulates the dual nature of narrative identified by A. Greimas, describing:

> an *apparent* level of narration [...] and an *immanent* level [...] at which narrativity is situated and organized prior to its manifestations. A common semiotic level is thus distinct from the linguistic level and is logically prior to it, whatever the language chosen for manifestation.[51]

Lyly's first story continued Gascoigne's 1573 disruption of the narrator and his simplistic moral world. As Catherine Bates argues, 'Lyly poses alternately as an arbiter of moral values and as a courtly entertainer specifically (it seems) in order to problematize our moral judgements'.[52] In previous prose fiction, a narrator told a story which occasionally incorporated the direct 'quotation' of his characters' voices. Lyly's *Anatomy*, in contrast, is dominated by his characters' monologues, conversations and epistles to the extent that the narrator rarely makes narrative statements at all. In consequence, comparatively little narrative action takes place during Lyly's first story, although this fact does not justify Hunter's claim that the story is a kind of anti-plot: on the contrary, as Scragg has noted, the *Anatomy* reworks the popular story paradigm of the choice between a woman's love and a man's friendship. But this interest in 'the conventional assumptions of a patriarchal Christian society' is predominantly presented to the reader through the matrix of the characters' speech rather than via a linear narrator, so that narrative, as in Gascoigne's work, is enacted by biased and unreliable characters.[53] Lyly's discursive intrusion into print prose fiction was determined by the multiplicity of his characters' voices, and not by a narrator aligned either with Painter's moral certainties or G.T.'s naive ambiguities.

Lyly's narrational voice is therefore much closer to Gascoigne's

G.T. than to Painter. But whereas G.T. cast his prose storytelling as an intermediary context or gloss to F.J.'s love poems, Lyly's narrator allows his characters to dominate the story from the start. Here, as Walter King suggested, Lyly's compositional mode is crucial to the structure of the story itself: 'Lyly is an innovator. For Lyly is adapting the rhetorical set-piece to narrative purposes.'[54] Lyly's introduction of Euphues at the beginning of the story takes two pages in Scragg's recent edition, but Lyly's many references to the classical and natural world require that the reader's imaginative engagement with the central character should also encompass a huge range of other characters, concepts and stories. Thus over these first two pages the narrator aligns the protagonist with a bewildering array of things in four sections: (1) Nature, Fortune, a rose, velvet and flour; (2) Venus, Helen and Paris, Aristippus, Lycurgus, Alexander, Cicero, Solomon and David; (3) colours, a razor, cloth and cambric; (4) an atheist, Ovid, Aristotle, Paris and Hector, and Flora and Diana (32–3). All of these people and objects are used to define Euphues in the first two pages alone, and demonstrate the way euphuistic allusions challenge a reader's ability to imagine or anticipate a unified and coherent character. The imaginative world of Lyly's story is therefore created within a dazzling matrix of intertextual information, what we might call the matter of euphuism itself, and, far from creating a static and stable world, Lyly's style requires the reader to dance around his many imaginative suggestions.[55] The reader's relationship with the fictive, narrated world depends upon a succession of appeals beyond the fictive world to the shared cultural knowledge of the period. This shared English culture foregrounds the supposed narrative world of Italy and Greece, but perhaps more importantly prevents a reader foregrounding the narrative world of Euphues alone.

As William Ringler shows, Lyly developed the writing techniques usually called euphuism by reworking the famous lecturing style of John Rainolds, whom he had heard in Oxford.[56] This source rooted euphuistic writing in a style associated both with oral delivery and with the comfortingly authoritative world of academia. But this aphoristic style, with its emphasis on *copia* (copiousness) and *exemplae* (multiple sources of authority), militates against the kind of simple narrative statement made in Painter's work. For Barish, Lyly's 'analytic imagination leads to successes of exposition [. . .] but it leaves him helpless to cope with the very different requirements of denouement'.[57] Barish here overlooks the fact that the endings of Lyly's prose fictions make good marketing sense (since they set up potential sequels) and unhelpfully locates euphuistic style within

Lyly's psychology (he is 'helpless'), but he does give an insight into the relationship of euphuistic expression to exposition.

Thus the narrator tells us that Euphues is 'of more wit than wealth, and yet of more wealth than wisdom', that Naples is 'of more pleasure than profit, and yet of more profit than piety', and that Lucilla is 'more fair than fortunate, and yet more fortunate than faithful', and in so doing he tells us more about the narration's discursive universe than he does about the characters and setting being narrated (32–3). These details help to determine the terms of narration rather than a narrated mimetic world imaginatively set out for the reader or listener. Lyly's parisonal syntax in these sentences makes clear that this is a work that sketches out words in order to demonstrate their contingency, not to determine or draw upon their fixed meanings: on the contrary, the syntax unfixes their meaning. Rather than describing Naples in physical terms, for example, the narrator sets up terminological hierarchies between pleasure, profit and piety that challenge the reader's sense of those words' meanings. They are posed, postulated and juxtaposed in a way that calls their contingent meanings into question.

The stylistic self-consciousness evident in Lyly's writing sets him apart from G.T., who at times affects a diction associated with improvised, oral delivery. Thus after F.J.'s and Elinor's first sexual encounter, G.T. explains that they were forced to part by the onset of morning: 'Wel, remedie was there none' (168). Two sentences later, F.J. reached the door of his room: 'Wel, *F.J.* having now recovered his chamber, he went to bedde' (168). The colloquial use of 'Wel' suggests the narrator's excitement with his material, as does his reference to F.J.'s rape of Elinor when 'he thrust hir through both hands, and etc.' (198). G.T.'s gossiping mode reinforces his claim that he is telling a true and controversial story, an imaginative reconstruction of a real event that has an emotive (and therefore mimetic) effect on the narrator. These offhand, apparently spontaneous words seem to be the equivalent of giving a narrative shrug.

Lyly's narrator, in contrast, rarely betrays an emotional relationship to his material. At the end of his sequel, *Euphues and His England*, he declares himself 'indifferent' to his characters' future fate. This supposed objectivity, however, does not preclude the narrator from suggesting that he is thoroughly convinced of the existence of his characters:

> For if I should meddle any further with the marriage of Philautus it might haply make him jealous, if with the melancholy of Euphues it might cause him to be choleric; so the one would take occasion to rub his head, sit his

> hat never so close, and the other offence to gall his heart, be his case never so quiet. (353)

The clausal control and self-conscious references typical of Lyly's style should not therefore be taken as a sign of lack of interest in the imaginative world of his stories; they are simply new ways for an author and his readers to relate to that narrated world. Storytelling is once again figured as a discursive intrusion, this time into the sexual lives and psychological humours of his characters, something we will see Lyly continuing in his plays. In contrast to G.T.'s sexual naivety, Lyly's narrator conceives of his male identity as potentially threatening to Philautus. He is himself part of the world he narrates. Hunter's description of Lyly's 'anatomical' narrative technique, a lack of interest in cause and effect, may have been intended as a helpful preparation for a modern reader expecting the narrative experience of a novel, but it misrepresented Lyly's storytelling, which would engage and excite his readers and his emulators until the last early modern reprint of his work in 1636.

Prose fiction miscellanies and the first storybook

Lyly's narrator is able to relate to his characters in this way because he has told their story across the space of two storybooks. This was Lyly's greatest innovation in his discursive intrusion into Tudor print storytelling, an intervention that transformed the market for such books. Previous storytelling volumes had anthologised a series of short stories. Lyly and his publisher Cawood intervened in this tradition by publishing England's first lengthy prose story, a story which comprised and publicised the whole of the book's contents (though, as we shall see in Chapter 2, the second half of the book is less a conventional narrative than a compendium of letters, tracts and dialogues produced by the fictional characters themselves). It is on the basis of a single-story book that Lyly's book was sold and bought, and, as the next chapter demonstrates, it is this new, Lylian form that would dominate prose fiction in the following decade and beyond. Claire Squires defines modern marketing as '*a form of representation and interpretation* [...] surrounding the production, dissemination and reception of texts' which involves '*multiple agencies* operating within the marketplace', agencies such as the reader, the publisher and the writer. Such marketing is 'a reactive and proactive process, one that begins with an assessment of perceived desires and moves on to a production and promotion of products that try to fulfil them'.[58]

For Squires, marketing represents '*the making of contemporary literature*' and is 'the creator of the literary marketplace'.[59] Such markets make literature at every level, as writers, publishers and book-buyers make decisions that are both reactive and inventive. This modern model is extremely useful for early modern scholars: Paul Voss has shown that 'sophisticated forms of advertising, [...] closely related to the modern notion of marketing and persuading, were developed in Elizabethan England'. Elizabethan publishers were equally reactive and proactive, as Voss shows:

> If an important change in consumers' habits materialized (such as fashionable book browsing), the printing press, acting in Eisenstein's phrase as 'an agent of change', could effectively respond to the situation. [...] The rise of advertising contributed to new methods of writing, printing, and promoting books, allowing the literate Elizabethan unprecedented opportunities in acquiring new knowledge.[60]

Early modern circumstances of literary composition, publication, marketing and reading were far less developed and bureaucratic than the term 'marketing' suggests, to the extent that terms such as 'marketing' and 'market' should be used with care.[61] But a publisher's decision to print a particular work, based in most cases upon their own reading of the manuscript, represents a proactive estimation of customer demand. To adapt Spivak's description of the author as 'a reader at the performance of writing', the publisher is reader at the point of manuscript purchase, print production and prospective marketing. Thus Tottell and Jones's decision to publish a collection of prose stories, Painter's *Palace of Pleasure*, and Cawood's decision to publish a book containing only a single story, Lyly's *Anatomy*, both constitute publisher innovation, the initiative to test out a market with a new bibliographical form. Certain publications, meanwhile, represent reactive versions of the same estimation, obvious examples being Pettie's *Petite Palace of Pettie his Pleasure* and the later *Euphues* books. The titles of these books rework and quote earlier publications whose reprints had demonstrated current and potentially continuing customer demand. And these marketing techniques became constitutive of Elizabethan literature in the manner Squires suggests, as marketing terms – most obviously *Palace*, *Anatomy* and *Euphues* – became compositional terms, organising the ways writers write and readers read.

These title pages do not just simply appear on the front of books. Extra copies were posted around London, so that the early modern title page was also a form of advertising poster.[62] Ronald McKerrow explains that title pages are 'an explanatory label affixed to the book by the printer or publisher', but their use beyond the book and around the city created 'an immediate advertising network', in Voss's words, and printers often reserved and set aside the type for title pages to facilitate the printing of additional copies should further promotion be deemed necessary.[63]

Shifts in book titles, then, witness shifts not only in marketing by stationers but in the ways writers and readers thought about books: they had compositional and receptive consequences. They record, and indeed helped to determine, changes in the ways readers, writers and marketing agents experienced printed prose storytelling. It is important to stress how profoundly these shifts affected compositional opportunities and decisions. Up until 1578, story miscellanies were the dominant kind of storytelling publication: Painter's *Palace* (1566, 1567), Fenton's *Discourses* (1567), Pettie's *Palace* (1576). From 1578, publications tended to mimic Lyly's new literary form, the single-story book: Lyly's *Euphues and His England* (1580), Anthony Munday's *Zelauto* (1580), Barnabe Riche's *Don Simonides* (1581, 1584), Greene's *Mamillia* (1583), and so on. The obvious exception, Riche's *Riche His Farewell to the Military Profession*, published in 1581, had already been written by July 1579, as this marketing shift was taking place.[64]

Some later books, such as Greene's *Planetomachia*, *Euphues His Censure to Philautus* and *Perimedes*, include a series of stories framed by an overarching story, and therefore house a miscellany structure reminiscent of Painter and Pettie within a structure associated with Lyly: a single story. Both Painter and Pettie would be republished in the 1580s. But from December 1578 the dominant form of fiction was the single-story book and these exceptions – a miscellany structure within a single story – only serve to demonstrate how pervasive the single-story book had become. With Lyly's *Anatomy*, then, everything changed, and it changed because of a shift in book title, story structure and economic success.

Gascoigne's focus on 'The Adventures of Master F.J.' demanded that his readers should invest interest in the central character, and the effect of this narrative demand was that the prose fiction became the most controversial part of the miscellany, as is evident from its extensive 1575 revision. In the *Anatomy* and again in *Euphues and His England*, Lyly made exactly the same demands of his readers. A final point to make about Gascoigne's title 'Adventures' is that it does not correspond with G.T.'s definition of the story. He proposes to link a sequence of poems with an explanation of 'the very proper occasion whereuppon it was written' (145). Where the title prioritises

F.J., G.T. prioritises the poems, and the story he tries to tell is merely intended to explain and contextualise these poems. Gascoigne's prose story therefore fits in amongst elements of a poetry miscellany: it is a fragmented, dispersed and parasitic narrative that supplements the otherwise generalised emotions associated with poems written for a commonplacing culture. And this narrative structure – a story told amongst poems – mirrors the place of F.J.'s 'Adventures' within the *Hundreth Sundrie Flowres*, a prose fiction within a poetry miscellany. The prose fiction's composition therefore repeats the bibliographical structure within which it came to be printed.

New bibliographical forms entailed new ways to think about books. Where earlier writers such as Painter constructed their readers as patrons engaged in an act of exchange, the experience of reading *Flowres* positioned the reader as a voyeur in somebody else's manuscript commonplace book. In his preface to gentlemen readers, by contrast, Lyly emphasised the book they were reading as one that might start 'on the stationer's stall' and would one day 'be broken in the haberdasher's shop' (30). In other words Lyly referred to the book as a book, an ephemeral and commercial object subject to the vagaries of fashion. For Gascoigne, meanwhile, his fiction was only a small part of a wider range of authorial modes and practices. The story of F.J. routinely teases the reader that the fiction is supposed to be a secret and has been published against the author's will, a strategy Pettie repeats in the *Petite Palace*. Gascoigne's wider authorial games in his anthology were developed within the fiction itself to create a set of disparate and fictionalised authorial personae. Whereas Painter occasionally intervenes to interpret his stories, Gascoigne's narration is already, by definition, an act of interpretation, since the prose storytelling is intended to explain and interpret the poems it contextualises. Since Gascoigne's narrator is himself so unreliable, moreover, the author forces his readers into an interpretative and sceptical position, demanding a reading technique at odds with the compliance expected by Painter's stories.

Gascoigne's biggest contribution to prose fiction, however, was the use of a single character at the centre of an extended, lengthy story. With his opaque, withholding and half-formed personality and his botched amorous intentions, F.J. is an obvious forerunner for Lyly's two characters, Euphues and Philautus. Salzman claims that Gascoigne's story exposes F.J. as a man 'far too fixed in his conception of himself, and of the role he desires to play (or at least be seen to play)', a claim that has important consequences for the next chapter's study of Lyly's character.[65]

Squires's claim that markets make literature is borne out by the extent to which book titles determined book composition. In these books, title-page metaphor is not confined to the title page alone. Painter repeatedly refers to his work as a palace, in the prefatory material of his first volume, at the start of his first story and again in the preface to his second volume. His promise that 'This boke is a very Court and Palace for al sortes to fixe their eies therein' demonstrates the courtly ambition of the miscellany author and his *Palace* (II, 157). Gascoigne's title-page language of *Flowres* was adapted in the work's revised reprint, *The Posies*, and the flower metaphor was employed again in this second version's contents, divided into 'Flowers', 'Herbs' and 'Weeds'. Lyly, meanwhile, casts himself as the anatomist of his *Anatomy*, comparing himself to a 'surgeon that maketh the anatomy', and 'him that [...] goeth about to make the Anatomy of Wit' (28). Title-page rhetoric therefore reflects both the marketing strategies of the book and the compositional procedures of the text, and is capable of organising the writing and projecting the reading of the whole work.

These title pages also register the increasing importance of a story's author, as Gascoigne's anonymous *Flowres* (1573) became *The Posies of George Gascoigne* (1575), and Painter's *Palace* (1566–67) became Pettie's *The Petite Palace of Pettie his Pleasure* (1576). By the 1580s, Gascoigne's miscellany had become *The Whole woorkes of George Gascoigne Esquyre*. In Evelyn Tribble's terms, these changes in title mark a transition from a medieval 'residual conception of authority' which was 'at odds with emergent market forces that begin to shape reading and writing'.[66] The imbrication of author and title in the three years before the publication of Lyly's work demonstrates readers' increasingly open attitudes to fiction books and their ever more visible authors. To put it another way, it demonstrates the extent to which marketing strategies had transformed the status of authors and readers within the nascent market for printed prose stories.

Conclusion

This chapter has asked basic questions of late Tudor prose fiction: what's a character, what's a story, and how do they exist within prose style and in relation to certain book titles? The single-story book is of course so fundamental to modern culture that it is difficult to appreciate how unusual Lyly's *Anatomy* was. In effect, his innovation has become invisible precisely because it was so influential.

But the single-story book enabled prose fiction to be written, marketed and sold in a smaller, and therefore cheaper, bibliographical form. In the *Anatomy* Lyly developed existing traditions within the print market to tell a story, and he drew especially on Gascoigne in focusing that story on the exploits of a single young man. But he broke from previous tradition by sustaining that story across the space of a single book, and he and his publisher then marketed that book in terms of its single story. Lyly's style revolutionised a narrator's relationship with the story, by destroying easy access to Painter's moralistic platitudes and developing the complex narrative strategies worked out by Gascoigne and his narrator who purported to 'imagine' events which he also insisted were based on fact. Lyly's compositional style gave far more space to his characters' voices than it did to his narrator, but the narrator was nevertheless implicated in the stories he told, casting himself, for example, as a potential rival to Philautus's happy marriage. Lyly therefore created the first major storybook, using an elusive and allusive style that nevertheless promised an extensive and imaginative fictional world.

Raven has recently emphasised the continuity of manuscript publication centuries after the introduction of print, claiming that 'The fundamental change' introduced by print was that 'Booksellers advanced marketing and extended the market'.[67] By reworking an existing and emergent market for printed prose fiction, Lyly and Cawood significantly extended the potential readership for English stories. The words *Anatomy* and *Euphues* became meaningful everyday terms, and would be increasingly reused as labels to market new books. As the next chapter demonstrates, the *Anatomy* and the names of its protagonist and its author had extensive consequences for late Elizabethan literary publishing. Lyly and Cawood had created new ways for readers, publishers and writers to think about storytelling.

Notes

1 Hunter and Bevington, *Campaspe: Sappho and Phao*, 18.
2 Hunter and Bevington, *Campaspe: Sappho and Phao*, 21; Peter Saccio, *The Court Comedies of John Lyly: A Study in Allegorical Dramaturgy* (Princeton: Princeton University Press, 1969), 31.
3 Devon L. Hodges, *Renaissance Fictions of Anatomy* (Amherst: University of Massachusetts Press, 1985), 2; Jonathan Sawday, *The Body Emblazoned: Dissection and the Human Body in Renaissance Culture* (London: Routledge, 1995), viii–ix.
4 Michael R. Best, 'Lyly's static drama', *Renaissance Drama* n.s. 1 (1968), 75–86.

5 For a discussion of this scene, see Scragg, *Metamorphosis*, 15–16.
6 On this topic more generally, see Helen Smith and Louise Wilson (eds), *Renaissance Paratexts* (Cambridge: Cambridge University Press, 2011).
7 William Shakespeare, *Henry V*, in Bate and Rasmussen, *The Complete Works*, V.0.3–6; George Peele, *The Love of King David and Fair Bethsabe* (London, 1599), G4v.
8 Mentz, *Romance for Sale*, 140.
9 Katharine Wilson, *Fictions of Authorship in Late Elizabethan Narratives: Euphues in Arcadia* (Oxford: Oxford University Press, 2006), 52.
10 Scragg, *Euphues*, 2.
11 Hunter, *Humanist as Courtier*, 72; Leah Guenther, '"To parley euphuism": fashioning English as a linguistic fad', *Renaissance Studies* 16:1 (March 2002), 24–35 (25–6).
12 Paul Salzman, *English Prose Fiction 1558–1700: A Critical History* (Oxford: Clarendon Press, 1985), 35 and 46–7.
13 Paul Salzman, 'Placing Tudor fiction', *Yearbook of English Studies* 38:1–2 (2008), 136–49 (148).
14 Ernest A. Baker, *The History of the English Novel*, 10 vols (London: Witherby, 1924–39), II, 11; William Lyon Phelps, *The Advance of the Novel in English* (New York: Dodd and Mead, 1916), 30.
15 See Alexandra Halasz, *The Marketplace of Print: Pamphlets and the Public Sphere in Early Modern England* (Cambridge: Cambridge University Press, 1997); Joad Raymond, *Pamphlets and Pamphleteering in Early Modern Britain* (Cambridge: Cambridge University Press, 2003).
16 Mary Augusta Scott, *Elizabethan Translations from the Italian* (Cambridge, MA: Harvard University Press, 1916), xl.
17 William Baldwin, *Beware the Cat: The First English Novel*, ed. William A. Ringler and Michael Flachmann (San Marino: Huntington Library, 1988), xxvi; compare Ringler, '*Beware the Cat* and the beginnings of English fiction', *Novel* 12 (1979), 113–26.
18 Compare Terence N. Bowers, 'The production and communication of knowledge in William Baldwin's *Beware the Cat*: toward a typographic culture', *Criticism* 33 (1991), 1–29.
19 James Raven, *The Business of Books: Booksellers and the English Book Trade 1450–1850* (London: Yale University Press, 2007), 47–8.
20 Robert W. Maslen, *Elizabethan Fictions: Espionage, Counter-Espionage and the Duplicity of Fiction in Early Elizabethan Prose Narratives* (Oxford: Clarendon Press, 1997), 90.
21 Raven, *Business of Books*, 42.
22 Sonia Massai, *Shakespeare and the Rise of the Editor* (Cambridge: Cambridge University Press, 2007), 201; Alan B. Farmer and Zachary Lesser, 'Vile arts: the marketing of English printed drama, 1512–1660', *Research Opportunities in Renaissance Drama* 39 (2000), 77–165 (78–9).
23 Richard Tottell, '*Songes and Sonettes*': *The Elizabethan Version*, ed. Paul A. Marquis (Tempe: Arizona Center for Medieval and Renaissance Studies, in conjunction with Renaissance English Text Society, 2007), xv–xvi.

24 Felix E. Schelling, *The Life and Writings of George Gascoigne With Three Poems Heretofore Not Reprinted* (1893; New York: Russell & Russell, 1967), 28.
25 Stewart Mottram, '"An empire of itself": Arthur as icon of an English empire, 1509–1547', in Elizabeth Archibald and David F. Johnson (eds), *Arthurian Literature 25* (Cambridge: D. S. Brewer, 2008), 154.
26 Anna Greening, 'Tottell, Richard', *Oxford Dictionary of National Biography* (Oxford: Oxford University Press, 2004) (www.oxforddnb.com, accessed 23.10.12).
27 William Painter, *The Palace of Pleasure*, ed. Joseph Jacobs, 3 vols. (London: David Nutt, 1890), I, xxxvi.
28 Jennifer Richards (ed.), *Early Modern Civil Discourses* (Basingstoke: Palgrave Macmillan, 2003), 1–9.
29 Maslen, *Elizabethan Fictions,* 87.
30 *A Critical Old-Spelling Edition of Richard Brome's 'A Mad Couple Well Match'd'* (1653), ed. Steen H. Spove (London: Garland Publishing, 1979), II.ii.147–9. I am grateful to Eleanor Lowe for bringing this reference to my attention.
31 For example, *Gabriel Harvey,* I, 189.
32 Wendy Wall, *The Imprint of Gender: Authorship and Publication in the English Renaissance* (Ithaca: Cornell University Press, 1993), 244.
33 Leah Knight, *Of Books and Botany in Early Modern England: Sixteenth-Century Plants and Print Culture* (Farnham: Ashgate, 2009), 4.
34 Yvonne Rodax, *The Real and the Ideal in the Novella* (Chapel Hill: University of North Carolina Press, 1968), 96.
35 J. Paul Hunter, *Before Novels: The Cultural Contexts of Eighteenth-Century English Fiction* (New York: Norton, 1990), 169–70.
36 *The Poems of George Chapman*, ed. Phyllis Brooks Bartlett (1941; New York: Russell & Russell, 1962), 175.
37 Jonathan Gil Harris, *Foreign Bodies and the Body Politic: Discourses of Social Pathology in Early Modern England* (Cambridge: Cambridge University Press, 1998), 20.
38 Richard Sugg, *Murder After Death: Literature and Anatomy in Early Modern England* (London: Cornell University Press, 2007), 206.
39 William Heckscher, *Rembrandt's Anatomy of Dr Nicholaas Tulp* (New York: New York University Press, 1958), 28.
40 D. F. McKenzie, *Making Meaning: 'Printers of the Mind' and Other Essays*, ed. Peter D. McDonald and Michael F. Suarez, S.J. (Amherst: University of Massachusetts Press, 2002), 251.
41 Mieke Bal, *Narratology: Introduction to the Theory of Narrative*, 2nd ed. (1985; Toronto: University of Toronto Press, 1997), 19–30.
42 Anne Lake Prescott, 'Making the Heptaméron English', in James M. Dutcher and Anne Lake Prescott (eds), *Renaissance Historicisms: Essays in Honor of Arthur F. Kinney* (Newark: University of Delaware Press, 2008), 73.
43 Constance C. Relihan, '"Dissordinate desire" and the construction of geographic otherness in the early modern novella', in Constance C. Relihan and Goran V. Stanivukovic (eds), *Prose Fiction and Early Modern Sexualities in England, 1570–1640* (Basingstoke: Palgrave Macmillan, 2004), 43.

44 Robert Weimann, *Shakespeare and the Popular Tradition in the Theater: Studies in the Social Dimension of Dramatic Form and Tradition*, ed. Robert Schwartz (London: Johns Hopkins University Press, 1978), 80–1.
45 George Gascoigne, *A Hundreth Sundrie Flowres*, ed. G. W. Pigman III (Oxford: Clarendon Press, 2000), 144–5.
46 Maslen, *Elizabethan Fictions*, 138.
47 Gillian Austen, *George Gascoigne* (Cambridge: D. S. Brewer, 2008), 69.
48 See, for example, Charles W. Smith, 'Structural and thematic unity in Gascoigne's *The Adventures of Master F.J.*', *Papers on Language and Literature* 2 (1966), 99–108; Lynette McGrath, 'Gascoigne's moral satire: the didactic use of convention in *The adventures passed by Master F.J.*', *JEGP* 70 (1971), 432–50.
49 Gascoigne, *Hundreth Sundrie Flowres*, 591.
50 Salzman, *English Prose Fiction*, 7 and 26.
51 Greimas, 'Éléments d'une grammaire narrative', quoted in and translated by Shlomith Rimmon-Kenan, *Narrative Fiction* (London: Methuen, 1983), 7.
52 Catherine Bates, *The Rhetoric of Courtship in Elizabethan Language and Literature* (Cambridge: Cambridge University Press, 1992), 95–6.
53 Scragg, *Euphues*, 7.
54 W. N. King, 'John Lyly and Elizabethan rhetoric', *SP* 522 (April 1955), 149–61 (161).
55 Compare W. S. Howell, *Logic and Rhetoric in England 1500–1700* (1956; New York: Russell & Russell, 1961), 24.
56 Ringler, 'The immediate source of Euphuism'.
57 Barish, 'Prose style', 34.
58 Claire Squires, *Marketing Literature: The Making of Contemporary Writing in Britain* (Basingstoke: Palgrave Macmillan, 2007), 3 (her emphasis).
59 Squires, *Marketing Literature*, 51 (her emphasis).
60 Paul J. Voss, 'Books for sale: advertising and patronage in late Elizabethan England', *Sixteenth Century Journal* 29 (1998), 733–56 (736 and 755–6), referring to Elizabeth Eisenstein, *The Printing Press as an Agent of Change: Communications and Cultural Transformations in Early Modern Europe*, 2 vols (Cambridge: Cambridge University Press, 1979).
61 David Harris Sacks, 'London's dominion: the metropolis, the market economy, and the state', in Lena Cowen Orlin (ed.), *Material London, ca. 1600* (Philadelphia: University of Pennsylvania Press, 2000), 21–2.
62 Zachary Lesser, 'Typographic nostalgia: popularity and the meanings of black letter', in Michael Denbo (ed.), *New Ways of Looking at Old Texts, IV: Papers of the Renaissance English Text Society 2002–2006* (Tempe: Arizona Center for Medieval and Renaissance Studies, in conjunction with Renaissance English Text Society, 2008), 284; Michael Saenger, *The Commodification of Textual Engagements in the English Renaissance* (Aldershot: Ashgate, 2006), 38.
63 McKerrow, *Introduction to Bibliography*, 91; Voss, 'Books for sale', 737.
64 Willy Maley, 'Riche, Barnabe', *Oxford Dictionary of National*

Biography (Oxford: Oxford University Press, 2004) (www.oxforddnb.com, accessed 23.10.12).

65 Salzman, *English Prose Fiction,* 34.

66 Evelyn B. Tribble, *Margins and Marginality: The Printed Page in Early Modern England* (Charlottesville: University Press of Virginia, 1993), 2.

67 Raven, *Business of Books*, 10.

CHAPTER 2

Euph culture: Lyly, Euphues and the market for single-story books (1578–94)

In 1588, ten years after Lyly's first book had been published, Robert Greene's prose fiction *Alcida: Greenes metamorphosis* appeared. As the latest version of the model of prose fiction innovated by Lyly and his publisher Cawood, *Alcida* makes numerous references to the tradition of which it formed a part. Its prose is heavily euphuistic, its story follows Greene's practice of privileging the female viewpoint and Lyly's practice of allowing soliloquy and dialogue to dominate narrative statement. Most obviously, it is a single-story book, following directly on from Lyly's *Anatomy*. Its prefatory material makes an appeal to Lyly's work with its references to 'the Anatomy of womens affections' and 'A cooling card', the name Lyly's Euphues gave to one of his compositions.[1] Eight years after Lyly had stopped writing his own prose fiction, he was still inspiring and promoting the fiction of others.

Lyly's importance to new work is made most obvious by an anonymous prefatory poem which constructs an authorial tradition giving rise to Lyly and Greene. Here Lyly is the climax to a list of English landmarks, beginning with the poets Chaucer, Gower and Lydgate, continued by the prose writers Ascham, Cheke and Gascoigne, and ending in Lyly and his disciple Greene:

> & alter
> Tullius Anglorum nunc vivens Lillius, illum
> Consequitur Grenus, praeclarus uterque Poeta.
> [and now Lyly lives, another, English Cicero, and Greene follows him, both men famous poets] (13, my translation)

Since Gascoigne was eligible to be included in the list of poets as well as prose writers, this poem offers particularly clear evidence for the argument, advanced in the previous chapter, of his visible importance in new developments in prose fiction. But most importantly here, ten years after the publication of the *Anatomy*, Lyly was 'praeclarus', pre-eminently famous, and had demonstrated that the English language could rival that of the greatest Latin orators. He had already attained the place allotted to him by Jonson's 1623 reference to 'our Lyly' and Blount's 1632 description of England's debt. By the late 1580s the dominance of the single-story book form which Cawood and Lyly had introduced was now obvious, and the claim that Greene followed Lyly was made within a book, Greene's *Alcida*, that had been created in Lyly's model.

Lyly and Cawood's bibliographical innovations have not been appreciated by modern scholars. Lyly's impact on the print market has been consistently downplayed within a critical discourse that continues to view – often unwittingly – the early modern period from a post-Shakespearean position. Our view is necessarily, of course, post-Shakespearean in a historical sense, but the ideological implications of our unhistoricised perception of early modern culture via Shakespeare have not been appreciated by scholars working with Lyly. Following the rise of bardolatry from at least the eighteenth century onwards, Shakespeare's contemporaries were forced into redistribution around him, with the result that Lyly became conceptually confined to the 1580s, as if to make way for what could then be defined as the first Shakespearean decade.

The reductive scope that this redistribution entailed is especially clear in the spatial terms with which John Dover Wilson described Lyly's canonical position in 1905. In the first monograph devoted to Lyly's works, the writer was depicted standing 'upon the threshold of modern English literature and at the very entrance to its splendid Elizabethan ante-room'.[2] Dover Wilson's language helps to explain the otherwise rather enigmatic preface to R. Warwick Bond's *Complete Works* (1902), 'Sad patience that waiteth at the doore'. Throughout Dover Wilson's book, Lyly's position on the 'threshold' and the imagery of the 'silver light of his little moon' are deployed to show that he was soon eclipsed by 'Shakespeare, the sun of our drama'. Dover Wilson enunciated the conceptualisation of Lyly 'at the very entrance to' the 'ante-room' of Elizabethan literature, spatially and temporally before 'the midday sun' of Shakespeare's glory, of which Lyly had 'no conception'.[3] These descriptions demonstrate the discursive conditions in which Lyly was discussed at the turn of the century: Lyly is quite literally boxed in by Shakespeare's overwhelming and inevitable presence. We are very far here from the *Alcida* poem in which 'now Lyly lives'.

As we have already seen, Hunter gave this idea its most authoritative and often-cited expression. Hunter's impact can be seen in the most interesting recent work on Lyly. Guenther and Wilson both cite Hunter in support of their belief that Lyly fell from grace. For Guenther, Lyly's work was 'a linguistic fad' inciting a 'Euphuistic frenzy', its 'initial colossal triumph' followed by '*Euphues*'s fall from favour'.[4] Wilson equally relies upon Hunter's work when she claims of 'Lyly's bestselling stories about Euphues' that 'by the end of the 1580s, *Euphues* (1578) was looking a little tired'.[5] Leah Scragg was the first to challenge Hunter and Bond in this regard, and thereby made the current book possible, but she nevertheless cites Hunter to argue that 'the euphuistic mode itself, moreover, ceased to be fashionable by the turn of the century', 'finding a new readership among the middle classes, rather than the intelligentsia and cultural elite towards whom they were initially directed'.[6] Whilst these writers disagree about the timing of Lyly's 'fall', fatigue or lack of fashion, Guenther and Wilson follow Hunter in tracing it to the late 1580s. This idea requires reconsideration. As Scragg argues, 'The dawning of the last decade of the sixteenth century [...] did not witness the abrupt collapse of Lyly's standing following a seismic shift in literary tastes'.[7] On the contrary, and as the prefatory poem to *Alcida* makes clear, the longevity of Lyly's appeal and influence was becoming clear to contemporary commentators, writers, publishers and readers only towards the end of the 1580s.

The continued description of Lyly's career in terms of initial success and imminent failure or lack of fashion is legitimised for all three writers by reference to Hunter's work, demonstrating his continued – and unchallenged – influence over current scholarship. And indeed the neat expressions that Hunter employed to summarise his paradigm of Lyly's sudden success and equally sudden failure (if that is the right word) can be seen to influence the way modern critics express their versions of the Hunter paradigm: compare Hunter's claim that 'Lyly's very success [...] was the source of his undoing' with Guenther's observation that 'during the last two decades of the sixteenth century' euphuism 'reached both its apex and its nadir'.[8] For both critics, what goes up must come down, especially if it encounters Shakespeare on the way up.

These claims that Lyly 'fell from favour', 'ceased to be fashionable' or became 'a little tired' are all made despite continued and even increasing levels of reprints, and we therefore need to ask for whom these scholars are speaking. Lyly was not forgotten after 1590 or 1600: even a conservative count of his publications show that sixteen editions of his prose fiction and ten editions of his plays were published between 1590 and 1636.[9] What Hunter identifies as a fall from favour rests on what he perceives to be a fall from elite favour, as Lyly's work increasingly reached a wide and more popular readership, though there is evidence that this popularity managed to be 'popular' *and* elite at the same time.[10] Certainly, the assumption that Lyly's later readers were less elite than his initial audience appears to underpin Hunter's claim, made in *The Spenser Encyclopedia*, that Lyly 'had to descend into the marketplace, play the buffoon, and ended by despising himself for having done so'.[11]

Despite Hunter's insistence on the 1580s-bound nature of Lyly's 'success', the majority of Lyly's plays were published in the 1590s, not the 1580s, as a direct result of the cultural import and impact of his authorship. In 1601, long after Hunter claims Lyly's name had lost its fame, the publisher William Wood expected to find customers for *Love's Metamorphosis*, which contains all the rhetorical tropes associated with euphuism, and he made sure to advertise Lyly's authorship on the title page, as William Jones had done with *Woman in the Moon* in 1597. These publications coincide with a famous use of Lyly by Shakespeare, when Falstaff uses Lyly's work to sound like Henry IV. Hunter and many others have read this moment as an example of parody, and thus as evidence of Lyly's fall from favour: indeed, Hunter twice describes this moment as 'the famous parody of Euphuism with which Falstaff amuses Hal and posterity'.[12] All modern editions of the play agree with Hunter, canonising this moment as Shakespeare's rejection of Lyly's model. In Bevington's edition of the play, he confirms that Falstaff parodies Lyly's 'affectation': 'Lyly's mannerisms were fashionable in the 1580s, but were becoming outdated by 1597'.[13]

But in performance, for this audience member at least, the obvious target of Falstaff's impersonation has been the monarch, and this moment in fact confirms that in the late 1590s the court continued to imitate Lyly's prose. This in turn endorses Blount's claim that the cadences and content of that prose became a common mode of speaking at court. If anything, this moment in *1 Henry IV* seems aimed at Elizabeth and her courtiers, not at Lyly; it parodies authority rather than authorship. In his impersonation of the king, Falstaff also paraphrases Sidney and Pettie, but no scholar has claimed this moment as a parody of those writers: as Chapter 5 suggests, there may be something uniquely threatening about the idea of Lyly's influence over Shakespeare. Jonson's *Every Man Out of His Humour* also provides confirmation of Lyly's continuing influence, this time over a much wider audience: the characters discuss 'as pure a phrase and [...] as choice figures [...] as be i' the *Arcadia*' and 'in Greene's works', whilst the 'proud mincing peat' Fallace (as Jonson describes her in his character sketch) quotes *Euphues and His England* to Master Brisk.[14] Once again, the satire appears to be directed at those who thoughtlessly repeat what they have read, inept commonplacers, rather than at Sidney, Greene or Lyly.

Lyly's plays were never part of a continued repertory system, but his work continued to be reworked and discussed right up until the Civil War, and his prose fiction continued to be reprinted at regular intervals until 1636. When Jonson named Lyly in the prefatory poem to Shakespeare's First Folio, Lyly was the only contemporary dramatist in the poem whose plays had not recently been in repertory (though Peter Blayney reminds us that Shakespeare himself had almost disappeared from the repertory by the time his collection was published).[15] But Jonson still assumed his readers' still-current knowledge of Lyly as playwright. Similarly, though Blount describes Lyly's plays in 1632 as forgotten masterpieces, he still casually refers to *Euphues and His England* in the full knowledge that his readers will recognise a literary triumph still in print fifty-two years after its first appearance. Peter Hausted's Latin play, *Senile Odium*, was performed at Cambridge in the late 1620s, and its modern editor is surprised to find 'the satire on Euphuism' in what he considers to be a 'very late' play. He suggests that this 'may signify that the fascination of such artificial and exaggerated styles was still potent at Cambridge'. On the contrary, this play appears to be further evidence that Lyly's work continued to be associated with English culture itself. Hausted confirms Blount's association of Lyly with Englishness: the character Euphues appears as 'Euphues Anglus', the Englishman, and rather less positively as 'literarum venator' (a 'word hunter') and 'nausidice' ('vomit-spewer'):

> At obsecro te, estne hic chirurgus ille Anglicus
> Qui ingenium anatomizat, quique nundinis his vernalibus
> Cum bibliorum mercatoribus huc venit?
> [But tell me, isn't he that English surgeon who anatomizes genius, and who at the spring market came here with the book merchants?][16]

Hausted quotes directly from both Lyly's prose fictions, and, though the satire against euphuism and the print market is vicious, this play, published a year after Blount's *Six Court Comedies*, confirms that Lyly's fame lasted far longer than Hunter suggests. Jonson's unfinished *The Sad Shepherd* reworks *Gallathea*, perhaps using Blount's new edition: in the late 1630s, then, Lyly was still a useful compositional resource.[17]

Perhaps the most useful text with which to consider Lyly's early modern reception is Francis Beaumont's *Knight of the Burning Pestle*. Editors have noted that the second edition of the play (1635) contains a new prologue which is a slightly modified version of Lyly's Blackfriars prologue to *Sapho and Phao*. As Sheldon Zitner summarises these additions,

> Q2 omits the Dedicatory Epistle to Keysay but adds an address to the readers decrying the fastidiousness of the age and insisting that the play has no intent to 'wrong anyone'. Further, it prints a prologue taken from Lyly's *Sapho and Phao*, which was among six Lyly plays reprinted in 1628 [*sic*].[18]

No editor has noted that, like the new prologue, the new address to Beaumont's readers that Zitner mentions is also taken from a Lyly play, the prologue to *Midas*. In other words, someone connected to the *Knight*'s reprinting read and reused two prologues printed in Blount's *Six Court Comedies*, providing further evidence of Lyly's continuing fame and rhetorical utility in the mid-1630s. J. W. Lever makes clear why no scholar has noticed the *Midas* material, when he explains that 'The "euphuistic" style' of the *Sapho and Phao* prologue, 'with its fanciful natural history and elaborate parallelisms, has, of course, nothing to do with Beaumont and was typical of Lyly's prose'.[19] In other words, the use of *Sapho and Phao* has been obvious because it conforms to nineteenth-century descriptions of euphuism: it is 'typical of Lyly's prose'. The *Midas* prologue, on the other hand, conforms less to what is presumed to be typical of Lyly's style, and its provenance has therefore been invisible to early modern scholars. Here is further evidence of the way Lyly's automatic association with euphuism has effaced his originality and continuing importance to early modern culture. In 1635, a publisher thought to mix together Lyly and Beaumont's authorship without any sense that the earlier writer could be reduced to or defined by euphuism, providing evidence for a previously unnoticed Jacobean and Caroline Lyly. We therefore need to discard the idea that Lyly's cultural status was immediately displaced or eclipsed by the early Shakespeare and instead consider this period in the light of Lyly's place in the print market, the importance of Euphues, euphuism and the boy company plays.

This book encompasses new primary material, since it assumes that the continued reprinting of Lyly's work from the 1570s to the 1630s, in conjunction with the printing and reprinting of Lyly's imitators, is itself a form of evidence.[20] Lesser and Farmer have noted that critics tend to overlook reprints, arguing that, although 'stationers, after all, could have repeatedly misread consumer demand', at the very least a reprint shows that 'the publisher anticipated continued demand for the book'. They remind us of the limits of reprinted texts as evidence, warning that 'reprint rates tell us neither the number of individual copies bought and sold nor the total capital invested in or profits earned from the sale of plays; without access to a comprehensive balance sheet for every early modern publication, this information cannot be known'.[21] But as Lesser elsewhere puts it, 'a reprint can be taken to indicate that the previous edition had either sold out or was about to sell out'.[22] We might note here that a lack of reprinting does not need to represent the failure of a particular text, though this is often how book historians describe texts that go into 'only' one edition. Such editions might represent a text that sold steadily but not spectacularly, or whose publisher no longer wished to be associated with it, or whose publisher or printer was now engaged with other projects. But we can say that a reprint indicates the publisher's projection of profit. For Jowett, 'the decision to reprint [. . .] would lie with the copy-holding stationer on the basis of his perception of demand'.[23] Lyly's unparalleled reprint history, therefore, tells us much about his publishers' perceptions of the marketplace: stationers expected new readers for Lyly and continued to do so for sixty years.

The unprecedented reprint rate of Lyly's prose fiction and plays has received little attention from Lyly scholars and from historians. Farmer and Lesser note the fact that '[r]eprint editions have been strangely absent from many earlier analyses of the print market', and this absence characterises approaches to Lyly's work.[24] For many early critics reprints represented popularity, and popularity represented the defining mark of an ephemeral and negligible work, the opposite of the literary: thus Margaret Schlauch dismissed Lyly's work as 'strangely popular', an attitude that may explain Hunter's insistence on Lyly's later irrelevance.[25] As Catherine Belsey makes clear, much of the purpose of literary criticism has been to celebrate that 'which is *not* minor, popular, ephemeral or trivial, as well as that which is not medicine, economics, history or, of course, politics'.[26] None of Shakespeare's works was reprinted at the rate of Lyly's two prose fictions, confirming the notion that a canonical work should preferably be a non-popular, and therefore elite object. This chapter considers one way in which Lyly's popularity created new forms of literature and permitted new kinds of authorial careers and reading experiences.

'Hard by the market place': Euphues *and modes of authorship*

Despite the common narrative by which Lyly's sudden success was followed by an equally sudden redundancy, in the 1580s Lyly's importance was only just beginning to be worked out. By 1583, Lyly had moved into the Blackfriars, where he rehearsed his plays and attended their performances near to St Paul's churchyard, which was issuing his prose fiction. He had written two prose works, the *Anatomy of Wit* and *Euphues and His England*, and at least two plays, *Campaspe* and *Sapho and Phao*. He may well have begun work on a new play, *Gallathea*.[27] In the previous five years, twelve editions of his two prose works had been printed, and the next year, 1584, would see his first two plays published in five separate editions.[28] Although he had moved into playwriting, by the middle of the 1580s the impact of his prose fiction was only just beginning to be felt as yet more book-buyers invested in – and writers and publishers emulated – his authorship.

This industry of Lylian emulation therefore has much to tell us about his transformation of literary culture. Many of Lyly's readers actively used and reused his work (to adapt William Sherman's expression) to compose and market publications of their own.[29] Thus, by 1583, Lyly's protagonist Euphues had jumped off the page and appeared on the title page of a book by Anthony Munday and was about to make a cameo in a book by Barnabe Riche. Stephen Gosson, who may well have known Lyly from their days in Canterbury, had reworked Lyly's style in two of his books, and Greene's first work, *Mamillia*, another imitation of Lyly, appeared at the latest by 1583, and perhaps in 1580 (the date it is entered into the Stationers' Register). All of this offers evidence of Lyly's immediate impact upon his contemporaries. Lyly's work also seems to have prompted, and certainly coincided with the sudden popularity of rhetorical self-consciousness in prose, for Thomas Wilson's study in Ciceronian rhetoric, *The Arte of Rhetorique*, which had first been published in 1553 and reprinted up to 1567, was suddenly printed again, after an interval of thirteen years, in 1580, 1584 and 1585. Wilson's publishers seem to be responding to, and therefore confirming, evidence of a renewed interested in rhetorical style in the late 1570s and 1580s.

These later prose fiction publications emulated Lyly's central and most important innovation, described in the previous chapter: a single narrative told across the space of a single book. James Raven calls Paul's churchyard 'the premier site of book publishing in

Britain' and 'the commercial hub of the English book trade': it was, for John Twyning, 'the unofficial cultural centre of early modern London', and therefore serves as an alternative to the court with which Hunter associated Lyly.[30] From here Lyly's works were disseminated and distributed as publishers sold their books on; from the Blackfriars Oxford's boys travelled to court, perhaps taking their plays further afield on tour. The market for print fiction, as defined by his own writing, was only just beginning to grow.

In order to reassess Lyly's impact on this print market in a manageable manner, this chapter is limited to what are described here as *Euphues* books: in other words, books that mention Euphues in their titles or on their title pages (it rarely being possible to delineate where a 'title' starts and the 'rest of the title page' begins). Ten books participated in this culture of emulative *Euphues* books by explicitly naming Lyly's character. Lyly's *Anatomy* (1578) and *Euphues and His England* (1580), of course, begin this process, but Munday's *Zelauto* (1580) may well have appeared before Lyly's sequel, making it either the second or third item in this sequence. *Zelauto* welcomes Euphues to England as part of its title: *Zelauto. The fountaine of fame* [...] *Given for a freendly entertainment to Euphues, at his late arivall into England.* This book therefore extended the visibility of Lyly's protagonist, helped to market Lyly's sequel (in which Euphues comes to England), and used Lyly's own marketability to sell itself. Book-buyers are tempted to spend money on *Zelauto* since it is a book Euphues has enjoyed.

The two parts of Riche's *Don Simonides* (1581 and 1584) are not *Euphues* books, but the second volume continued the narration of Lyly's story by including both Euphues and Philautus as part of its narrative. Greene's *Euphues His Censure to Philautus* (1587) and Lodge's *Rosalind: Euphues golden legacie* (1590) each continue the Munday marketing strategy by mentioning Euphues, and both pose as publications of manuscripts written by Euphues himself. Each writer then went on to present his next work as a publication of a manuscript written by Lyly's other fictional characters in response to Euphues: Greene's *Menaphon: Camillas alarum to slumbering Euphues, in his melancholie cell at Silexedra* (1589) and Lodge's *Euphues Shadow* (1592). The final *Euphues* book, John Dickenson's *Arisbas: Euphues amidst his slumbers* (1594), engages far less with Lyly's work at a compositional level, using Sidney's *Arcadia,* newly available in print, as its major source, but the Dickenson book nevertheless uses Lyly, not Sidney, as the principal means of title-page promotion. Indeed, of all the *Euphues* books Dickenson best exposes the way in which Lyly's work is used on title pages by these writers, since his use of Euphues is intended only for the book-buyer, not for the book reader. Euphues had become a marketing device and a narrative impetus that took peculiar hold over those of Lyly's readers with their own authorial or publishing ambition.

The other half of Lyly's first title, the *Anatomy*, had introduced the concept of anatomy to a non-scientific market. Stubbes's *Anatomy of Abuses* (1583), Nashe's *Anatomy of Absurdity* (1589) and Robert Burton's *Anatomy of Melancholy* (1621) are but the more familiar of a host of anatomy books that were published following Lyly's first work, which also included Greene's *Arbasto: The Anatomie of Abuses*. The word suddenly became common fare in plays as well, passing from Lodge's prose fiction *Rosalind* into *As You Like It*, for example. A word that was previously reserved to scientific discourse had become 'Englished' (to return to George Chapman's wording) by Lyly's work. Lyly's use of the word introduced it to the print market as a marketing term, and to general English usage where, as we shall see, its associations with spectacle became linked to a genre of performance, the humour play, that Lyly helped to create in *The Woman in the Moon*. Lyly's first work, *Euphues: The Anatomy of Wit*, offered two new words with which to think about prose publication, *Euphues* and *Anatomy*, and we shall see that its very syntax offered a third way to signify printed prose fiction.

The *Anatomy* had been published in 1578 with a title page that presented Euphues as an allegorical figure, advertising a book 'wherin are conteined the delights that Wit followeth in his youth, by the pleasantnesse of love, and the hap-pinesse he reapeth in age, by the perfectnesse of Wisdome'. This narrative description is potentially misleading, suggesting as it does a narrative in which Euphues moves from youth to age and from love to wisdom. Although Euphues himself claims to have made such a 'progression', we are strongly encouraged to be suspicious of his self-congratulation, and the latter part of the book is mediated not through narrative but through texts 'written' by the characters themselves. At no point does the narrator confirm that Euphues does achieve happiness or wisdom. Indeed many modern editions of Lyly's first work have misrepresented its form by excluding the non-narrative sections, so that Charles Whitworth has remarked that, until Leah Scragg's 2003 edition, scholars were encouraged to read only a 'truncated and denatured' version of the text.[31] For at least the last century, many scholars have been reading one of the most popular texts of the period in an edition which represented less than half of the early modern text (*Euphues and His England*, meanwhile, has never been printed in its own right). But the most significant point here is that the *Anatomy* title page makes Euphues an allegorical figure for 'Wyt', and therefore the object of anatomy.

Cawood and Lyly's second publication, *Euphues and His England*, also offered a description of its contents, but that description is notably less allegorical and more invested in narrative: 'CONTAINING his [in other words, Euphues'] voyage and adventures, myxed with sundry pretie discourses of honest Love, the discription of the countrey, the Court, and the manners of that Isle'. This is a very different summary, its focus on 'adventures' aligning the work with Gascoigne's story and distinguishing it from the *Anatomy*'s title page wit-allegory. Indeed this summary captures the structural complexity of Lyly's second work, since its reference to a voyage suggests a linear story, whereas the 'adventures, myxed' suggests the book's use of patterned, intertwined inset narratives. Whereas the first pages of the *Anatomy* set out the character of Euphues before presenting a dialogue between him and Eubulus, in the opening to *Euphues and His England* Euphues tells Philautus a story which itself contains several instances of storytelling. This difference characterises the whole of the two works, the *Anatomy* a combination of narrative statements and character oration or letter-writing, *Euphues and His England* a blending of these two forms which emphasises their blending. This title page therefore gestures towards the narrative structure of the work in a way that the *Anatomy* title page did not.

But the most important change in the new title is the more prominent position of Euphues himself. Where the *Anatomy* Euphues had to share space with his 'subtitle' *The Anatomy of Wit*, the new book is simply called *Euphues and His England*: the protagonist has taken over the title page and even claimed some kind of ownership over England.[32] Whereas the *Anatomy* narrative summary displaced (and helped to explain) Euphues with his allegorical persona 'Wyt', the *Euphues and His England* summary promises prospective book-buyers 'his voyage and adventures'. Following the success of his first book, customers are expected to invest in another instalment of Euphues' life-story. In this transition Lyly's authorship changes from the earlier anatomist to a fictional biographer, and Euphues changes from an allegorical figure of wit to something much closer to a mimetic, representational character. This is an important transition which creates the possibilities of a *Euphues* culture: a book market culture in which customers might be expected to be excited about and invest in the latest *Euphues* book.

'another face to Euphues': the 1579 revisions of Euphues: The Anatomy of Wit

At the end of the *Anatomy* Lyly had projected the writing of *Euphues and His England*, and from 1579 new reprints of the *Anatomy* furthered this advertisement for the forthcoming sequel in an appended letter describing Euphues currently at sea and on his way to England. All new reprints of the *Anatomy* contained a set of additions and expansions to the 1578 text, but the only addition obvious at first glance is this appended letter: since Lyly explains that the letter is written 'to offer a defence where I was mistaken', it is self-evidently presented to the reader as an addition to the amended text (151). This letter appears to have troubled the publisher Cawood or someone else involved in the publication, since it appears with the prefatory material in the first revised edition, only to be moved to the back of the book in the next edition. In the last 1579 edition and in all subsequent editions, the letter was restored to the work's prefatory material.[33] The movement of the letter from the front to the back of the book and back again appears to reveal anxiety on the part of the publisher over the exact function of the letter which, after all, ambiguously combined the virtues of advertising the topicality and vibrancy of Lyly's work at the same time as it acknowledged its potential to create controversy and division. If Cawood and Lyly colluded in their courtly or social ambitions, Cawood may well have had a highly ambivalent response to the lucrative but controversial work he now owned.[34]

Less obvious additions reveal that Lyly decided to revise the ways in which readers encountered his protagonist. In the 1578 original, Euphues is introduced as a gifted man with flaws. In the course of this introduction, Lyly marshals no fewer than eleven examples to illustrate this point, so that his readers encounter the eccentricity of the euphuistic fictive world at the same time as they meet Euphues. In the opening of the book, stretching just over the first page, three sections illustrate Euphues' ambiguous nature: Lyly compares him to the rose's prickle and flawed velvet; to Venus and her mole, Helen and her scar, Aristippus's wart and Lycurgus's wren; and to Alexander's alcoholism, Cicero's vanity, Solomon's wantonness and David's murderousness (32–3). This introduction concludes with a summary of Euphues' character and the inevitable life-story he is about to experience:

> Which [examples] appeared well in this Euphues, whose wit being like wax apt to receive any impression, and having the bridle in his own hands either to use the rein or the spur, disdaining counsel, leaving his country, loathing his old acquaintance, thought either by wit to obtain some conquest, or by shame to abide some conflict, and leaving the rule of reason, rashly ran unto destruction.[35] (4)

Thus Lyly's careful exposition of Euphues' ambiguous character traits leads him into a brief summary of the rather less ambiguous storyline: Euphues will run into destruction. This summary of the story, however, is not particularly helpful for the reader, since Euphues does not run into anything approaching destruction. He may betray his best friend, he may be betrayed by his lover and he may even become an academic, but none of these narrative predicaments appear to qualify as outright destruction. For some early modern readers, Euphues' moral degradation might presage his spiritual destruction, but the text does not insist on such a reading. Certainly Lyly implies a narrative conclusion that the text will ultimately refuse.

Lyly himself may have noticed this problem, for this is the first passage in the *Anatomy* to be amended in the 1579 and later versions. Euphues now:

> thought either by wit to obtain some conquest or by shame to abide some conflict; *who, preferring fancy before friends, and his present humour before honour to come, laid reason in water, being too salt for his taste, and followed unbridled affection, most pleasant for his tooth.* (33, italics mark emendation)

By removing the reference to Euphues' destruction, Lyly revises the reader's expectation of the narrative, and indeed revises the introduction so that it more accurately represents the story to follow. But Lyly's revision has a rather more profound impact upon his story, for whereas a meditation on Euphues' contrary personality was resolved by the 1578 narrator's reassurance of Euphues' comeuppance, the revised version suppresses resolution and reassurance. Moreover, rather than resolving the contrary aspects of Euphues' personality, the revised version perpetuates and extends the ambiguous protagonist. Instead of 'leaving the rule of reason', as he did in 1578, Euphues 'puts it into water', a metaphor that refers to the soaking of meat to remove strong flavours. As elsewhere in Lyly's writing, the water metaphor works to mystify the content of Lyly's work, as when the Blackfriars *Campaspe* epilogue told the audience: 'Our exercises must be as your judgement is, resembling water, which is always of the same colour into what it runneth' (136). This epilogue informs the audience that their responses determine the meaning of the play, and in his 1579 revisions of the *Anatomy* Lyly puts Euphues into water, removing the narrative hints about his character and story and requiring readers to make their own judgement.

This process can be seen again in the next addition to the 1578 text. In that edition, Euphues' voice was not heard directly until he replied to the long address by Eubulus, so that the reader did not encounter the protagonist's direct voice until several pages into the work. In the revised version, Euphues is heard replying to an earlier (and anonymous) interlocutor:

> Who, being demanded of one what countryman he was, he answered, 'What countryman am I not? If I be in Crete, I can lie; if in Greece, I can shift; if in Italy, I can court it. If thou ask whose son I am also, I ask thee whose son I am not. I can carouse with Alexander, abstain with Romulus, eat with the Epicure, fast with the Stoic, sleep with Endymion, watch with Chrysippus', using these speeches and other like. (34–5)

This is the new protagonist Lyly presented to his readers from 1579 onwards, a character emptied of stable characteristics.[36] The earlier reference to reason 'laid [...] in water' prepared the reader for a diluted, osmotic figure, but the man speaking here celebrates his endlessly protean, performative personality. Nancy Selleck suggests that 'Where we see objectification as undermining, even catastrophic, for selfhood, English Renaissance writers could see it as constitutive and crucial – a problem perhaps, but also a solution'.[37] Lyly's Euphues is a character who anticipates and celebrates the adaptable, uncentred self.

In *The Scholemaster* (1570), Roger Ascham puts forward the putative and exemplary Euphues as the gifted schoolboy whom the teacher must guide well. Euphues 'is he, that is apte by goodnes of witte, and appliable by readiness of will, to learning, having all other qualities of the minde and partes of the bodie'.[38] Lyly uses Ascham's Euphues to objectify selfhood, to return to Selleck's terms. Particularly in his 1579 revisions, he makes Euphues a blank canvas, bearing good but also unfortunate qualities, somebody able to pose in various authorial guises, something Lyly himself delights in in *Pap with an Hatchet*. Euphues' celebration of his own performative brilliance is a major constituent of his impact on early modern readers and his appeal to later writers: he invites inventive reading. His unstable character permitted new writers and publishers to define and redefine their own social and professional identities around him.

To put it another way, Lyly's difficult and playful writing style anticipates the kind of 'active' reading technique that Anthony Grafton, Lisa Jardine and William Sherman have recently discovered in the early modern period, projecting the text as the 'site of an active and biased appropriation of the author's material'.[39] Although Lyly requires the kind of reading practices studied by these scholars, he has not yet fallen into their view. Although all reading might be described as a form of speculative and active interpretation of an otherwise indeterminate and negative text, and early modern pedagogy advanced a 'radically analytical' reading style, Lyly's rhetorical and narrative opacity was particularly provocative of reader response, as the history of Lylian imitation reveals.[40] Arthur Kinney describes Lyly 'struggling toward a language that can embody a reliable statement of virtue [...] and we are asked to search too', and although Kinney sees Lyly's search as an essentially moral one, it is also the case that Lyly's writing actively disturbs the moral certainties of humanism and encourages readers to share this scepticism.[41]

In his 1579 emendations, Lyly suppressed details of Euphues' already mysterious identity. Stephen Dobranski has argued that 'apparently unfinished works [...] reinforced Renaissance practices of active reading'. Lyly's text is not 'unfinished' in this sense; if anything, its revisions appear to suggest that it is 'more finished'. But these revisions repressed narrative detail in a way that appears to have provoked active readers and writers alike. As Dobranski puts it, these 'omissions' are 'deliberate holes [that] establish an author's authority and enhance rather than diminish meaning'; 'all these omissions remain evocatively present; something may be missing, but its absence is palpable'. In Lyly's case, Euphues' protean and allusive character is not so much evocative as provocative, prompting readers to define and continue his story in an example of the relationship between 'an individual author and a collaborative community'.[42] As Annabel Patterson observes, 'authors who build ambiguity into their works have no control over what happens to them later', and as we have seen Lyly constantly figured his writing and his plays as a product of readerly or audience imagination.[43] Lyly's work and its immediate reception are perhaps the most overt – and most often overlooked – example of what Kinney calls the 'potential multiplicity of perspective' figured into early modern composition and calling for the interpretative and 'intervening' function of the reader.[44]

Lyly's presentation of character particularly distinguished him as a storyteller. Austen Saker's *Narbonus* (1580) exploits the single-story book innovated by Lyly and Cawood and is an early example of a work closely modelled on Lyly's *Anatomy* in structure, narrative and style. Nevertheless, it affords the opportunity to isolate Lyly's peculiarity as a narrator. Saker's narrator is often emotionally involved in his own story, crying 'alas' as he tells it, for example, which might remind us of Gascoigne's G.T. and his chatty use of 'Wel'.[45] He repeatedly reflects ahead to later stages in the narrative, as when Narbonus's uncle is described as a man 'as glad to heare his [nephew's] wise answers, as hee was afterwards sorry for his lewde behaviour', or when Fidelia's eagerness to meet her beloved is accompanied by the narrator's reflection that had she 'knowen hir mariage day had bin so farre off, she woulde not have made such hast' (Di and Pii). Saker's narrator constantly flirts with the reader about upcoming narrative events.

In contrast, Lyly's narration rarely encourages the reader to reflect on how the story will progress, and there is little room in the *Anatomy* for this kind of narrative reflection. As we have already seen, Lyly's 1579 revisions actively suppress such predictions. In a technique that adapts Gascoigne's use of G.T., Lyly's narrator interrupts the monologues and dialogues that make up the bulk of the *Anatomy* but fails to offer authorial solutions to them, as when he ends the standoff between Eubulus and Euphues with a lengthy digression to his readership: 'Here ye may behold, gentlemen, how lewdly wit standeth in his own light' (42). This gloss on the story interrupts rather than explains its narrative sequence, turning it into a kind of euphuistic example from which the reader must deduce his or her conclusions, whereas Saker's narrator assumes that the reader shares his emotional and intellectual absorption into the process of narrative itself. Lyly's narrative instead encourages and produces the readers' alienation from the story.

The difference between Saker and Lyly is particularly obvious when Saker reworks Lyly's narrative. When Saker's Narbonus returns from Wittenberg and has to meet his disappointed uncle, he begins a speech but is unable to continue because 'his thoughts so troubled his giltie conscience, as he could not speake any more, or utter the effect of his meaning' (Fiii). This moment reworks the dinner party scene in *Anatomy* when Euphues is unable to continue his speech on love, a moment that Lyly represents only via Euphues' speech (in other words, without a narrator's intervention or explanation):

> You shall pardon me, Mistress Lucilla, for this time, if this abruptly I finish my discourse. It is neither for want of good will, or lack of proof, but that I feel in myself such alteration that I can scarcely utter one word. Ah Euphues, Euphues! (51)

The narrator provides no explanation for this moment, but Euphues himself, in the course of a later soliloquy, offers an obvious clue. He reveals that he has fallen in love with Lucilla, so that readers have the means necessary to deduce what has happened without the narrator's help. But what is significant is that Saker explained to his readers the reason for Narbonus's sudden silence, taking them into the 'thoughts' of his protagonist. Lyly, on the other hand, refuses any narrational support for the same event, and his only narrative comment, that '[t]he gentlewomen were struck into such a quandary with this sudden change', mirrors the state of his readership, who without narrational support are at this stage likewise left in a quandary (51).

In *Sapho and Phao*, Lyly similarly forced his audience, and later his readers, to deduce the reason behind Sapho's illness, when the courtier Trachinus says, 'Sapho is fallen sudden sick. I cannot guess the cause' (III.i.1–2). In neither case is it difficult to understand what has happened, but what is significant is the fact that the narrator and playwright do not spell out character motivation or plot. The dearth of narrative detail in Lyly's story cannot be explained by the difference between modern and early modern attitudes to fiction telling, since Saker's story, like many by Painter, Pettie and Sidney and indeed many of the stories of the Bible, attests to an early modern interest in a carefully crafted and clearly explained narrative. Rather, the absence of narrative detail in the *Anatomy* is testimony to its predominant interest in the process of communication itself, forcing its readers to read actively.

This technique for forcing a reader into a supplementary position was a major part of the attraction Lyly held for later writers and readers. We have already seen how the first speech in the 1579 *Anatomy* showed Euphues defining himself as psychologically protean, able to construct and rearrange his identity to suit whatever situation is before him, but Lyly's narrative conclusion to this speech, 'using these speeches *and other like*', tells us that the printed speech does not quite reflect what Euphues 'really' said (35, my emphasis). At the same time that Euphues claims psychological slipperiness, the narrator promotes the unreliability of his reported speech. For many of his more recent readers, these moments are symptomatic of Lyly's failure as a storyteller, yet they could also be understood as prose equivalents of the games Jonathan Goldberg locates in Spenser's *Faerie Queene*, a poem that reinvents itself before the reader's eyes.[46]

This compositional technique is the narrative equivalent of a problem Lyly brings up in his preface to the female readers of

Euphues and His England, in which Arachne is told that her tapestry, which depicts a rainbow, is at fault because it does not depict all the colours of the rainbow:

> Unto whom she replied, 'If the colours lack thou lookest for, thou must imagine that they are on the other side of the cloth; for in the sky we can discern but one side of the rainbow, and what colours are in the other, see we cannot, guess we may'. (161)

Arachne casts the limitations of representation as an impetus for the onlooker to 'imagine'. The revised edition of the *Anatomy* shows Lyly deliberately suppressing character detail and definition for Euphues, and thereby forcing his readers into a position of supplementary imagination. Lyly appeals to the imagination, but he does so by means of the suppression of detail, a fact that has major implications for his plays as well as his fiction. Other writers' responses to Euphues might be read not only as exploiting the productive absence of a psychologically defined character in their own stories but also as an anxious response to close off the radical instability of Lyly's narrational technique. David Margolies suggests that 'Lyly's famous style, more than the mere decoration it became for many of his imitators, is the artistic embodiment of a world view'.[47] This view of a mutable and unpredictable universe encompassing a mutable and unpredictable self was tamed by those who adapted Lyly's style and stories. The future imitations and commodifications of Lyly's work can be read as an attempt to respond to the protean nature of Euphues and his peculiarly challenging storytelling style.

In a study of twentieth-century archetypal characters, Will Brooker suggests that certain figures such as Batman, James Bond and Robin Hood are distinct from Sherlock Holmes, Hamlet and Don Quixote in that they represent

> cultural icons, whose meanings long ago escaped the anchorage of whatever 'original' text brought them into being, and whose identity is no longer inseparably tied to an individual author [...] but exists somewhere above and between a multiplicity of varied and often contradictory incarnations.[48]

In the 1580s and early 1590s, writers and publishers attempted to use Lyly and Euphues as cultural icons, and the rest of this chapter demonstrates the complex way in which Euphues was both distinct from and representative of Lylian authorship.

Across Lyly's first book, the writer uses different formulae to refer to the text itself, revealing productive tensions in its meaning and significance. References in the prefatory material to 'the Anatomy of wit' have transformed, at the close of the work, into references to 'the first part of *Euphues*', inviting readers to invest in the sequel. Similarly, the book was entered in the Stationers' Register as 'the Anotomie of witt', but was published as *Euphues: The Anatomy of Wit*. These changes and alterations might be read as a developing marketing strategy or a changing conception of the work at the point of composition, either way producing a successive emphasis on the character who will define both of Lyly's books (and a good deal of other books by other writers). This inference is confirmed by the epistle to the Oxford scholars that is the most substantive addition to the 'Corrected and augmented' second edition of the *Anatomy*. Lyly's future work, of course, dropped the concept of the anatomy of wit, and the epistle to the Oxford scholars that was appended to the second and later reprints of the *Anatomy* refers only to Euphues' subsequent biography ('Euphues at his arrival (I am assured) will view Oxford [...]. He is now on the seas'), extending Euphues' biography into the future work and ignoring the thematic concern of the previous work with wit-anatomisation (151). If the change in emphasis from the preface's anatomy to the final reference to the first part of *Euphues* is indicative of a change in compositional as well as marketing strategy, then the *Anatomy* is a transitional document, a work that produces, but was also produced by, a project to create a sequence of *Euphues* books.

'for Euphues' sake': developing new single-story prose books

Lyly's conceit that Euphues was a real person with an ongoing biography began at the end of the 1578 edition and drew on Gascoigne's 1573 tale of F.J. It was drawn out at greater length and with greater insistence in the epistle added to the 1579 and later editions at a time when other writers were beginning to consider the advantages of this fictional creation to their own authorial personae. The first non-Lylian text to present itself as a *Euphues* book was by Anthony Munday, working, like Lyly, for the Earl of Oxford and recently returned from Italy. *Zelauto* presents itself on its title page, in its preface and in its ending as a 'welcome' for Euphues 'into England'. Munday's book colludes with Lyly's marketing strategies but, in so doing, shows the marketing potential of Lyly's work for other writers, demonstrating how Euphues' ongoing biography and protean identity could be used to promote another author's book and define another author's corpus.

Munday articulates his book as an interaction with Lylian

authorship, and indeed acknowledges what a provocative concept that is:

> Againe, some will be inquisitive, why I am so willing to welcome *Euphues* into England? he beeying so excellent: and my selfe so simple? If *Euphues* so wisely dooth wish you beware, and to prevent the perilles that heedelesse heades may have, wishing youth likewise to frame their fancies so fit, that no crooked chaunces doo happen to harme them: Then like that *Lilly* whose sent is so sweete, and favour his freend who wisheth your welfare. And although my wit be so weake: that I cannot welcome as I would, and my skyll to simple to gratifye so gentle a gueast: I trust my good will shall plead me a pardon, & my honest intent be nothing misliked.[49]

Munday canonises Lyly's nascent authorship whilst inserting himself within it. Lyly's first work had been published only in December 1578, and so it might have been possible, in 1580, for bookshop customers to associate the character Euphues with Ascham or even Plato. Munday's preface makes clear that readers are expected to think of Lyly when they read the word 'Euphues' on Munday's title page: 'If *Euphues* so wisely dooth wish you beware, [...] Then like that *Lilly*'. And his preface also reveals the compositional and marketing boon Munday hopes to gain from Lyly's influence: readers asked to 'like that *Lilly*' are also requested to 'favour his freend'. But it was 'that *Lilly*' whose name seems to have sold books. Despite its reference to Euphues, *Zelauto* does not seem to have been reprinted, whilst in 1581 the *Anatomy* went through its seventh edition in its third full year, and *Euphues and His England* was published for the fourth and fifth time in 1581 and 1582. In a pattern which we will see reoccur, a very specific combination of Euphues and Lyly seems to have fuelled these later reprints; the combination of Euphues and Munday did not initiate such a reprinting process.

In 1584, the second part of Barnabe Riche's *Don Simonides* continued the story of Euphues and Philautus as part of its own narrative. Riche's two volumes appeared either side of reprints of Lyly's work, demonstrating the continued vibrancy of the single-story book model Riche emulated and quoted, and the Euphues story he continued. Where Munday mentioned Euphues on his title page and in his preface but did not include him as a character in *Zelauto*, Riche worked him into his story but did not advertise his presence on his title page. Thus Munday's book corroborated and furthered the cultural interest in Euphues as a character whose name sold books, whilst Riche confirmed the character's imaginative, compositional and narratological interest.

Riche's extension of Euphues' story encouraged later developments that took place in the texts and on the title pages of later books by Greene and Lodge. Lodge himself wrote a preface to Riche's first volume, enmeshing himself early into the culture of *Euphues*. Riche's first book developed the character of Simonides that showed the author's assimilation of Lyly's work, but it is the second volume of Riche's book which continues the story of Euphues, calling the *Don Simonides* project 'the Anotomy of wanton youth, seasoned with ouer late repentance' (Aiv). The character Simonides is told to search out 'this Euphues' in Athens, 'who is curious in describyng the Anotomie of wit' (Liii).

Simonides is figured as a second Euphues, one who has 'tried suche like path waies as once did Euphues': 'Simonides is now he whome Euphues was once' (Oii). At a time when Euphues was the most lucrative and visible character in the print market, it is easy to see why a writer and publisher would want to make such a claim of their new character. When Simonides comes to Athens, he hears from a passing scholar 'how at that very instaunt, *Euphues* was come from the Mount Silexsedra into the Citie, and was lodged hard by the Market place', a telling description of a character so buoyant in the early print literature market (Miv). And Euphues' first speech in Riche's book refers to both Alexander and the Sybil, characters Lyly had staged that year in front of the queen and whose stories had then been published in multiple editions, creating strange and complex networks in the early canon of Lyly's writing (Oii).

By 1583, then, twelve editions of Lyly's prose fiction had been printed, and both Munday and Riche had participated in the movement to emulate and rework them. These specific emulations of Lyly's work – a *Euphues* book and a book containing Euphues the character – played out against wider manifestations of Lyly's influence that lie beyond the remit of this chapter: Gosson's *Ephemerides*, for example, with its use of euphuistic techniques, and Greene's first work *Mamillia*, which not only reworks euphuism but was also one of the first imitations of the innovative single-story book structure. Munday's *Euphues* book was obviously carefully timed to coincide with *Euphues and His England*, to which it refers on the title page: whichever book was published first, each book helps to market the other. In 1580 Munday's *Zelauto* was accompanied by two editions of the *Anatomy* and three of the new Lyly book, *Euphues and His England*. In the following year, when the first *Don Simonides* volume appeared, Cawood published each book once again, and in 1582 he issued another edition of the more recent book, *Euphues and His England*. Lyly's impact on the print market and its consumers was immediate and extraordinary, and he was helping writers find new ways to compose and structure stories. These stories, in turn, helped to market Lyly's two *Euphues* books.

In 1583, the year that Lyly began work in the theatre, Cawood issued no new edition of the prose fiction. Instead, he extended Lyly's authorship into the poetry market, printing Lyly's prefatory epistle to Thomas Watson's innovative sonnet collection *Hekatompathia*. Watson's own preface to the Earl of Oxford describes how 'Alexander the Great, passing on a time by the workeshop of Apelles, curiouslie surveyed some of his doings'.[50] In so doing, Watson refers not only to the scenario which opens Lyly's *Anatomy of Wit* and reappears throughout the prose fiction but also to the storyline to Lyly's first play, *Campaspe*, staged by Oxford's boys, thereby making complex use of Lyly's authorship and Oxford's authority. Lyly's preface to Watson teases the reader with reference to unpublished material, promising Watson a glimpse of material 'which I woulde be loth the printer should see' (B1v). Given the number of writers who were about to publish their own stories and claim them to have been written by or for Euphues in manuscript, Lyly anticipates his contemporaries' games with publication and his authorship. Lyly's preface therefore endorses Watson's volume of poetry whilst also taking the opportunity to refer teasingly to future Lyly publications. Perhaps more intriguingly, Lyly's preface provides a testimony to the experience of being published: 'for that my fancies being never so crooked [the printer] would put them in streight lines, unfit for my humor, necessarie for his art, who setteth downe, blinde, in as many letters as seeing' (B1v).

It is impossible to explain why Cawood stopped printing new editions of Lyly's work in 1583 or why he might have started to issue new editions again from 1585, although that year he registered his rights to a Lyly play, *Gallathea*. But when he did start to reissue Lyly's work, Cawood pursued what we might read as a determined marketing strategy in which he published first the *Anatomy* and then its sequel, using one volume to set up and promote the other. This pattern is evident from 1585 to 1588, when he published the *Anatomy* (1585, 1587) and then *Euphues and His England* (1586, 1588).

Determining Cawood's agency here is clearly speculative, but changes in Lyly's authorial standing and in the print market itself certainly help to situate the decision to reprint the prose fiction. Firstly, Cawood's dominant position in Paul's churchyard placed him near the Blackfriars theatre where Lyly rehearsed and staged his first two plays, in a commercial theatre whose plays were justified as rehearsals open to the public before being seen at court.[51] Lyly's currency in the print market would certainly have ensured wide interest in his theatrical productions, an interest that would be stunningly confirmed in 1584 when his plays became the first to be published immediately after their stage debut, the first to go through a series of reprints and the first to do so within a single year. The theatrical and print response to Lyly's plays may therefore have prompted Cawood to reissue his prose fiction.

But Cawood may well have been influenced in his decision by wider movements in the print market. Thus the appearances of Munday's book in 1580 and Riche's two volumes in 1581 and 1584 both demonstrated the market valence of Euphues as a character and a story, and may have suggested to Cawood a continued market for the original *Euphues* books. But the much more numerous imitations of Lyly's bibliographical form, a single-story book, particularly Greene's multiple publications from at least 1583 to 1585, also suggested a continued market for new reprints of Lyly's work. Greene, Munday and Gosson reflected an even wider early emulation of Lyly's work, through their use of euphuistic composition. Finally, the mid-part of the decade saw three further developments that indicated Lyly's topicality: Webbe's 1586 praise of Lyly's 'singular eloquence' (worthy of Demosthenes and Cicero), the reprinting of Pettie's miscellany, which in 1576 had anticipated many of the rhetorical tricks characteristic of euphuism, and the publication of Rainolds's Latin lectures, themselves highly euphuistic. It would be fruitless to claim any one of these events in particular as reasons for Cawood's decision to start republishing Lyly's two works one after the other, but collectively they attest to a growing climate which made Lyly's work ever more commercially viable.

It was during this second stage of publication of Lyly's *Euphues* books that Greene intruded himself (to use Lyly's image) into *Euphues* writing. All of Greene's early books had shown the result of Lyly's impact: Greene is the author who most thoroughly reworked, rethought and remarketed Lyly's mode of expression. In 1583–84 all of Greene's titles re-enacted the syntax of Lyly's first publication, a classical name followed by two nouns, one the genitive of the other: as with Munday's syntactical copy, *Zelauto: The Fountain of Fame*, so Greene produced *Mamillia: A Mirrour or Looking-Glasse for the Ladies of England* (1583), *Arbasto: The Anatomie of Fortune* (1584), *Gwydonius: The Carde of Fancie* (1584; reprinted 1587) and *Morando: The Tritameron of Love* (1584; reprinted with a second part 1587). Newcomb defines this combination of an unfamiliar exotic initial word with an explanatory, almost hermeneutical subtitle as 'a protagonist's name and a fanciful genre name exploring a broad theme', helpfully emphasising the novelty of naming a book after its protagonist.[52] Greene's *Arbasto: The Anatomie of Fortune* provides further evidence that the word 'anatomy' was associated with Lyly, Euphues, euphuism and the single-story book. Some of Greene's works were published by men intimately involved in the publication of Lyly's work: *Mamillia* printed by Thomas Dawson, the man who the following year printed the five editions of *Campaspe* and *Sapho and Phao*; *Gwydonius* printed by Thomas East, who was Cawood's printer for the Lyly *Euphues* books until 1588; and *Morando* co-printed by John Charlewood, who would later print *Endymion* and *Gallathea* for Joan Brome in 1591–92. Given the extension of Lyly's influence into wider, non-Lylian books, East's involvement with *Gwydonius* is particularly striking, since his role as Cawood's principle printer would have brought Greene's euphuistic interventions particularly close to Cawood's attention and may have encouraged the latter to renew reprints of Lyly's work.

Greene's first *Euphues* book appeared in 1587. Although Greene reworked Lyly's legacy from his very first publication, imitating both euphuistic compositional techniques and Lyly's title syntax, he did not start to refer to Lyly's protagonist on his title pages until the second phase of Cawood's reprints of Lyly's work. Lyly's enigmatic first title had been followed by the more prosaic, self-explanatory *Euphues and His England*, and Greene's *Euphues His Censure to Philautus* likewise presents prospective book-buyers with a title that would make immediate sense. By 1580, Lyly's second title suggested that the word 'Euphues' itself was assumed to 'make sense': unlike Mamillia, Zelauto or Arbasto, it no longer required to be unpacked by an explanatory subtitle. Greene's title not only shows that Euphues made sense as a marketing tool but further suggests that the secondary Lylian character Philautus was expected to be familiar to bookshop customers, demonstrating the extent to which Lyly had penetrated book-reading culture.

Although none of the *Euphues* books written by Lyly's imitators continues Euphues' story in their main narratives (unlike Riche's *Don Simonides*, which does not name Euphues on its title page but gives him a cameo role in the story itself), Greene's *Euphues* work uses Lyly's character as an authorial framing device as well as a marketing tool. The Euphues story is in effect used both as an external site of narration, in which Euphues either 'writes' or 'reads' the story of the book, and as a form of publicity, in which Euphues fictionally produces, and actually promotes, Greene's book. But the relation of the character Euphues to the contents of the book his name promotes is often opaque. For example, *Euphues his Censure to Philautus* is a narrative geared towards advice for a military man, and Euphues makes an almost comically inappropriate authority on this particular topic.

Greene dedicates the work to the Earl of Essex, suggesting that the Euphues and Philautus story was being co-opted well beyond the fiction market and interwoven into the young Essex's courtly and military ambitions. Greene hopes that 'as Alexander did vouchsafe of Myson's rude and unpolished picture of Mars', so Essex will accept Greene's book, a simile that happily constructs Essex as a great military leader and Greene as his honoured artist. Writing at a time when Essex was only beginning to establish himself at court, Greene claims that he 'by happe chaunced on some parte of Euphues counsell touching the perfection of a souldier, sent from Silexedra his melancholie cell to his friende Philautus new chosen generall of certaine forces[.]'[53] Greene assumes that Essex and a wider readership will remember Euphues, Silexedra and Philautus, an assumption implicitly underpinning the title of Greene's work, and recasts Euphues as an author of a considerable body of work, since the current book is only 'some part of Euphues' counsel'. In the coming years the manuscript output of Silexedra would provide material for some of the most often republished editions of Paul's churchyard.

The epistle demonstrates the Lylian terminology which Greene uses to imagine his own authorship. He describes his work as a 'homelie gyfte, unperfect as the halfe formed counterfaite of Apelles', but the modesty of this remark is tempered by the implicit comparison between Apelles and Greene (a further reference to Alexander places this anecdote firmly in a Lylian discursive universe). Lyly's own insistent references to Apelles, which begins from the very start of the *Anatomy* and culminate in the painter's role in *Campaspe*, further imbricate Lyly into Greene's self-figuration as Apelles. Greene also writes a short epistle 'To the reader', repeating the claim that 'by chance some of Euphues loose papers came to my hand' (VI, 154).

But this epistle is principally important for its long second sentence, which is printed as a continuation of the previous sentence in the original edition, but in fact represents a second, discrete grammatical unit. Between them, these two sentences make up the rest of the epistle:

> conjecturing with my selfe the opynion of the man would bee not onely authenticall, but pleasing, and that the tyme required such a discourse, as necessarie: I thought not to conceale his censure, but to participate what I had to your courteous favours, although intended by him for the pryvate use of his deerest friend, hoping as ever I have done to find your courteous acceptation, and that you will for Euphues sake vouchsafe of the matter, and in requitall of my travell make some favorable conjecture of my good meaning: which hoping to obtayne, I rest satisfied. (VI, 154)

This is a long, difficult sentence, atypical of Greene's more common euphuistic control in this period. It also represents the clearest single articulation of Euphues' 'canonisation', his 'authenticall' status and his function as a figure who will authenticate the real author Greene: 'for Euphues sake vouchsafe of the matter'. The consistency of the fiction (that the book was authored by Euphues) is difficult and unnecessary for Greene to sustain, but his reference to 'my good meaning' does not so much destroy the artifice as imbricate Greene's authorship further with Euphues'. Euphues' 'opynion' bolsters the authorship of the real Elizabethan writer; but, equally, that real Elizabethan writer is able to cast himself as Euphues' publisher (his 'participate[r]'), disseminating that which the fictional author 'intended [...] for [...] private use'. Greene here reworks a formula familiar from G.T.'s request that the F.J. manuscript should not be 'ma[d]e [...] common' by being printed (Pigman, 144), and Pettie's request that the *Petite Pallace* manuscript be 'use[d ...] to your owne private pleasure'.[54] Greene articulates his act of authorship, fictionally figured as publication, as an attempt to find 'courteous acceptation' and 'favourable conjecture' by publishing Euphues' authentic opinion.

Euphues' authentic opinion would be published again in 1590 in Lodge's *Rosalind: Euphues Golden Legacie*, two years after Cawood's most recent reprint of Lyly's *Euphues and His England.* Lodge's *Rosalind* was printed by Thomas Orwin, who the next year printed Lyly's first two plays for the publisher William Brome. Orwin's publication may well have helped to prompt Cawood to reprint *Euphues and His England* again in 1592. Lodge's day-job as a sailor means that, despite its pose as a printed version of a manuscript written at Silexedra, this particular *Euphues* book may have been written off the shore of Peru.

The work has a particularly complex relationship, not just to Lyly's *Euphues* works but with his canon and authorship as a whole. In an epistle to 'Gentlemen Readers', Lodge denies writing in 'the pleasing vaine of any eloquent Orator'.[55] The euphuistic emulation of Lyly's prose and the title-page claim to be *Euphues Golden Legacy* both seem to counter Lodge's modesty: like Greene's association with Apelles, Lodge patently aims towards Lyly's status as the Demosthenes and Cicero of his generation. The epistle echoes Lyly's epistle to Lord Delaware in the *Anatomy*, with its allusions to 'Coblers' and the 'latchet', its insistence on the author's reluctance to attempt style and 'matters above my capacitie' (95). As the introduction made clear, Lyly's interest in 'matters above' the author's or speaker's 'capacitie' had been a defining characteristic of his authorship. Allusions to the wider Lylian canon may be evident in Lodge's defence of his book against 'any squinteied asse, that hath mighty eares to conceive with *Midis*, and yet little reason to judge', a reference to the Midas legend staged by Lyly's company the previous year and published two years later (95). This is particularly striking in a work that self-consciously reworks Lyly's *Gallathea* two years before it was published (suggesting that Lodge saw the play in performance or had access to a manuscript).

In an innovation upon Greene's conceit that Euphues had written the main body of text of *Euphues his Censure* for Philautus, Lodge includes a preface by Euphues himself to Philautus, explaining that the work is intended for Philautus's sons. As with Greene, this 'Scedule' makes clear Lodge's canonisation of Lyly's first work, a canonisation intended to have positive, transformative effects upon Lodge's own authorship. In 'The Schedule Annexed to Euphues' Testament, the Tenor of His Legacy, the Token of His Love' (the words Lodge uses to describe his own book), Philautus's sons, and by extension any other reader, 'shall find Love anatomized by Euphues with as lively colors as in Apelles' tables: roses to whip him when he is wanton, reasons to withstand him when he is wily' (96). This short sentence works up a number of intertextual relationships with Lyly's canon. The phrase 'Love anatomized by *Euphues*' is an obvious allusion to Lyly's first work, and points up the fact that love, rather than wit, is here the subject of anatomisation. The reference to Apelles repeats the move made by Greene to associate himself with the painter, and thus with Lyly, and may or may not reflect the appearance of Apelles in Lyly's first play. But Lyly's second play appears to underpin the proverbial reference to 'roses to whip him', particularly in the context of an assault upon Love:

> VENUS And as for you, sir boy, I will teach you how to run away: you shall be stripped from top to toe, and whipped with nettles, not roses.[56]
>
> (*Sapho and Phao*, V.ii.78–81)

Pointedly, the anatomy in Lodge's book is enacted *by* Euphues *upon* Love, which may imply that this is how Lodge read the logic of Lyly's title *Euphues: The Anatomy of Wit*. Although the syntactical relations of the phrase *Euphues*: *The Anatomy of Wit* do not clarify whether Euphues is the agent or the object of anatomy, the title page and, later, the work's narrator, refer to Euphues *as* Wit, strongly implying that the character is the object of anatomisation. Here we seem to have another example of Lodge's reception of Lyly's *Anatomy* being at odds with the meaning apparently encoded in Lyly's text, or of the way Lyly's emulators attempt to solve syntactic ambiguities in their source text.[57]

Euphues' schedule ends with the signature 'Euphues dying to live' (96), and Lodge and Greene (in his 1590 *Euphues* book, *Menaphon*) both take advantage of the death of this particular author. Euphues' final message, 'If any man find this scroll send it to Philautus in England', is obviously part of the fictional conceit of Euphues' authorship, but it also seems to demonstrate the extent to which Lodge, secluded at sea, identified with that authorship and Euphues' seclusion at Silexedra (96). Euphues is not mentioned once throughout the entire main body of the text of *Rosalind*, but the work ends with an 'audience' address that reprises Euphues' authorship: 'Here, gentlemen, you may see [...] Euphues' Golden Legacy' (227). But whereas Greene 'thought not to conceale [Euphues'] censure, but to participate [that is, publish] what I had', Lodge's participation in Euphues' authorship is rather more miscellaneous (*Euphues His Censure*, VI, 154). The speaker of this final address signs himself 'T. Lodge', and the gentlemen he addresses are presumably not Philautus's fictive sons but Lodge's conjectured readership: 'If you gather any fruits by this legacy, speak well of Euphues for writing it and me for fetching it' (228).

The final new *Euphues* book, Dickenson's *Arisbas: Euphues Amidst His Slumbers,* was published in 1594, in the midst of a new spate of Lyly publications. The past three years had seen six Lyly plays published and one new edition of *Euphues and His England*. In the next three years *Arisbas* was followed by three new editions of the prose fiction and two Lyly plays. But despite its investment in this publication history and its status as a *Euphues* book, *Arisbas* assimilates the prose fiction of Sidney, whom Dickenson praises in his preface, far more than it uses Lyly as a traditional kind of compositional source.[58] Dickenson's own comment on his work's structure is ample evidence of his distance from a Lylian narrative aesthetic:

> I have observed that Poetical method in my discourse, which the best & most approved Authors of the ancientest and most famous languages have alwaies used & allowed, beginning in medio, & afterward at occasions, unfolding former accidents.[59]

There is not enough story in either of Lyly's prose fictions to begin *in medio*: the technique presupposes the kind of linear narrative complexity that Sidney embraced. The ancient and famous authors Dickenson praises in his preface are allowed into Lyly's text only with the ambivalence and contingency characteristic of his writing, but this very dissimilarity and discontinuity between the two writers shows up the importance of Dickenson's *Euphues* title. The title is, in other words, motivated only by marketplace exigency; its meaning is intended for the book-buyer, not for its reader. That said, relationships between the book and the Lyly canon may be detected: despite the Arcadian setting, Dickenson refers to the Earth using the unusual name, Tellus (a central character in *Endymion*, published two years before), and Arisbas's love interest is called Timoclea, an opening character in *Campaspe* (republished three years before).

Dickenson, then, employs the word 'Euphues' on his title page even though his authorship accommodates, but never seriously engages, the Lylian canon. This is in contrast to Greene and Lodge, who between them sketch out Euphues (in Greene's terms) as an 'authentical' author, with whose 'discourse' Greene hopes to 'participate', 'hoping [...] to find your courteous acceptation' and set out his own 'good meaning' (*Euphues His Censure,* VI, 154). Greene's willingness to 'participate' in Euphues' discourse demonstrates how thoroughly Lyly had defined the prose fiction market. Lodge analogously begs his readers, at the end of *Rosalind*, 'If you gather any fruits by this legacy, speak well of Euphues for writing it and me for fetching it' (228). Lyly feared his readers would deem him a 'fool [that] hath intruded himself to discourse of wit', but Greene and Lodge found Lyly's intrusion opened up and anatomised discourse opportunities, displaying authorial possibilities for narrative and narration (29).

When Riche's Simonides discovers Euphues 'hard by the Market place', a basic perception about the utility of Lyly's character is uncovered. He was a market force that sold books, fuelled discussion about style and story, and buoyed contemporary constructions of authorship by permitting writers to pose as publisher-agents to his work. But it was only when Euphues' name was joined with Lyly's that books began to sell at an unprecedented rate, in a demonstration of the 'growing [...] name recognition that came with the spread of print culture'.[60] In this way Lyly and the prose fiction market anticipated the development Chartier identifies with the early 1700s in which a publication's value was dependent on its visible and signifying author.[61] Cecile Jagodzinski has argued that the increasing visibility of authorship was the result of readers and their investment in the development of authorial individuality, and this chapter has shown a particularly active kind of reader, the reader who writes a continuation of a previous writer's work.[62] Given recent interest in the history of reading, we might want to rethink the use of source material by later writers as a major part of that history.

Conclusion

Sherman has noted that 'The interaction of texts and readers has in recent years emerged as one of the most central subjects of theory and research in the humanities'.[63] This chapter has traced the reader- or user-responses of a very particular group of agents: those readers who chose to emulate Lyly and Cawood in their compositions and publications. Narrative theorists have recently emphasised the reader as a narrative agent, as when Robert Scholes suggests:

> I should like to employ the word 'narrativity' to refer to the process by which a perceiver actively constructs a story from the fictional data provided by any narrative medium. A fiction is presented to us in the form of narration (a narrative text) that guides us as our own active narrativity seeks to complete the process that will achieve a story.[64]

Lyly's emulators were also, then, Lyly's narrative users. In order to write an *Anatomy*, an author needs to open up and pull apart the anatomical subject. This metaphor for corporeal intervention fits with Lyly's prefatory concept of discursive intrusion, an authorial intervention that opens up and pulls apart its linguistic, textually bound topic. An anatomist performed his work for the benefit of an audience, with pedagogical intent, and, although it is unlikely that Lyly intended to empower his readers to create their own writing, his *Anatomy* clearly demonstrated new terms and modes of authorship, comprehensible and marketable ways of composing new writing and new speech.

This chapter has looked only at books with Euphues in their title or their narratives, and has confined itself to showing Lyly's dominant market position up to the mid-1590s, but at least that demonstration has begun to sketch out an alternative reading to the paradigm that sees Lyly's impact as superficial and short-lived. On the contrary, Lyly's place in the print fiction market was dynamic and fundamental to constructing paradigms of print storytelling that continued into seventeenth-century pamphlet and novelistic traditions, and, as we shall see, it helped to produce a new kind of authority for printed drama. Green has claimed that

> Much the most common method of acquiring profitable texts was to gain control of the works of an author of proven popularity, or to seek new authors whose texts might in turn become best-sellers or steady sellers [. . .] especially where a new author's style or material was similar to that of a proven best-seller. [. . .] A less honest but increasingly common solution was to commission works which were so similar to successful ones that they might be mistaken for them.[65]

Lyly's place within such a history is both important and unrealised, and he dominated reading habits both in his own right and via the many writers who emulated or used him. Critics tend to see the 1580s and 1590s as a period dominated by Spenser, Sidney, Marlowe and Shakespeare, as when Gavin Alexander puts forward the 1590s as 'a decade in which Sidney dominated literary culture'. Patrick Cheney has recently charted Shakespeare's 'professional response to the most famous model of authorship available in Elizabethan England: the laureate self-fashioning of Edmund Spenser'.[66] But Spenser's authorial games may not have been as famous in their own time as we now think, and there is certainly less evidence of his cultural ubiquity in the 1580s in comparison to that of Lyly. Cheney's work productively places Shakespeare in 'a professional dialogue between a Spenserian and a Marlovian aesthetics', but that conversation may have been an aside during a much larger debate about authorship, narrative, style and character engendered by Lyly's prose fiction.[67] The middle section of this book considers these questions in relation to Lylian drama.

Notes

1 Robert Greene, *The Life and Complete Works in Prose and Verse of Robert Greene*, ed. Alexander B. Grosart, 15 vols (1881–86; New York: Russell & Russell, 1964), IX, 7. Unless otherwise stated, all quotations from Greene are taken from this edition.
2 John Dover Wilson, *John Lyly* (Cambridge: Macmillan and Bowes, 1905), 3.
3 Dover Wilson, *John Lyly*, 9 and 138–9.
4 Guenther, 'To parley euphuism', 25–6.
5 Katharine Wilson, 'Transplanting Lillies: Greene, tyrants and tragical comedies', in Kirk Melnikoff and Edward Gieskes (eds), *Writing Robert Greene: Essays on England's First Notorious Professional Writer* (Aldershot: Ashgate, 2008), 189.

6 Scragg, *Euphues*, 18.
7 Scragg, 'Victim of fashion', 214.
8 Hunter, *Humanist as Courtier*, 285; Guenther, 'To parley euphuism', 25.
9 These figures count the 'doubled' editions of Lyly's prose fiction published in 1617, 1623, 1630 and 1636 as only one edition each, and similarly count Blount's *Six Court Comedies* as a single dramatic publication.
10 For further interrogation of the term 'popular', see Andy Kesson and Emma Smith, 'Towards a definition of print popularity', in Kesson and Smith (eds), *The Elizabethan Top Ten: Defining Print Popularity in Early Modern England* (Aldershot: Ashgate, 2013).
11 Hunter, 'John Lyly', in A. C. Hamilton (gen. ed.), *The Spenser Encyclopedia* (London: Routledge, 1990), 443.
12 Hunter, *Humanist as Courtier*, 284 and 287.
13 *Henry IV Part 1*, ed. David Bevington (Oxford: Oxford University Press, 1987), II.iv.373–4n. and 386–8n. Compare the editors' comments on this passage in *The First Part of King Henry IV*, ed. Herbert Weil and Judith Weil (Cambridge: Cambridge University Press, 1997), II.iv.331–3n.
14 *Every Man Out*, II.i.506–9, 'Characters', l. 55 and V.iii.512.
15 Blayney, *The First Folio of Shakespeare* (Washington, DC: Folger Library Publications, 1991), 2.
16 Peter Hausted, *Senile Odium*, ed. and tr. Laurens J. Mills (Bloomington: Indiana University Press, 1949), 9, I.iv and I.vi (Mills's translation). There are no line numbers in Mills's edition.
17 My thanks to Eugene Giddens for discussing his work for the edition of the play, with Anne Barton, in *The Cambridge Edition of the Works of Ben Jonson*, ed. David Bevington, Martin Butler and Ian Donaldson, 7 vols (Cambridge: Cambridge University Press, 2012), VII.
18 *The Knight of the Burning Pestle*, ed. Sheldon P. Zitner (Manchester: Manchester University Press, 2004), 5.
19 *The Knight of the Burning Pestle*, ed. J. W. Lever (London: Longmans, 1962), 111.
20 Compare Scragg on 1590s reprints of Lyly's work ('Victim of fashion', 214).
21 Alan B. Farmer and Zachary Lesser, 'The popularity of playbooks revisited', *Shakespeare Quarterly* 56:1 (Spring 2005), 1–32 (5).
22 Zachary Lesser, 'Playbooks', in Joad Raymond (ed.), *The Oxford History of Popular Print Culture, vol. 1: Cheap Print in Britain and Ireland to 1660* (Oxford: Oxford University Press, 2011), 526.
23 Jowett, *Shakespeare and Text*, 10.
24 Farmer and Lesser, 'Popularity', 7.
25 Margaret Schlauch, *Antecedents of the English Novel 1400–1600* (London: Oxford University Press, 1963), 185.
26 Catherine Belsey, 'Literature, history, politics', *Literature and History* 9 (1983), 17–26, rpt in Richard Wilson and Richard Dutton (eds), *New Historicism and Renaissance Drama* (London: Longman, 1992), 40 (her italics).
27 See [John Lyly], *Gallathea*, ed. Leah Scragg (Oxford: Oxford University Press, 1998), ix.
28 On the two editions of *Sapho and Phao*, only recently identified by

Bevington as such, see Bevington, 'The first edition of John Lyly's *Sappho and Phao* (1584)', *Studies in Bibliography* 42 (1989), 187–99.

29 William Sherman, *Used Books: Marking Readers in Renaissance England* (Philadelphia: University of Pennsylvania Press, 2008).

30 Raven, *Business of Books*, 26–8; John Twyning, *London Dispossessed: Literature and Social Space in the Early Modern City* (London: Macmillan, 1998), 123.

31 Charles Whitworth, 'Reviews', *Cahiers Élizabéthains* 66 (2004), 77–80 (79).

32 Compare Andrew Hadfield, 'From English to British literature: John Lyly's *Euphues* and the 1590 *The Faerie Queene*', in *Shakespeare, Spenser and the Matter of Britain* (Basingstoke: Palgrave Macmillan, 2004), esp. 109, and, more generally, Richard Helgerson, *Forms of Nationhood: The Elizabethan Writing of England* (Chicago: University of Chicago Press, 1992), 1 and 33.

33 Scragg, *Euphues*, 21.

34 Daniel Javitch, *Poetry and Courtliness in Renaissance England* (Princeton: Princeton University Press, 1978).

35 References to the 1578 edition are taken from John Lyly, *Selected Prose and Dramatic Work*, ed. Leah Scragg (Manchester: Carcanet Press, 1997).

36 Compare King, 'John Lyly and Elizabethan rhetoric', 153.

37 Nancy Selleck, *The Interpersonal Idiom in Shakespeare, Donne, and Early Modern Culture* (Basingstoke: Palgrave Macmillan, 2008), 8–9.

38 Roger Ascham, *The Scholemaster* (London: printed by John Day, 1570), Diiiv.

39 Anthony Grafton and Lisa Jardine, '"Studied for action": how Gabriel Harvey read his Livy', *Past and Present* 129 (1990), 30–78 (30); William H. Sherman, *John Dee: The Politics of Reading and Writing in the English Reniassance* (Amherst: University of Massachusetts Press, 1995), 65.

40 Eugene R. Kintgen, *Reading in Tudor England* (Pittsburgh: University of Pittsburgh Press, 1996), 182.

41 Arthur F. Kinney, *Humanist Poetics: Thought, Rhetoric and Fiction in Sixteenth-Century England* (Amherst: University of Massachusetts Press, 1986), 178.

42 Stephen B. Dobranski, *Readers and Authorship in Early Modern England* (Cambridge: Cambridge University Press, 2005), 2–3 and 6.

43 Annabel Patterson, *Censorship and Interpretation: The Conditions of Writing and Reading in Early Modern England* (Madison: University of Wisconsin Press, 1984), 18.

44 Arthur F. Kinney (ed.), *The Cambridge Companion to English Literature, 1500–1600* (Cambridge: Cambridge University Press, 2000), 5.

45 Austen Saker, *Narbonus: The Laberynth of Libertie* (London: Richard Jones, 1580), Biiiv.

46 Jonathan Goldberg, *Endlesse Worke: Spenser and the Structures of Discourse* (Baltimore: Johns Hopkins University Press, 1981), 24–5.

47 David Margolies, *Novel and Society in Elizabethan England* (London: Croom Helm, 1985), 46.

48 Will Brooker, *Batman Unmasked: Analyzing a Cultural Icon* (London: Continuum Books, 2001), 9.
49 Anthony Munday, *Zelauto: The Fountaine of Fame*, ed. Jack Stillinger (Carbondale: Southern Illinois University Press, 1963), 7–8.
50 Thomas Watson, *The Hekatompathia; or, Passionate Centurie of Love (1582)*, ed. S. K. Heninger, Jr (Gainesville, FL: Scholars' Facsimiles & Reprints, 1964), A3.
51 For Cawood's dominant position in Paul's churchyard, see Ryrie, 'Cawood'.
52 Newcomb, *Reading Popular Romance*, 48.
53 Grosart, *Greene*, VI, 151–2.
54 George Pettie, *A Petite Pallace of Pettie his Pleasure*, ed. Herbert Hartman (London: Oxford University Press, 1938), 5.
55 Robert Greene, *Rosalind: Euphues Golden Legacy*, ed. Donald Beecher (Ottawa: Dovehouse Editions, 1997), 95.
56 R. W. Dent, *Proverbial Language in English Drama Exclusive of Shakespeare, 1495–1616: An Index* (London: University of California, 1984), W280.2, T436, N135.1.
57 Catherine Bates, '"A large occasion of discourse": John Lyly and the art of civil conversation', *Review of English Studies* n.s. 42 (1991), 469–86 (469–70).
58 Robert H. F. Carver, *The Protean Ass: The Metamorphoses of Apuleius from Antiquity to the Renaissance* (Oxford: Oxford University Press, 2008), 335–6; Constance C. Relihan, *Cosmographical Glasses: Geographic Discourse, Gender and Elizabethan Fiction* (Kent, OH: Kent State University Press, 2004), 62–8.
59 John Dickenson, *Arisbas, Euphues amidst his slumbers* (London: Thomas Woodcocke, 1594), Aiiv.
60 Dobranski, *Readers and Authorship*, 7.
61 Roger Chartier, *The Order of Books: Readers, Authors, and Libraries in Europe Between the Fourteenth and Eighteenth Centuries*, tr. Lydia G. Cochrane (Stanford: Stanford University Press, 1994), 37–9.
62 Cecile M. Jagodzinski, *Privacy and Print: Reading and Writing in Seventeenth-Century England* (Charlottesville: University of Virginia Press, 1999), 11.
63 Sherman, *John Dee*, 53.
64 Robert Scholes, *Semiotics and Interpretation* (New Haven: Yale University Press, 1982), 60.
65 Green, *Print and Protestantism*, 17–18.
66 Gavin Alexander, *Writing After Sidney: The Literary Response to Sir Philip Sidney 1586–1640* (Oxford: Oxford University Press, 2006), xix; Patrick Cheney, 'Perdita, Pastorella and the romance of literary form: Shakespeare's counter-Spenserian authorship', in J. B. Lethbridge (ed.), *Shakespeare and Spenser: Attractive Opposites* (Manchester: Manchester University Press, 2008), 123.
67 Patrick Cheney, *Shakespeare, National Poet-Playwright* (Cambridge: Cambridge University Press, 2004), 9.

PART II

Lyly, performance and print

CHAPTER 3

'Whatsoever we present': Lyly's elusive theatre (1583–c.1590)

At the start of the second act of Noel Coward's *The Vortex*, a long stage direction sets out the choreography necessary for the play. Coward ends his directions with a postscript which is unlikely to have made him popular backstage: '*This scene will probably be exceedingly difficult to produce, but is absolutely indispensable*'.[1] Lyly might well have said the same of his plays. From the start of his playwriting career, he experimented with the abilities of his boy actors, asking them to dance, tumble and sing in his first play, *Campaspe*. But soon Lyly showed his willingness to test out the limits of performance: old characters have their youth restored to them on stage, an aspen tree grows and then turns into a witch, stones and a stick turn golden, asses' ears sprout and then fall off and three nymphs turn into a stone, a rose and a bird respectively, only to have their original shapes restored to them in a heavenly shower. No wonder Lyly's prologues and epilogues compare his plays to demonic conjurations and dancing fairies. These scenes must have been exceedingly difficult to produce, but the company apparently felt them to be absolutely indispensable. This chapter asks questions about Lyly's onstage worlds to determine his impact on early modern dramaturgy, both as represented in the theatre and in the printed versions of his plays. It also shows ways in which this dramaturgy suggests continuity with the prose fiction.

As the next chapter demonstrates, the printing of Lyly's plays was an important moment in the development of an early modern market for play books. Without this market, we would have lost almost all traces of early modern theatre, and, as is often the case in this period, the printed versions of Lyly's plays are our only record of the content of his dramatic work. But the printed record provides only a partial and a distorted witness to the play worlds created on stage, and we therefore need to treat the texts we have with proper caution. Lyly himself seems to play with this boundary between the onstage world and its representation in a book in *Love's Metamorphosis*, when a siren attempts to seduce a young man on the seafront. The boy, Petulius, is rescued by his shape-shifting girlfriend Protea, who disguises herself as the ghost of the Greek hero Odysseus. In order to describe the fictional role of the theatre's stage, the text names a small range of props that define the seashore at which the scene takes place, such as a rock, a mirror and a comb, and the characters refer to parts of the onstage and offstage world: 'this shore', 'this rock', 'the sea' and 'this thicket' (IV.ii.51.0, 25, 87–8 and 101). With their words, their props, their costumes and their whereabouts, the actors, in McMillin's terms, '*are* the scenic design, in the patterns of motion and colour', their deictic language helping to establish the physicality of the fictional world.[2] But when Protea leads Petulius away from the siren, she tells him to 'Follow me at this door, and out at the other' (IV.ii.112). In an era before beach-huts, this is not a reference to the fictive seaside that the text, props and actors had otherwise consistently constructed, but rather to the theatre space itself. Removing her disguise and revealing herself to be Protea, the character also removes the disguise of the stage, ignoring its fictional, metaphorical meaning and referring instead to its architectural and theatrical reality. It is very difficult to know whether this sentence records a moment of metatheatricality in the playhouse or shows us that Lyly's plays were adapted for publication: to put it another way, this line may be an internal stage direction for the actor reading before performance or for the reader reading in the absence of performance.

This book has shown Lyly's 'discursive intrusion' into a nascent prose fiction tradition, but it is not possible to make a comparable study of Lyly's use of contemporary models for playwriting. Whereas the prose fiction could be compared to earlier models, such as Painter, Pettie and Gascoigne, few plays survive from the 1570s and early 1580s, making it difficult to investigate Lyly's impact on his contemporaries in quite the same way. But although the historical record does not permit us to grasp the way Lyly worked with the models around him, he certainly had to engage with existing dramatic models. Though we have few extant plays from this period, Lyly's plays were written alongside a thriving culture of play composition: William Ingram estimates that more than two hundred plays were written during the 1570s alone.[3] Almost all of those plays are now lost, and subsequent plays, including those of Shakespeare, could easily have been lost were it not for the important model Lyly set when he saw a majority of his plays into print. As a consequence of the poor record of survival of earlier plays, this chapter cannot compare Lyly's work to earlier models in a way possible with his prose fiction, and therefore seeks to investigate his dramaturgy on its own terms, emphasising its particularly influential and provocative nature. John Lyly's dramaturgical stories are as elusive and protean as his prose fiction, and, at the same time that his character Euphues was being reworked and commodified by print writers and publishers, Lyly reworked and innovated ways to create fictional worlds and characters in the theatre. Lyly's plays made an enormous impact on those who saw and read them, and this chapter assesses that impact at the level of audience addresses, performative rhetoric and the establishment of character and fictional worlds.

Lyly's plays have suffered from the same post-Shakespearean prism that refracts our perception of the prose fiction. They continue to suffer from a general lack of interest in 1580s theatre: as Sally-Beth MacLean and McMillin put it, 'Theatre historians have not thought much about the London theatre of 1583', the year that Lyly's first two plays entered the Blackfriars repertory.[4] MacLean and McMillin have ensured a renewed interest in 1580s adult performance, but the most recent work on the Queen's Men, a collection edited by Helen Ostovich, Holger Schott Syme and Andrew Griffin, claims the Queen's Men to be 'the company that dominated the English theatrical world between 1583 and the early 1590s' without considering the claims of the child companies that staged plays by Lyly, Marlowe, Peele and others in the same period.[5] Indeed, this entire decade is, Paul Whitfield White suggests, a 'perplexing decade for theater historians', and, despite efforts by scholars such as William Ingram and Janette Dillon, scholarship remains remarkably uninterested in the period in which new theatre companies moved from a reliance solely on old touring plays and began to market themselves as purveyors of new plays in new buildings. As Whitfield White points out, Lyly is 'the one major English playwright for whom we have extant plays extending across the decade of the eighties', and as such he offers us an excellent point from which to begin work on this overlooked decade.[6]

Lyly's plays have never enjoyed a full-scale, modern professional production, and scholars have therefore largely been working in the dark when it comes to describing his work on stage. Even Shakespeare scholarship has only recently started to take performance seriously as a form of research.[7] Given the tendency to minimise Lyly's achievements in order to heighten those of

Shakespeare, it is no surprise that Lyly's plays are most often described as old-fashioned or medieval, static and unnatural. Thus W. W. Greg quoted a Lylian monologue to demonstrate that the 'unsuitability of his style for dramatic purposes' was 'painfully evident, and, as may be imagined, the effect is even less happy in the case of dialogue'. Michael Best influentially described 'Lyly's static drama' as rooted in an 'inconclusive plot', rather than moving from an opening 'motivation' towards a 'conflict which is [then] resolved in action'. For Best, Lyly favours 'discussion rather than action'.[8] Hunter makes clear that such interpretations are coloured by anachronistic expectations of realism: 'In the obviousness of its rhythmical and conceptual organisation, Lyly's [dramatic] prose is certainly pushed far beyond the limits of realism and cannot be thought to reflect the business language of any particular community.'[9]

A wide variety of Lylian scholars follow Best in describing Lyly's dramaturgy as static. Saccio described Lyly as a dramatist 'avoiding the development of plot'. One of Lyly's most astute critics, Jocelyn Powell, referred to 'stasis' as 'Lyly's great dramatic discovery' but paradoxically defines it in terms of Lyly's use of 'a continually changing visual pattern', 'the play of sight, solo, ensemble, dialogue; and [...] a consequent play of rhythm'.[10] Reviewing these statements about static Lyly, Hunter claimed that '[t]he unusual critical agreement on this point is, fortunately for all concerned, shared by Lyly himself'; and in support of this claim he quoted the epilogue to *Sapho and Phao* and its reference to the play's conclusion as 'an end where we first began'. Best agrees and adds, 'not only does *Sapho and Phao* remain static, ending where it began, but *Endimion* begins and ends with the same complimentary [*sic*] situation'.[11] And in his edition of the play, Bevington quotes the epilogue's 'labyrinth of conceits' and calls the play 'a static drama', 'the very opposite of narrative drama'.[12] As Hunter says, scholarly consensus here is unusually strong.

But as we have already seen in relation to his prose fiction, Lyly's work is not 'the very opposite of narrative'. Lyly repeatedly encourages readers and audiences to treat his texts with suspicion, and the epilogue to *Sapho and Phao* merits such suspicion: the play does not end as it first began.[13] Just as Lyly asks the audience of *Endymion* to overlook the implications of his story, so he asks the *Sapho* audience to ignore ways in which stories change characters. Sapho may still 'sway her sceptre in her brave court' by the end of the play, just as Phao describes her at the beginning, but Cupid has switched allegiances from Venus to Sapho, and Phao himself is no longer 'a ferryman' or 'a free man' (I.i.9, 1). The change in Phao's position is highlighted by the fact that he begins and ends the play: he tells the audience at the start of the play of his 'content', 'quiet' and lack of ambition, and he tells them at its close of his intent to abandon his ferry in order to 'Range rather over the world' and 'entreat for death' (I.i.1–2; V.iii.16–17). Certainly for Phao, Lyly's 'labyrinth of conceits' entails emotive movement, not intellectual stasis.

Bevington's description of this scene as a 'signification of a concluding harmony' seems therefore to privilege Lyly's statements in the epilogue over the actual content of the final scene, or the well-being of the high-status monarch over the suffering of the working-class ferryboy.[14] This ending might prompt scholars to reconsider the play's genre: Lyly's plays are not called comedies until 1632, and they are given this label by the same publisher who helped to create the Shakespeare First Folio's problematic generic boundaries. Indeed genre itself is an unexamined idea in the 1580s, characterised by flux rather than certainty. *Sapho and Phao* was published in 1584 and in 1591 with no generic support for its readers, and the language of labyrinthine conceit might well denote bewildering and disconcerting movement: 'a dance of a fairy in a circle', as Lyly also describes the play (10). The epilogue not only tells the audience they have been moved (in both senses of the word), but informs them that they are now lost and will need to rescue themselves from the conclusion of the story: 'And so we wish every one of you a thread to lead you out of the doubts wherewith we leave you entangled' (11–13). The later imposition of genre on this play has helped to gloss over the implications of this ending.

As the play's male protagonist, Phao epitomises this sense of movement, change and doubt. When Venus first sees him, she describes his readiness for movement, saying to Cupid, 'Come away, and behold the ferry boy ready to conduct us' (I.i.55–6). As he bids 'farewell, Sicily!' and goes 'wherever I wander', Phao is defined not by stasis but by itinerancy, a quality implicit from the start of the play in his profession as ferryman as well as his movement from the ferry to Sibylla's cave, to Sapho's court and then into self-imposed banishment. The dramatic logic of movement was built into the early indoor theatres, dominated as they were by stage houses that framed the performance space.[15] This is a theatrical structure unfamiliar to early modern scholars, who are more used to considering the spatial dynamics of the outdoor theatres. Lyly repeatedly uses this stage structure to set up oppositional spaces on stage, from Alexander's court and Diogenes' tub in *Campaspe* to Cynthia's court and the lunary bank in *Endymion.* Alexander's efforts to persuade Diogenes to leave his tub and cross the stage to the court dominate much of the story and the spatial logic of the earlier play, and it is Cynthia's decision to leave her court and travel to the lunary bank that resolves much of the story in the later play. Both stories play out in spatial terms: having failed to visit Endymion previously, Cynthia's journey across the stage is a physical, kinetic kind of climax, whilst Alexander's attempts to persuade Diogenes to come to court ironically entail frequent visits from the court to Diogenes. Scholars have read these scripts and complained about the lack of story, but story in Lylian drama is written into the choreography of the space rather than the logic of character statements. Lyly exploited the locational meaning of the stage by writing a dramaturgy of movement into the script, creating what James Thomas has called (in relation to all kinds of drama) '*indigenous blocking*', textually implicit movement.[16] As we shall see throughout this chapter, Lyly's scripts routinely demand movement, gesture and rhythm from the actors speaking their lines. But since we have now heard the epilogue to *Sapho and Phao* describe the play as a 'labyrinth of conceits', 'a dance of a fairy in a circle', phrases which stress 'the doubts wherewith we leave you entangled', we should now turn to Lyly's audience addresses and consider the ways they represent his art.

'Agrippa his shadows': Lyly describes performance

Many of Lyly's plays provide audience addresses in the form of prologue and epilogue, and the earlier printed plays offer the reader a choice of such addresses: a reader opening the 1584 *Campaspe* finds first 'The prologue at Blackfriars' and then, over the page, 'The prologue at the court'. This seems to carry a dual function, firstly of emphasising to the reader the importance of performance space to the script that follows, whilst also troubling that importance by emphasising the script's mobility from one performance space to another. We might also consider the combination of a court prologue and a more public prologue within the space of a relatively cheap book as indicative of the way Lyly transcended distinctions between elite and popular culture. The court prologue emphasises this shift by worrying that 'our bird which fluttered by twilight, seeming a swan' at the Blackfriars will now 'be proved a bat set against the sun' – that is, exposed as a flawed play when performed before such an illustrious audience (1–2). The reader is asked to think about the impact of performance circumstances on the meaning of the play, and asked to choose how to navigate two prologues and two epilogues that frame and renegotiate the script.

It is therefore particularly significant that Lyly's prologues and epilogues insistently interrogate the meaning of performance, in ways which may take his contemporary audience and modern readers by surprise. Thus, speaking before the court debut of *Campaspe*, Lyly's prologue told the audience that 'Appion, raising Homer from Hell, demanded only who was his father; and we, calling Alexander from his grave, seek only who was his love' (10–13). Despite his modern associations with sycophancy and conformity, Lyly's debut at court presented itself as an act of necromancy, as confirmed by the next sentence of the prologue:

> Whatsoever we present we wish it may be thought the dancing of Agrippa his shadows, who in the moment they were seen were of any shape one would conceive, or lynxes, who, having a quick sight to discern, have a short memory to forget. (13–16)

The passage is typical of Lyly's ability to say provocative, surprising and dissident things under the cover of authenticating references to humanist culture. The reference to lynxes relies on Erasmus's description of these animals as quick-sighted but equipped with desultory memory skills, which Lyly found in the same passage from which he took the reference to Appion. But these uses of humanistic learning are combined with a reference to Agrippa and his 'shadows', these being the kind of supernatural spirits Puck refers to when he calls Oberon 'king of shadows'. Lyly here describes his play with reference to the same necromancer that Marlowe's Dr Faustus would later hope to emulate and outdo. Lyly compared his second play to dancing fairies, but his first play is here compared to the raising of dancing demons.

With his hope that the play 'may be *thought* the dancing of Agrippa his shadows', Lyly links the audience's mental processing of a play to ideas he first adumbrated in his prose fiction. In *Euphues and His England*, the lover Philautus approaches the magician Psellus to obtain potions which will make his beloved fall in love with him, but the magician tells him:

> if you have so great confidence in my cunning as you protest, it may be that your strong imagination shall work that in you which my art cannot; for it is a principle among us that a vehement thought is more available than the virtue of our figures, forms, or characters. (253)

Psellus emphasises the immunity of the mind from magic: those who 'imagine that the mind is either by incantation or excantation to be ruled are as far from truth as the east from the west' (261). In much the same way, Lyly in his court prologue to *Campaspe* throws emphasis upon what 'may be thought' by the audience, what 'shape one would conceive', and not upon the mimetic powers of Agrippa and his shadows (who presumably stand for Lyly and his actors). It is the believing and imagining audience members who must determine the effect of the magic, and in this way the audience are both empowered by and blamed for the play they are about to see.

This prologue provides evidence for the tactical way in which Lyly deployed euphuism, that strange combination of deliberative prose style combined with unusual analogies and examples, to make statements that might otherwise be impossible. No editor of the play has commented on the way the prologue slips out of syntactic control. It begins by offering to define the play itself ('Whatsoever we present'), but it ends instead by defining the audience ('lynxes, who, having a quick sight to discern'). This transition from the play to the audience means that the reference to Agrippa's shadows is a reference to the audience members as well as – or instead of – the actors. The conception of the play, its physical shape and its conceptual meaning are the responsibility of those who 'conceive' it, the audience. Under cover of humanist commonplacing and a lengthy and labyrinthine sentence structure, Lyly tacitly shifts the referent of his statement, locating the meaning of performance not in the words of the script, the movement of the actors or the process of the story but in the audience's response.

The prologue to Lyly's next play, performed during the same court season, reuses these ideas. The speaker, who Bevington suggests was Lyly himself, repeats the phrase 'Whatsoever we present' from the *Campaspe* prologue.[17] This time, however, the performance is located not in the responses of the entire audience but solely in the mind of the queen:

> Whatsoever we present, whether it be tedious (which we fear) or toyish (which we doubt), sweet or sour, absolute or imperfect, or whatsoever, in all humbleness we all, and I on knee for all, entreat that your Highness imagine yourself to be in a deep dream that, staying the conclusion, in your rising your Majesty vouchsafe but to say, 'And so you awaked'. (12–18)

Once again, a Lyly prologue tries to define this 'Whatsoever we present', and once again the sentence concludes by locating the 'whatsoever' within the perception of the audience itself. The queen must 'imagine' just as the lynxes 'discern' and Agrippa's onlookers 'conceive', and these verbal affinities between *Campaspe* and *Sapho and Phao* insist on the production of dramatic meaning as the provenance of the audience – though this time only one audience member, the queen, is invested with the power to create meaning.

Despite the similarity between the two prologues, the second play revises the idea as it recycles it. Whereas Lyly managed to define 'Whatsoever we present' in *Campaspe* as something conceived and discerned by onlookers, in *Sapho and Phao* the speaker awkwardly returns to the word that began the sentence ('sweet or sour, absolute or imperfect, or whatsoever'). This repetition of the word marks the centre of the sentence as Lyly once again switches focus from the production to the audience, though he this time locates the play in the mind of the audience's most privileged member. Since the play is cast as the queen's dream, the very vagueness of 'whatsoever' suggests something unreal, even ghostly, created in the mind of the beholder. Whether described in terms of the raising of Alexander's ghost in *Campaspe* or Elizabeth's supposed dream in *Sapho and Phao*, Lyly's first two plays are introduced as something indefinable and supernatural, the imaginative responsibility of the audience's quick and cunning minds.

As we have seen, the printed versions of these plays contained prologues for their two different venues, and Lyly explains to the plays' audiences and later readership that the change in performance space entailed a change in the play's meaning: 'We are ashamed that our bird which fluttered by twilight, seeming a swan, should be proved a bat set against the sun'. This sun, of course, is Elizabeth, and her presence is figured as transformative: the play will seem different in her presence. But the Blackfriars audience of *Campaspe* is also told that they define the play, for 'Our exercise [the performance] must be as your judgment is, resembling water, which is always of the same colour into what it runneth' (epilogue, 4–6). Lyly's statement that Elizabeth will shine on the play and reveal its limitations represents conventional praise of the monarch (a convention the play's story does much to unpack and challenge), but his description of the play as water running into the audience's judgment is not conventional. It throws emphasis upon the function of the audience within dramaturgical meaning, an emphasis made all the more explicit when the plays were printed and the reader came across two prologues for two different spaces. The play's appearance and meaning is repeatedly ascribed to, and claimed to be determined by, the audience's imagination.

Discussing 'the connection between dramaturgy and the imagination', Catherine Richardson turns to Katherine Eisaman Maus, for whom all early modern drama was 'radically synecdochic', urging or forcing its audiences into using 'partial and limited presentation as a basis for conjecture about what is undisplayed or undisplayable'. Richardson responds thus:

> a theatre which relies upon conjecture suggests a broad and fruitful interaction between narrative suggestion and audience imagination [...]. It raises the question, can we begin to reconstruct how and what the audience might have imagined?[18]

Richardson and Maus both describe how the public theatre tradition developed from the late 1580s onwards, and are therefore thinking neither of Lyly's work nor of the indoor theatre. Their interest in audience imagination tallies with perhaps the most famous early modern enunciation of dramaturgy, the *Henry V* prologue, which asks its audience to interact with and imaginatively transform the material limitations of the play, collaboratively and imaginatively supplementing Maus's 'synecdochic' dramaturgy to achieve the desired effect. As Richardson puts it elsewhere, props on the onstage world encourage audiences to 'complete the representation from memory', by seeing a table and the actors around it as a room, for example.[19] This is a local example of the general principle spelt out by Weimann, that 'In the Elizabethan theatre, the imaginary play-world and the material world of Elizabethan playing constitute different, although of course partially overlapping registers of perception, enjoyment, and involvement'.[20] Lyly's work anticipates these ideas but also maps out something bolder and more bizarre, at least to anybody used to thinking of performance as the product of authors, actors or directors, when he claims it to be the imaginative responsibility of the audience only. This brings his dramatic theory into line with his prose fiction practice, where the revisions to the *Anatomy* show Lyly suppressing narrative information in order to force his readers to supplement his stories imaginatively.

Modern directors and specialists often describe theatre performance as a collaborative process, in contrast to cinema or television. The Shared Experience director, Mike Alfreds, for example, talks about a 'willing complicity' of theatre practitioners and audience members. As Stephen Purcell puts it,

> actors create the imaginative world of the play in full acknowledgement of its fictional nature, and by implication, request the audience's complicity

> in establishing the illusion. Alfreds recounts how this realisation made him appreciate that actors and audience 'shared in an act of imagination – were, in fact, brought together by it'[.][21]

It is hard to argue with the idea that theatre takes place around a mutual and collaborative imaginative system, and we therefore need to ask why Lyly attempts to locate dramatic meaning solely in the interpretative faculties of the audience. This may, for example, be early modern deference, determined by hierarchical thinking. But, more importantly, Lyly's insistence that whatever 'shape[s]' the audience 'conceive' during the production are their responsibility alone relinquishes that responsibility for himself and his company. This relegation, not just of the meaning but the 'shape' and identity of performance, clearly has socio-political implications; it releases, or tries to release, the company from the responsibility of performance. Tied to the elusive and secretive nature of Lylian stylistic composition, his pronouncements on dramaturgy in *Campaspe* and *Sapho and Phao* offer us interpretative positions from which to read the plays themselves. But it is important to note the limitations of the idea that meaning proceeds exclusively from an audience. The very fact that Lyly's audience addresses make statements about his plays' meanings demonstrates that meaning cannot come solely from the audience, and shows Lyly negotiating tensions between the stage and the audience who watch it. Just as Lyly's prose fiction made unusual and disturbing demands of his readers, so he characterises his plays as peculiarly audience-derived.

Two Lyly plays feature scenes in which characters sleep and dream, and these scenes once again show the playwright confronting the audience with interpretative challenges, since these dream narratives are offered to the audience without authoritative explanation. In this respect they resemble the second half of the *Anatomy*, with its absence of a narrator or any other guide to interpretation, and show Lyly making use of the lessons he learnt in the process of revising his first work. In *Sapho and Phao*, Sapho experiences a lengthy dream that patently encodes her fears about the consequences of her love for Phao. But Sapho's dream is interrupted, and therefore given no conclusion, and her subsequent description of it to her waiting-maids initiates a scene in which each maid discusses the meaning of dreams. Sapho returns to her bed in order to continue her dream, suggesting to the audience a later explanation of this dream's meaning, but it is not mentioned again. In *Endymion*, the audience actually see a dumb show of Endymion's dream, and he later retells it to Cynthia and her court. Cynthia promises that the soothsayer 'Gyptes at our better leisure shall expound it' – but he does not (V.i.103–4). In both plays, the dreams are composed of threatening images that articulate fears about sexuality and power, and so are especially provocative in court performance in front of a queen who had recently abandoned prolonged marriage negotiations and begun to promote herself as the Virgin Queen. These dreams are further tied to the real queen in the audience by the *Sapho and Phao* court prologue which begged Elizabeth to imagine the play as her own 'deep dream' and 'to say', at its conclusion, 'And so you awaked' (16–18). This image of the play as a dream, like the dreams in the plays' stories, devolves meaning over to the audience.

In his audience addresses, as well as in the plays themselves, Lyly developed a theory and practice of dramaturgy as something ephemeral in the elusive quality of the images it presented and the responsibility of audience members' imagination. Indeed William West claims Lyly as the first English playwright to express 'the theatre's indeterminacy', producing an 'uncertainty built in to performance'.[22] Again and again, spectacle is described by Lyly as 'of any shape one would conceive', as water which is 'always of the same colour into what it runneth', as something in which the audience's 'strong imagination shall work that in you which my art cannot'. If, as Psellus put it in *Euphues and His England*, 'a vehement thought is more available than the virtue of our figures, forms, or characters', then Lyly made sure that the figures, forms and characters he presented on stage prompted vehement thoughts within his audiences' imaginations.

'[W]ords melt wits like wax': euphuism onstage[23]

Although Lyly's claim that audiences are entirely responsible for the onstage worlds seems a deliberate overstatement of the performance process, his use of dreams in plays is an example of the way his theory determines dramaturgical practice. By the time he came to write plays, Lyly was already celebrated for his unusual, unexpected and allusive prose style, and this style shared with the performance theory an emphasis on the role of the listener or reader in the determination of meaning. As a playwright, Lyly continued to deploy and develop this prose style, but, since some of the first readers of a new play are actors, these stylistic games had very different implications once they were used within the script of a play.

In *Campaspe*, Alexander the Great confronts the philosopher Diogenes who has refused to come to pay homage to the king. Leah

Scragg notes: 'Alexander's superficially straightforward observation to Diogenes, "Thou shalt live no longer than I will" [. . .] is capable of both benign and malign constructions.'[24] The double meaning in Alexander's statement to Diogenes, which hinges on the meaning of the word 'will', means that the king is either acknowledging that both men will one day die or threatening to have the philosopher executed. This means that a single line in their conversation makes demands of the actor playing Alexander that will affect his entire performance. Lyly's rhetorical style in his prose fiction had been associated by his readers with wittiness, trickiness and verbal dexterity, and it is developed here to delegate decisions about meaning to a very particular kind of reader, the actor.

Scragg has traced the way the structures of euphuistic prose came to govern the way Lyly structured his plays, in particular opposing characters, speeches and scenes against one another. But this is not the only way that euphuistic technique and performance interrelated. Once Lyly began to adapt his prose to the stage, he had to use it to define 'real' characters within a fictional world. The prose fiction had experimented with the readers' engagement with the story by playing on the protean elements of Euphues' personality, but, unlike readers' relationship with Euphues, audiences could actually see the bodies of the actors who represented Lyly's stage characters. The writer of *The Anatomy of Wit* suddenly had real anatomies to describe and define, a fact that threw his writing into a new relationship with the fictional but now partially physicalised world it depicted. As Lyly became more confident writing for real bodies, his depiction of psychological interiority became more explorative, and the few modern actors who have performed Lyly's plays have described their surprise at discovering the physical movement written into his prose, the gestural nature of euphuistic clauses. Recent performance has confirmed Barish's claim that 'Lyly's techniques of marking out divisions of thought and subdividing his material in parallel sequences not only contribute to clarity of outline, they affect gesture and delivery, dictating stage motion, enforcing pauses and accents'.[25] Early modern prose therefore has implications for the construction of stage space, just as stage space had implications for the development of prose.

A good example of this uneasy fusion between dialogue and action can be seen in *Campaspe*, in which both Alexander and Diogenes are described to the audience at some length before they enter the stage. The play starts with a discussion of Alexander in relation to his father by the army officers Clitus and Parmenio, whilst the messenger

Melippus later describes an encounter with Diogenes in a long speech that includes a reported dialogue within an audience address. Melippus tells the audience that:

> I came to [. . .] an old obscure fellow who, sitting in a tub turned towards the sun, read Greek to a young boy. Him when I willed to appear before Alexander, he answered, 'If Alexander would fain see me, let him come to me; if learn of me, let him come to me; whatsoever it be, let him come to me'. 'Why', said I, 'he is a king'. He answered, 'Why, I am a philosopher'. (I.iii.14–20)

In both cases, Alexander and Diogenes are detailed to the audience in relation to an authority figure. Alexander is measured against his father, and Diogenes the philosopher is opposed to Alexander the king. Both characters are thus introduced in antithetical terms familiar to anyone who had read Lyly's prose fiction ('none more witty than Euphues, yet at the first none more wicked', *Euphues*, 33). Indeed the continuity of the style provides one way that the audience might be aware of the play's authorship, and that Lyly's authorship offered itself as a hermeneutical key to the play. But in Lyly's plays, there are no equivalents to the narrator who mediated between the characters in the prose fiction: the audience alone are left to arbitrate between characters' antithetical positions.

As they open the play with a dispute, Clitus and Parmenio demonstrate a high degree of tension within Alexander's supposedly harmonious court, just as Diogenes demonstrates the limitations of Alexander's power over his subjects. The audience are left to draw conclusions about characters and the way they are described, and these conclusions themselves have implications for the representation of monarchy and its power. In the staged dialogue between Clitus and Parmenio, and the offstage dialogue reported to the audience by Melippus, familiar antithetical structures are adapted from print storytelling to anticipate the entrance of central characters. Alexander and Diogenes may be described in oppositional terms, but each regularly talks to and about the other: opposites do not so much attract as begin to affect one other.

The evolution in Lyly's use of euphuistic prose to define character may be seen in the difference between an earlier stage character, Sibylla in *Sapho and Phao* (performed in 1583) and Fidelia in *Love's Metamorphosis* (performed in the later 1580s). Both women tell a biographical story to explain the predicament in which they find themselves, and for anyone unfamiliar with these plays it is worth stressing how unusual these predicaments are: Sibylla is hundreds of centuries old, and Fidelia is a tree. Sibylla begins her story to Phao in this manner:

> When I was young as you now are – I speak it without boasting – I was beautiful; for Phoebus in his godhead sought to get my maidenhead. But I, fond wench, receiving a benefit from above, began to wax squeamish beneath, not unlike to asolis, which being made green by heavenly drops shrinketh into the ground when there fall showers, or the Syrian mud, which being made white chalk by the sun never ceaseth rolling till it lie in the shadow. (II.i.45–51)

This passage contains many of the patterns associated with euphuism: alliteration ('young', 'you'; 'boasting', 'beautiful'), rhyme ('godhead', 'maidenhead'), syntactical balance ('above [...] beneath') and esoteric humanist knowledge (asolis and Syrian mud). The euphuistic imagery is appropriate, since the amorous advances of Phoebus, god of the sun, are characterised in terms of weather: 'showers' and 'the sun'. But suitable or not, their effect is to delay, rather than advance, the linear telling of the story.

Fidelia in *Love's Metamorphosis* starts to speak in rather different circumstances. Erisichthon has begun to cut down Ceres' sacred tree, at which point the tree unexpectedly begins to protest with this address to its assailant:

> Monster of men, hate of the heavens, and to the earth a burden, what hath chaste Fidelia committed? It is thy spite, Cupid, that, having no power to wound my unspotted mind, procurest means to mangle my tender body and by violence to gash those sides that enclose a heart dedicate to virtue. Or is it that savage satyr, that feeding his sensual appetite upon lust, seeketh now to quench it with blood, that, being without hope to attain my love, he may with cruelty end my life? (I.ii.107–15)

Everything here is geared towards eliciting the audience's interest. A talking and talkative tree, after all, is a theatrical coup in itself. And in its speech, the tree, slowly emerging as a character, defines herself almost without meaning to (Lyly's dramaturgy defies the use of consistent pronouns here). Whereas Sibylla deliberatively proposed a story to Phao ('we will beguile the time with some story [...] Then hearken to my tale', II.i.25–6, 39), the wounded and dying Fidelia does not intend to tell a story at all. Instead, she rails upon her assailant, and in the process of railing reveals for the audience information about her character and her past.

The two speeches are in many ways very similar. Fidelia's immediate reference to herself as 'chaste Fidelia' identifies her as one of Lyly's many stage virgins. And whereas Sibylla foregrounded her story on Phoebus' amatory advances, Fidelia mentions 'that savage satyr' almost as an afterthought of her lament. Both speeches are developed from sources in Ovid's *Metamorphosis*, and both foreground a story of metamorphosis in which a once beautiful maiden is now unrecognisably monstrous. But Fidelia relates her story as an incidental part of a wider speech, whereas Sibylla told a story that was frequently interrupted by her conventional use of euphuistic imagery. By the time Lyly wrote *Love's Metamorphosis*, he had adapted euphuism so that it could inform, rather than interrupt, the definition of character and story. As Paul Parnell puts it, Lyly had become 'interested in representing real people with human foibles at the same time that he embodies abstract ideas in a few dominant traits. This means that at one time a character will be presented symbolically, at another realistically.'[26] Lyly's dramaturgical development helped to show contemporaries how a character's backstory could be established in the process of the play's own linear narrative.

An intermediate stage in this development is evident in *Gallathea*. In a speech that Scragg has repeatedly used to demonstrate the evolution of euphuism into a dramatic mode, the shepherd Tityrus tells his daughter the reason he has disguised her as a boy.[27] The play opens with the two characters seeking shade 'under this fair oak, by whose broad leaves being defended from the warm beams we may enjoy the fresh air' (I.i.1–4). But as Tityrus tells his story to his daughter, it emerges that Gallathea is in imminent danger of being 'brought unto this tree, and here being bound' to await the monster Agar (I.i.48–9). Tityrus's euphuistic words transform the tree from a place of shelter to the site of sacrifice.

Tityrus further explains that 'where thou seest a heap of small pebble stood a stately temple of white marble', and that the pastoral setting of the play had once been flooded, so that 'Then might you see ships sail where sheep fed, anchors cast where ploughs go, fishermen throw their nets where husbandmen sow their corn' (I.i.15–16, 33–5). Written down, these phrases are familiar forms of euphuistic opposition. But, uttered before an audience who can see the props and settings to which they refer, these phrases transform the potential meaning of the stage world. The tree which Tityrus and Gallathea sought for shelter has become an imminent site of execution, and the rest of the stage, with its apparently insignificant 'heap of small pebble', is at risk of flooding. As Scragg puts it, Lyly's 'oppositions and ambiguities' are

> further extended to embrace the stage properties that define the physical arena in which the action is set. [...] A lengthy speech by Tityrus invites

> both his internal and his external audience to imagine an alternative landscape to that with which they are presented, promoting a view of the world as unstable and capable of metamorphosis to an opposite state.[28]

The flow of Sibylla's story was interrupted by euphuistic imagery, whereas Fidelia's euphuistic lament included narrative information that informed the audience about the character's backstory, as if incidentally arising from the lament itself. In *Gallathea*, Lyly can be seen adapting euphuistic expression so that it could transform the potential meanings of stage props. In turn, the audience are not permitted to assume that any part of the play world is quite what it seems to be, a dramaturgical attitude that prepares them for the alarming revelation that the tree in *Love's Metamorphosis* is also a nymph. This development is a realisation of the insight set out in Lyly's very first publication, *The Anatomy of Wit*, when the narrator quotes the clever young men of his day: 'For', say they, '[...] neither is there anything but that hath his contraries' (43). The transition of euphuistic composition and expression from the printed prose story to a staged, dramatic form of storytelling therefore had implications both for the construction of stage character and rhetorical form. In his confrontation with Eubulus at the start of the *Anatomy*, Euphues was able to answer his interlocutor point by point. By the time he came to write his first play, however, Lyly was able to create Alexander, a character whose single sentences are capable of more than one interpretation: 'Thou shalt live no longer than I will.'

Alexander's reference to his ability to execute Diogenes underlines euphuism's new relationship on stage to the creation of characters who, unlike Euphues, are represented by the real bodies of actors. Suddenly euphuistic expression has consequences for the real, mortal bodies of humans. Sibylla tells a story to explain why she is still alive, despite being many centuries old. Tityrus tells a story to explain why Gallathea is in danger of her life. Fidelia tells a story as she dies. In this way, euphuism ceased to have implications merely for an author's verbal dexterity, his wittiness or trickiness in Nashe's or Harvey's terms, and instead came to define, and be defined by, characters represented by the physicality of boy actors. In consequence, its relationship with the real bodies on stage and the fictive bodies they tried to represent changed.

Lyly's onstage euphuism therefore constitutes a radical blend of 'variegated uses of performance' of the sort that Weimann divides between 'presentational' and 'representational' modes of performance. Presentational performance is turned out towards the audience and 'derives its primary strength from the immediacy of the physical act of histrionic delivery'. Representational performance is turned in towards the material stage that supports the fictive world, and 'is vitally connected with the imaginary product and effect of rendering absent meanings, ideas, and images of artificial persons' thoughts and actions'. In reality performance involves a blending of these two modes, so that 'the symbolic and the apparently material [...] are vitally and contradictorily implicated' in the production of partially imagined and partially visualised space.[29] Onstage euphuism was forced to adapt to describe a world that was now partially visible to the audience. The rhetorical games of prose fiction now had to square with physical bodies on stage, and Lyly increasingly found ways to progress and to explain his plays' stories in a way that defined the characters onstage.

'Herein hath Nature gone beyond herself': creating character on stage[30]

Some time around 1600, Shakespeare created a character who claimed himself to 'have that within which passeth show' (*Hamlet*, I.ii.85). Writing in the immediate wake of the recent vogue for humour plays, Shakespeare adapted their new emphasis on the discordant relationship between a character's body and personality to create Hamlet, a character whose 'anachronistic inwardness', an 'interiority' that 'remains [...] gestural', would subsequently influence nineteenth-century theories of psychology.[31] As Eleanor Lowe suggests in her critical edition of Chapman's *A Humorous Day's Mirth*, the humour play genre is anticipated by Lyly's *The Woman in the Moon*, and, as we have seen, the writer had already demonstrated an interest in humoural psychology in his prose fiction.[32] In this play the goddess Nature creates the first woman, and the seven planets, jealous of this new creation, resolve to 'signorize awhile' in her mind, a project which produces numerous uses of the word 'humour' to describe Pandora's state of mind (I.i.135). She is made melancholy, and cannot 'sift that humour from her heart'; she is made proud, demanding that her acquaintances 'fittest my humour' (I.i.221; II.i.112). Elsewhere Mars tells us that 'jealous humour croweth in [Juno's] brain', and Pandora ends the play being asked to decide 'the humours that content me best' (II.i.164; V.i.315). Pandora is created when the four elements are moulded into her body:

> The matter first, when it was void of form,
> Was purest water, earth, and air, and fire [. . .].
> Now fire be turned to choler, air to blood,
> Water to humour purer than itself,
> And earth to flesh more clear than crystal rock.
> (I.i.61–72)

This represents a variation on an image used towards the end of his playwriting career, the creation of a character on stage. We have already seen that the character Fidelia is created on stage. As Erisichthon hacks down Ceres' sacred tree, the nymph Nisa observes that 'the tree poureth blood, and I hear a voice' (*Love's Metamorphosis*, I.ii.102–3). Fidelia's ensuing speech then sketches out the character's backstory, and the scene repeats a tradition in Lyly's plays of giving the longest speeches to the least mobile characters on stage. In *Campaspe*, Diogenes abuses the Athenians at great length, either from within or by his tub (IV.i). In *Sapho and Phao*, the play's longest speeches (by some way) are given to Sibylla, who is not confined within a small space but whose identity as an aged crone presumably restricted the actor's characterisation to slow and painful movements (II.i and II.iv). In the Shakespeare Institute 2007 production, these speeches proved the most troublesome part of the play, in terms of both their staging and the purely pragmatic process of learning them.[33]

But Lyly, apparently, did not encounter the same difficulty, for in *Gallathea* he once again assigned the play's two longest speeches to an immobile character, the virgin Hebe, who is forced to deliver them whilst tied to the play's central tree. Hebe anticipates Fidelia's long speech in *Love's Metamorphosis* in that she, too, has not hitherto been introduced to the audience, nor does she appear again. In the portrayal of both virgins, Lyly required his actors (or actor) to establish their characters within the space of one or two long speeches, at the same time as he ensured that neither actor was able to move his body: Hebe is tied to a tree, and Fidelia actually is a tree (and the actor was therefore partially, perhaps entirely, invisible).

It should be added that the static nature of these speeches in no way confirms the view that Lyly's dramaturgy as a whole is static. Rather, Lyly exploits the considerable dramaturgical power of a character who is still as they speak, making them what Janette Dillon calls 'a centre of contained activity-in-stillness'.[34] Paul Allain estimates that seven-tenths of dramatic action takes place in time rather than space, charging stillness with a 'latent energy' which is vitally important for drama.[35] And in each case, although the speaker is physically compromised, they are provided with an onstage audience required to respond to what they hear. In *Campaspe*, Diogenes angers the Athenians; their angry reply needs to be set up by non-verbal responses during the speech. In *Sapho and Phao*, Sibylla is offering advice to the helpless Phao, who is at first bewildered by the beauty Venus has given him, and then painfully in love with Sapho. In both their scenes, his replies indicate urgent attention ('I attend', 'I pray, tell on'), helpless interjection ('What will you have me do?') and he describes his respect for Sibylla's wisdom in physical terms, promising to 'hang at your mouth till you have finished your discourse' (II.i.42, 64, 97; II.iv.59–60). These moments confirm the arguments put forward earlier in this book, in relation to the prose fiction, that the act of storytelling is emotive and transformative in Lyly's stories.

In *Gallathea*, the wretched Hebe is surrounded by villagers who all hope she will be molested by the monster so that their village will be saved: their attention is divided, presumably, between Hebe's speech and their lookout for the tardy monster. In the two staged readings I have seen of this play, their responses to Hebe's speech have met with delighted laughter, in particular the Augur's disappointed line, 'The monster is not come', which seems to require the early modern equivalent of checking your watch for the time (V.ii.61). In *Love's Metamorphosis*, meanwhile, Ceres' nymphs hear Fidelia's lament with 'grief' (I.ii.155). All these responses to the speeches suggest that they have been heard with visible emotion, either anger, surprise or desperation. All four speeches are given by characters defined by their physical immobility, but their emotive effect upon other onstage characters is always urgently physical and kinetic.

The creation of a woman on stage in *The Woman in the Moon* is in some ways the opposite of these earlier moments. Whereas they constituted moments in which a still character spoke at great length, Pandora begins as an image that can move but cannot speak. She is first brought on stage by the drawing of a curtain, revealing a tableau which is unorthodox, perhaps unparalleled in early modern drama, in its suggestion of onstage nudity: '*They draw the curtains from before Nature's shop, where stands an image clad, and some unclad. They bring forth the clothed image*' (I.i.56.1–2).

After Nature gives the 'image' life, a stage direction describes how '*The image walks about fearfully*' (I.i.77.1). Like the aged Diogenes and Sibylla, both of whom dwell on death, and like the virgins Hebe and Fidelia, both of whom anticipate death, the image is at the limits of mortality, but, in contrast to these earlier figures, Pandora is about to begin her life.

Pandora is a complex character in many ways, foremost of which is the fact that she is in control of her own personality only at the very start and end of the play. Michael Best's view that 'At no time is Pandora a character' only serves to demonstrate the innovation of Lyly's play.[36] As she is given the power to speak, a stage direction notes that she '*kneels*' to Nature, and her address, 'Hail heavenly queen, the author of all good', sets out her total submission to the female deity who rules the mortal and immortal realms of the play (I.i.87). At the play's conclusion, Pandora is restored to her own wits, and she once again addresses Nature in submissive terms: 'Fair Nature, let thy handmaid dwell with [Cynthia]' (V.i.306). During the rest of the play, the various planets infiltrate Pandora's mind and it is under their influence that she scolds, attacks and deceives, actions that the play makes clear are rooted not in her own identity as a character but in the agency of the planets. Her later actions, then, as when a stage direction describes how '*She plays the vixen with everything about her*', suggest that the character is capable of hysterical frenzy, but only as a result of the mind-altering affect of the planet's malign influence (I.i.176.1). As Scragg says, 'The rapid shifts of disposition that Pandora undergoes through the influence of the planets make far greater demands on the performer than any other Lylian role'.[37] They also raise questions, as did Lyly's representations of Euphues, about what an early modern character is.

In his creation of characters, Lyly developed a stylistic expression and a dramaturgical fluidity that enabled him to define character by movement, language and effect upon other people in the play. An interest in the emotional effect of long speeches delivered by immobile speakers to silent but responsive onstage characters developed into two instances in which he created (and, in one case, killed) characters on stage. In *Love's Metamorphosis*, a felled tree comes to life and announces its identity as a virginal nymph; in *The Woman in the Moon*, a clothed image is brought on stage, given sentience and then the power of speech, and finally infiltrated by the psychological characteristics of seven allegorical planets. It is no accident that these two plays have the only conceptual titles in Lyly's canon: all his other plays are named after a particular character, but in these plays characters are defined not by their names but by concepts or places foregrounded in the title, metamorphosis and the Moon. Eumedies explained in *Endymion*, 'There was never any so peevish to imagine the Moon [...] capable of [...] shape of a mistress', and the Moon, 'constant in nothing but inconstancy', is another figure for metamorphosis (I.i.23–4). These plays do not stage well-known, archetypal characters like Alexander the Great or Endymion; instead, they present protean and unpredictable characters. Fidelia in her status between woman and tree makes an obvious metamorphic image, and Pandora is the closest the early modern stage came to representing an entirely contingent and unfixed personality. In these characters and these plays, Lyly resisted any sense of stable and demonstrable character.

Lucy Munro has reminded us that 'An obvious area in which a staged reading of a play becomes a theatrical interpretation is the casting', and recent readings have revealed performance choices available in Lyly's texts.[38] At the Globe's staged reading of *Love's Metamorphosis* (2008), James Wallace cast the same actress, Rebecca Todd, as both Fidelia and Protea. This is a doubling that the structure of the play invites, since Fidelia is dead after the first act, and Protea enters for the first time in the second scene of Act 3. But beyond this pragmatic feature, the two characters are the play's most impressive female characters and their identities reinforce and renegotiate one another. Fidelia is so named for her chastity, but has been physically transformed; Protea is so named for her ability to change shape, but is also a faithful lover. The play as a whole recasts chastity as a form of faithful but sexual love, making fidelity protean. Wallace therefore discovered a potential for doubling that enunciates the fluid relationship between the characters and their wider allegorical significance. As Scragg points out in her edition of the play, Protea is a departure from Lyly's source, Ovid's *Metamorphosis*, and from 'the conventional model of exemplary female behaviour, in that though still unmarried she is no longer a virgin'.[39] Protea looks back on her sexual relationship with Neptune in terms of complicity (whereas in Ovid's version she had been raped), and this willing premarital sexual experience is not presented to the audience as a reason to vilify her character. On the contrary, she emerges as the play's only pragmatic and resourceful character. Protea's love for Petulius, then, is not a conventional kind of fidelity, since she cannot offer him her chastity, but it is nevertheless presented to the audience by Cupid himself as 'faithful love' (V.iv.27). Protea's brand of fidelity requires the audience to rethink notions of female chastity, so that the play *Love's Metamorphosis* enacts a metamorphosis on the early modern conceptualisation of love itself.[40] In a play in which fidelity is protean and protean characters are faithful, Lyly can once again be seen to be experimenting with the interiority of his characters.

Protea is first introduced on stage with her father, who names her twice in his first speech, inviting the audience to speculate on her name's meaning (III.ii.1, 9). Such speculation would be further fuelled by the terms with which Protea indicates her willingness to help her father – 'Chop and change me' – and she soon prays to Neptune for the power to change into 'any shape wherein I may be safe' (III.ii.21, 34–5). The audience do not see her first transformation, but she describes herself turned into 'a fisherman on the shore' in terms of a prop and a costume: 'an angle in my hand, and on my shoulder a net' (III.ii.4–6). Later turning into Odysseus, Protea appears on stage and is described in terms of her 'dim eyes', 'doting age', 'silver hairs' and 'crooked age': the siren calls her 'That old man' (IV.ii.76–84). At the Globe's staged reading, an older male actor represented Odysseus, and Lyly's productions of the play may well have used another actor, perhaps a man, to play Protea's new 'shape'. But the boy playing Protea may simply have been given a disguise which could quickly be removed, since in other Lyly plays sudden costume changes and other physical transformations apparently took place on stage. Either way, as Alan Dessen argues, an 'emphasis upon the choice, not the solution', is vital when discussing early modern staging.[41] It is therefore significant that the character who refers directly to the stage doors, rather than to the seaside, is herself a figure of protean transformation. The slip between the fictive and the real stage worlds is figured by the one character in the play who has the power to transform herself into different shapes.

Hunter observes that the page boy characters at the end of *Gallathea* are employed as wedding singers, and thus 'recover their identity not simply as characters in the play but as choirboy actors in their own right'.[42] This movement from the identity of the character to the identity of the actor anticipates Gallathea's move away from the rest of the cast and towards the audience in order to speak the epilogue, 'Go all, 'tis I only that conclude all', where it is not clear whether the speaker is character or actor (1). By his third play, then, Lyly was experimenting with the relationship between actor and character. In his next play, *Endymion*, he had Bagoa transformed into an onstage tree and back again; in *Midas*, onstage reeds seem to 'bow down, as though they listened to our talk', and later report back the conversation they had heard (IV.ii.69–70). By the time he wrote *Love's Metamorphosis* and *The Woman in the Moon* Lyly was regularly blurring the line between actor, character, prop and set. As Scragg notes, Fidelia 'occupies a liminal position between a setting and a part'. Scragg later extrapolates the significance of this development in Lylian dramaturgy:

> The intellectual arena evoked through the on-stage structures of

> *Campaspe* and *Sappho and Phao* has thus given way in *Love's Metamorphosis* to a world much closer to that of Ovidian myth, in which human and non-human forms are interchangeable, and processes of mutation and elision are constantly at work.[43]

Scragg has also noted the new significance of special effects in Lyly's later plays: whereas the tree in *Gallathea* might take on different meanings throughout the play, and the tree in *Endymion* might transform into a relatively minor character, the tree in *Love's Metamorphosis* is associated in the first act with every level of the plot.[44] By the time he wrote *The Woman in the Moon*, Lyly was beginning to develop new modes for the representation and exploration of onstage interiority.

The Woman in the Moon was published in 1597, becoming the first play to be published with Lyly's name on the title page. The appearance of Lyly's name makes sense during the third phase of Lyly's publishing history: the Bromes had published five Lyly plays from 1591 to 1592 and Cuthbert Burby published *Mother Bombie* in 1594 and 1598. In the same years Cawood printed editions of *Euphues and His England* (1592) and the *Anatomy* (1595), and printed both works in 1597. Lyly's name thus appeared on *The Woman in the Moon* title page in the same year that it was helping to sell his *Euphues* books, and publishers seemed to have realised that Lyly's earlier plays were selling well because of the identity of the author, even though his name had not yet appeared on the title page. And evidence for the impact of Lyly's name on the reception of *The Woman in the Moon* in print may be evident in the immediate interest in humour plays. The play's printer published Chapman's *Blind Beggar of Alexandria* the following year, and Chapman himself completed his next play, *An Humorous Day's Mirth*, often claimed as the first humours play; Lyly's experiments with character and humours, made available in print in 1597, either initiated or coincided with late Elizabethan innovations in onstage character identity.

Lyly's role in introducing humours theory to the stage should not be that surprising in view of his interest in anatomisation. Just as Lyly's prose composition was transformed when it came to define characters embodied by actors, so the protean concept of character developed in Lyly's *Euphues* books shifted once characters were represented on stage. The subtitle of Lyly's first book, *The Anatomy of Wit*, had implied a particular relation of body to soul, but Lyly and his readers had been free to imagine Euphues' bodily and mental identity. Carolyn Ruth Swift has identified in Lyly's earlier play

Endymion an emphasis upon 'The difficulty of understanding reality' and 'the demonstration of deceptive perceptions'.[45] Drawing on humours theory, itself a theory of the relationship of body and mind, Lyly developed new ways to stage characters who could be transformed by the world around them. The only director to have worked with all of Lyly's extant plays, James Wallace, claims that 'Lyly's influence can also be seen in Shakespeare's characters, who fashion themselves through choices made in the theatrical moment, rather than being presented as fixed emblems of vice or virtue'.[46] In this way Lyly helped to discover ways of representing spontaneous thought on stage.

'Cupid, what hast thou done?': representing love on stage[47]

Lyly's authorial investment in character emotion, movement and thought can perhaps best be demonstrated by tracing the career of a single character. Cupid appears in more plays than any other Lyly character: indeed, along with his roles in *Sapho and Phao*, *Gallathea* and *Love's Metamorphosis*, he has a small part in *The Woman in the Moon* (speaking two lines of blank verse and singing a song), and therefore appears in exactly half of Lyly's plays. This makes him the most dominant character in any early modern playwright's work. There are other characters who make regular appearances in the work of a single playwright, most obviously Shakespeare's Queen Margaret in the *Henry VI* plays and *Richard III* and Falstaff in the *Henry IV* plays and *The Merry Wives of Windsor*. But even in those Lyly plays in which he does not appear as a character, Cupid is a textual presence, mentioned in the dialogue of *Endymion* and *Midas*, and in the songs of *Campaspe* and *Mother Bombie*. Even in plays where he is not visibly on stage he appears to be in the minds of Lyly's characters, and always within Lyly's discursive range.[48]

This consistent appearance of the same classical figure invites a study of the representation of love, the emotion over which Cupid holds sway, and it allows a more precise study of the evolution – or discontinuity – in the representation of what might at first be presupposed to be the 'same character' Cupid. It is possible to build on Scragg's previous work to show that Cupid is as protean in Lyly's plays as Protea herself, and Lyly's engagement with the limits of Cupid's interiority and physicality continue the games the writer played with the character Euphues across the original and revised versions of his prose fiction.[49] In *Sapho and Phao*, Cupid is a boy who follows behind his mother and follows her orders. When Cupid and Venus visit Vulcan, Cupid's place within his family is made abundantly clear:

VENUS Come, Cupid, Vulcan's flames must quench Venus' fires. Vulcan?
VULCAN Who?
VENUS Venus.
VULCAN Ho, ho! Venus!
VENUS Come, sweet Vulcan, thou knowest how sweet thou hast found Venus[.]

(IV.iv.1–6)

Although Venus enters with an order to Cupid to 'Come', their meeting with Vulcan initiates a conversation between Cupid's parents in which they name each other seven times in seven quarto lines. Cupid's stepfather, however, appears to ignore the small boy completely. He seems all but invisible to his parents, an invisibility which is very visible to the theatre audience. Venus's order, 'Come, Cupid', underscores his dramaturgical position behind his mother, following her movements just as he follows her orders. At the end of this scene, in which Vulcan makes new arrows for Cupid, Venus says, 'Come, Cupid, receive with thy father's instruments thy mother's instructions', a line that encloses the boy within a parental regimen and leaves him no agency of his own (V.i.1–2).

At the start of *Sapho and Phao*, when Venus reveals her plan to attack Sapho's chastity, Cupid had worried that his involvement in his mother's plan would result in his punishment:

CUPID Mother, they say [Sapho] hath her thoughts in a string, that she conquers affections and sendeth love up and down upon errands. I am afraid she will yerk me if I hit her.

(I.i.45–7)

These fears are groundless, since Sapho entices rather than threatens him in the end. But they accurately describe Cupid's fate in Lyly's next play, in which the boy *is* conquered and led up and down upon errands.

Cupid first enters *Gallathea* on his own; he is now independent of his mother. His initial encounter with a nymph suggests that she does not recognise who he is ('Fair boy, or god, or whatever you be'), and, as a member of Diana's virginal train, she also claims to be ignorant of the meaning of love ('Love, good sir? What mean you by it? Or what do you call it?', I.ii.16–17). This passage establishes that Cupid is still played by one of the smaller boys in Lyly's various companies, since in relation to the boy playing the nymph he is considered to be a 'fair boy' (I.ii.3). This first Cupid scene is organised around questions about his identity, his entrance appearing to prompt discursive uncertainty.

In *Gallathea* Cupid is a comically malignant figure who forces Diana's nymphs to fall in love because one of them calls him a 'little god' (I.ii.32). When the nymph leaves, Cupid speaks directly to the audience, something he did not do during *Sapho and Phao*: 'Diana, and thou, and all thine, shall know that Cupid is a great god' (I.ii.33–4). Cupid later addresses the audience again, and is still upset to be called a little boy. Promising that 'whilst I truant from my mother, I will use some tyranny in these woods', he uses alliteration to convert the childish state of truancy into the monarchical might of tyranny (II.ii.10–11). In *Sapho and Phao* Cupid accepted and deferred to his mother's description of him as a 'peevish boy', and accepted Sapho's mothering banter (I.i.48). In *Gallathea*, he has developed a size complex, and the character Cupid seems perturbed by the size of the boy who plays him.

Cupid suffers no qualms about his size in *Love's Metamorphosis*. In this play Cupid no longer follows his mother to Syracusa nor wanders alone in a wood. He is now the presiding deity of the play and the proud owner of a temple, one of the two stage houses that define the play's stage space. Previously defined by movement, Cupid now represents a particular space, visible to the audience even when he is not on stage. Greg Walker has shown how early Tudor court drama 'demonstrates in kinetic and spatial terms the social and political rank of each character'.[50] In spatial, kinetic terms, the earlier Cupid followed; now characters come to him, in an indication of his growing conceptual importance.

This new onstage status is reflected in the language with which he is addressed: 'Thou great god Cupid, whom the gods regard and men reverence', whom 'Jove doth worship, Neptune reverence, and all the gods tremble at' (II.i.93–4; IV.i.63–4). In Lyly's two previous plays, Cupid's power was clearly subservient to other gods, to Venus and Diana, and this subservience was defined in part by his size, the 'peevish boy', the 'little god'. There is no clear reference to Cupid's size in *Love's Metamorphosis*, which makes it difficult to reflect on the actor's identity, but this very absence of reference shows that the discourse of boyishness and littleness has ended. In this context, the ambiguity of 'great' in the phrase 'thou great god Cupid' may suggest that Cupid's growth in status is accompanied by a growth in stature, and these physical changes in Cupid's dramaturgy are in turn accompanied by changes in the conceptualisation of his deity. In *Gallathea*, the nymph failed to recognise Cupid and did not understand the word 'love'. In *Love's Metamorphosis*, Cupid is the local celebrity, and the play's title articulates the metamorphosis of the status of the concept of love and the god of love.

Another, apparently subordinate god, Ceres, comments on the new representation of Cupid in the play. Turning directly to the audience, she says: 'They that think it strange for chastity to humble itself to Cupid know neither the power of love nor the nature of virginity, th'one having absolute authority to command, the other difficulty to resist' (II.i.46–50). The Cupid whom Sapho won over to the side of chastity now holds sway over chastity. Ceres' nymph Nisa immediately reviews the traditional image of Cupid with scorn:

> I have heard him described at the full, and, as I imagined, foolishly. First, that he should be a god blind and naked, with wings, with bow, with arrows, with firebrands; swimming sometimes in the sea, and playing sometimes on the shore; with many other devices which the painters, being the poets' apes, have taken as great pains to shadow as they to lie. (II.i.59–65)

Scragg argues that Lyly's earlier play, *Sapho and Phao*, had shown chastity triumph over love, when the virginal Sapho took control over Cupid, and that the new play, *Love's Metamorphosis,* argues instead that chastity should submit to the power of love.[51] In fact, in *Sapho and Phao* Sapho usurps Venus's power over Cupid with the words, 'I myself will be the queen of love', and tells Venus proudly: 'Cupid is mine; he hath given me his arrows, and I will give him a new bow to shoot in' (V.ii.28, 62). In other words, *Sapho and Phao* already prefigures a reconciliation between chastity and love, one which accords with a vision of Elizabeth's court in which a virginal queen directs the love-affairs of others.

The difference in *Love's Metamorphosis*, as can readily be seen in Ceres' speech, is that virginity 'must be humble' to love, not the other way around: love has 'absolute authority to command'. In order to assert this new dramaturgy, Lyly has Ceres directly explain this to the audience, and has Nisa scornfully articulate the conventional image of Cupid, the image Lyly had previously staged in *Sapho and Phao* and *Gallathea*. It is a measure of the difference in Lyly's presentation of this character that Nisa should be so well informed of Cupid's traditional accoutrements in a play which seems to reject them, whilst the nymph in *Gallathea* was unable to recognise Cupid from his emblematic attire. Submitting this image to a sceptical dismemberment, Nisa prepares the way for the authority figure she, Ceres and the audience are about to meet, Love metamorphosed. The conceptual changes discussed by the characters are grounded in the physical whereabouts and greater dramaturgical status of Cupid himself.

Yet despite this bodily, dramaturgical and conceptual metamorphosis, Cupid's power still suffers from a sense of contingency; it even seems to diminish as his stage presence grows. Cupid is worshipped by the god Ceres, but it is only after he grants her wishes that she describes him as 'like a god' (II.i.150–1). Three foresters also worship Cupid, but they agree amongst themselves that if Cupid fails to grant their request, 'Then he is no god' (III.i.193). The ability of mortals to decide on whether or not Cupid is a god seems to raise doubt about the issue, and the claim that Cupid is 'like a god' puts this idea as a simile rather than a straightforward statement. The 'deity' that Venus hoped to 'be shown' in *Sapho and Phao* still requires demonstration in *Love's Metamorphosis*, and characters seem to recognise his deity only when it is used in their favour.

Cupid's authority seems even more circumscribed in the play's ending. During the play three of Ceres' nymphs refuse to fall in love (in a direct reference to the plot of *Gallathea*), and Cupid therefore punishes them. Released from punishment at the end of the play, however, the nymphs persist in refusing to fall in love, prompting Cupid into an outbreak of anger.

> What have we here? Hath punishment made you perverse? – Ceres, I vow here, by my sweet mother Venus, that if they yield not I will turn them again: not to flowers, or stones, or birds, but to monsters, no less filthy to be seen than to be named hateful. (V.iv.112–16)

In *Gallathea*, Cupid determined to turn his 'truancy' into 'tyranny', and in *Love's Metamorphosis* he achieves his aim, speaking with tyrannous anger and power. Yet the speech demonstrates the limits of his tyranny, since his ability to punish has only made the nymphs more perverse, less likely to yield to love, and his only recourse now is to threaten further punishment, turning the nymphs into monsters.

This threat may seem to mark out the might of Cupid's power, but it also demonstrates that Cupid's power has changed. In *Sapho and Phao* and *Gallathea*, Cupid was able to enforce love. Although all the characters in *Love's Metamorphosis* assume that Cupid still exercises power over love, he never once demonstrates this power, and in the midst of his angry powerlessness he invokes, for the only time in the play, 'my sweet mother Venus'. Ceres was, in other words, wrong to claim for Cupid an 'absolute authority to command'. He defers to his mother still, and has if anything less power in the later play.

This return to Venus returns us to the first entrance of Venus and Cupid in *Sapho and Phao*, when Venus determined to demonstrate what she called Cupid's 'deity', a deity Cupid himself tried to assert in *Gallathea*. The Cupid in *Love's Metamorphosis* is clearly not the same kind of boy that entered with Venus in *Sapho and Phao*. He appears to be bigger or more physically imposing and is the high-status figure of the play to whom characters defer. But as all this happened, the nature and extent of his deity changed and contracted. Taken together, the three texts suggest that the boy playing Cupid grew up, or that the part of Cupid was played by different and progressively bigger boys in the three plays. But this metamorphosis in the material presentation of the character, in his size and the status conferred by his onstage temple, was accompanied by odd ambivalences about the mythic power of Cupid in all three plays.

Cupid's contingent power has an obvious applicability to the Elizabethan court that watched Lyly's plays at a time when the import of Elizabeth's decision not to marry became ever more fractious. Lyly himself makes the urgent relation of play world to audience obvious by repeatedly staging his stories in a court world dominated, just like his court audience, by a female, virginal monarch. Earlier Lyly scholars have tried to construct elaborate allegorical anagrams from his plays: Endymion represented the Earls of Leicester or of Oxford, for example, or Phao was an image of the Duke of Anjou. This is deeply unhelpful, and overlooks the fact that every member of Lyly's court audience faced the problems encountered by a Phao or Endymion, who each have to decide how to situate themselves in relation to the supposedly irresistible queen in the room before them. In other words, although critics have been wrong to demand precise and overt allegorical equations between characters and Elizabethan politicians, their sense that Lyly's plays gestured towards their audiences speaks to the genuinely gestural function of Lylian drama, its incessant interest with the Elizabeth who, though off stage, was just as visible to the audience as the actors on stage. Louis Montrose describes Elizabeth as 'the woman who has the prerogative of a goddess, who is authorized to be out of place', and Lyly's plays stage the uncertainty felt by courtiers and citizens alike for Elizabeth and her mythic self-projection.[52]

The investment of Lyly's frequent portrayals of a virginal monarchical figure in the realities of Elizabethan sexual politics can easily be demonstrated, as Susanne Scholz has recently demonstrated in relation to *Endymion*.[53] Again and again, Lyly's monarchs complain when their courtiers fail to take them into their confidences. 'You might have made me a counsel of your loves', says Ceres in *Love's Metamorphosis* (V.iv.14), and in Lyly's first play, *Campaspe*, Alexander the Great complains to Campaspe and Apelles, 'Methinks I might have been made privy to your affection; though my counsel had not been necessary, yet my countenance [approval] might have been thought requisite' (V.iv.108–10). Lyly's monarchs, like Elizabeth, claimed absolute authority to command over their own and others' love affairs at court; and Lyly's monarchs, much like Elizabeth, frequently discovered that this authority was not absolute, was contingent and clumsy and had continually to be played out and reinforced.[54]

To state the very obvious, Cupid's importance in Lylian drama seems predicated on his size, on his littleness; there is a visual, iconographical attraction in a small boy responsible for the erotic impulse out of which dynasties were founded and confounded. Cupid's productive, destructive and contingent power charts out the importance of love and the manipulation of sexuality at court, with all its political, economic, familial and personal implications. Lyly exploited Cupid's gestural, ideological function in a court that had come to anxiously valorise Elizabeth's decision not to marry at the same time that it promoted dynastic stability for its courtiers. Lyly staged the continent boundary between eroticism and chastity in an onstage court for a court audience that increasingly came to fetishise virginity and sexualise chastity.

Early twentieth-century readings of Lyly's allegorical intent read allegorical authorial statement where there was instead an implicit and elusive relationship. Best explained these allegorical readings when he paraphrased their assumptions thus: 'we clearly do not have a character, so perhaps we have an abstraction', and clarified his own mediation between these two possibilities: 'Lyly creates neither character nor specific allegory'.[55] As Parnell implies when he suggests that Lyly's allegory does not permit 'us to say that Cynthia "is" Elizabeth, or that Midas "is" King Philip', Lyly's plays are not so much allegorical as euphuistic in their relationship with the court that watched them.[56] Just as the prose style posits ideas against one another in problematic ways, so Lyly's stage confronted the audience with worlds that seemed all too familiar. When Cupid says 'whilst I truant from my mother, I will use some tyranny in these woods', the syntax, alliteration and internal rhyme call attention to the two words 'truant' and 'tyranny'. One word is posited against the other, and Cupid's intention is to make one activity become the other. That is the relation Lylian drama bears to its courtly audience: it does not set out to be viewed or read as an allegorical jigsaw-puzzle, but instead posits the fictional world it presents against a courtly audience that is itself partly fictional, partly mediated through symbols and discourse that appeal to the imagination. In Lyly's indoor theatres and whenever his scripts were read in books, wider audiences and readers were invited to see this relationship between fictional and real courts at one remove. The career of the god of love in Lyly's plays therefore holds a euphuistic rather than an allegorical sway over the audience, as the story prompts a radical reconsideration of the real world that watches it.

This reflexive function, reiterating but also renegotiating the relationship between a virginal court and an erotic court, can be seen in all three plays that include Cupid, most obviously in the boy in *Sapho and Phao* who followed behind his mother, and was eventually won over to Sapho's side; the boy in *Gallathea* who wandered on his own and was eventually forced to submit to Diana; and the boy or man in *Love's Metamorphosis* who held physical sway over the dramatic world but whose power seemed curiously contingent. John Astington insists on the interpretative effect of a female monarch, her female companions, maids of honour and the wives and daughters of her leading nobles upon the performance they watched.[57] The failure of love to articulate a clear role in Sapho's court, the surreptitious and seditious intent of love in Diana's court and the visually impressive but somehow limited role of love in *Love's Metamorphosis* all bespeak the shifting concepts of love, sexuality and chastity in the court that invested in these stories. As Tiffany Stern suggests, 'The fact that the audience was crammed into the same world as the actors and equally visible will also have shaped productions. Unsurprisingly, the story of stage and audience frequently meld together'.[58] The protean ways in which Cupid is staged represents on a small level the kind of magical staging Lyly claims to present in his audience addresses, demanding the interpretive faculties of the audience.

Conclusion

With his emphasis upon the 'vehement thought' of his audience members, Lyly aimed to create onstage worlds that were allusive and playful, requiring active and imaginative participation. But euphuistic prose composition shifted once it came to be used to describe physical bodies visible to the audience. This shift in the relationship between a character's speech, their backstory and the play's narrative seems in turn to have led Lyly to focus on characters who come into life on stage: Fidelia and Pandora. The figure of Cupid, meanwhile, shows how a protean concept of character initially developed in Lyly's prose fiction continued to dominate his stories, as the small boy's changing body came to define different conceptualisations of love, chastity and desire.

With his complex relationship to his audiences, his characters and their speech, Lyly's plays anticipated many of the concerns of later dramatists. His concern with 'diverse significations' was reflected in the multiple audience addresses written for different performance venues, and these addresses were printed together in early editions of his plays, promoting the function of audience reception amongst his early readers. As the next chapter shows, these dramatic ideas moved from the stage to the page as Lyly's plays helped to create and define a new market for printed plays.

Notes

1 Noel Coward, *The Vortex* (London: Methuen, 2002), 28.

2 Scott McMillin, 'Middleton's theatres', in Gary Taylor and John Lavagnino (gen. eds), *The Collected Works of Thomas Middleton* (Oxford: Oxford University Press, 2007), 83 (his emphasis).

3 William Ingram, *The Business of Playing: The Beginning of Adult Professional Theater in Elizabethan London* (Ithaca: Cornell University Press, 1992), 240.

4 Scott McMillin and Sally-Beth MacLean, *The Queen's Men and Their Plays, 1583–1603* (Cambridge: Cambridge University Press, 1998), 1.

5 Ostovich et al., *Locating the Queen's Men*, 4.

6 Ingram, *Business of Playing*, Janette Dillon, *The Cambridge Introduction to Early English Theatre* (Cambridge: Cambridge University Press, 2006); Whitfield White, 'Playing companies', 265 and 277.

7 For examples of this work not mentioned elsewhere, see Christie Carson and Farah Karim-Cooper (eds), *Shakespeare's Globe: A Theatrical Experiment* (Cambridge: Cambridge University Press, 2008); Bridget Escolme, *Talking to the Audience: Shakespeare, Performance, Self* (Abingdon: Routledge, 2005); Robert Shaughnessy, *The Shakespeare Effect: A History of Twentieth-Century Performance* (Basingstoke: Palgrave, 2002); and James Stredder, *The North Face of Shakespeare: Activities for Teaching the Plays* (2004; Cambridge: Cambridge University Press, 2009).

8 W. W. Greg, *Pastoral Poetry and Pastoral Drama* (London: A. H. Bullen, 1906), 226; Best, 'Lyly's static drama', 75–6; Michael R. Best, 'The staging and production of the plays of John Lyly', *Theatre Research, Recherches Theatrales* 9:2 (1968), 104–17 (104).

9 Hunter, *Campaspe*, 23.
10 Saccio, *Court Comedies*, 30; Jocelyn Powell, 'John Lyly and the language of play', in John Russell Brown and Bernard Harris (gen. eds), *Elizabethan Theatre 9* (London: Edward Arnold, 1966), 157–8.
11 Hunter and Bevington, *Campaspe: Sappho and Phao,* 17; Best, 'Lyly's static drama', 76.
12 Hunter and Bevington, *Campaspe: Sappho and Phao*, 189.
13 For another challenge to 'static' Lyly, see Kent Cartwright, 'The confusions of *Gallathea*: John Lyly as popular dramatist', *Comparative Drama* 32 (1998), 207–39.
14 John Lyly, *'Galatea' and 'Midas'*, ed. G. K. Hunter and David Bevington (Manchester: Manchester University Press, 2000), 142.
15 Best, 'The staging and production'.
16 James Thomas, *Script Analysis for Actors, Directors, and Designers*, 2nd ed. (1992; Oxford: Focal Press, 1999), 42 (his italics).
17 Hunter and Bevington, *Campaspe: Sappho and Phao*, 204.
18 Catherine Richardson, *Domestic Life and Domestic Tragedy in Early Modern England: The Material Life of the Household* (Manchester: Manchester University Press, 2006), 5 and 7; Katharine Eisaman Maus, *Inwardness and Theater in the English Renaissance* (Chicago: University of Chicago Press, 1995), 32.
19 Catherine Richardson, 'Properties of domestic life: the table in Heywood's *A Woman Killed With Kindness*', in Jonathan Gil Harris and Nastasha Korda (eds), *Staged Properties in Early Modern English Drama* (Cambridge: Cambridge University Press, 2002), 143.
20 Robert Weimann, *Author's Pen and Actor's Voice: Playing and Writing in Shakespeare's Theatre*, ed. Helen Higbee and William West (Cambridge: Cambridge University Press, 2000), 10.
21 Mike Alfreds, *A Shared Experience: The Actor as Story-Teller* (Dartington: Dartington College of Arts, 1979), 4; Stephen Purcell, *Popular Shakespeare: Simulation and Subversion on the Modern Stage* (Basingstoke: Palgrave Macmillan, 2009), 144.
22 William West, *Theatres and Encyclopedias in Early Modern Europe* (Cambridge: Cambridge University Press, 2002), 121.
23 *Campaspe*: Hunter and Bevington, *Campaspe: Sappho and Phao*, III.ii.49.
24 Leah Scragg, 'John Lyly and the politics of language', *Essays in Criticism* 55:1 (2005), 17–38 (18–19).
25 Barish, 'Prose style', 34.
26 Paul E. Parnell, 'Moral allegory in Lyly's *Love's Metamorphosis*', *Studies in Philology* 52:1 (January 1955), 1–16 (2).
27 Scragg, *Metamorphosis*, 15–16; 'Introduction' to Lyly, *Selected Prose*, xviii–xix; 'Speaking pictures: style and spectacle in Lylian comedy', *English Studies* 86:4 (August 2005), 298–311 (301).
28 Scragg, 'Speaking pictures', 301–2.
29 Weimann, *Author's Voice and Actor's Pen*, 11–12.
30 John Lyly, *The Woman in the Moon*, ed. Leah Scragg, Revels Plays (Manchester: Manchester University Press, 2006), I.i.78.
31 Francis Barker, *The Tremulous Private Body: Essays on Subjection* (London: Methuen, 1984), 23 and 36.
32 Eleanor Lowe, 'A critical edition of George Chapman's *The Comedy of*

Humours, later printed as *An Humorous Day's Mirth*' (unpublished doctoral thesis, University of Birmingham, 2004), 23–4.

33 I am grateful to Kelley Costigan for discussing her experience of this role with me.

34 Janette Dillon, *The Language of Space in Court Performance, 1400–1625* (Cambridge: Cambridge University Press, 2010), 56.

35 Paul Allain, *The Art of Stillness: The Theater Practice of Tadashi Suzuki* (Basingstoke: Palgrave Macmillan, 2002), 157; compare Robert Benedetti, *The Actor at Work: An Introduction to the Skills of Acting* (1970; Englewood Cliffs, NJ: Prentice-Hall, 1998), 15, 30 and 148.

36 Best, 'Lyly's static drama', 82.

37 Scragg, *Woman in the Moon*, 34.

38 Lucy Munro, 'Read Not Dead: a review article', *Shakespeare Bulletin* 22.1 (Spring 2004), 23–40 (30).

39 Scragg, *Love's Metamorphosis*, 33.

40 For a general discussion of Lyly's representation of love, see Michael Shapiro, *Children of the Revels: The Boy Companies of Shakespeare's Time and Their Plays* (New York: Columbia University Press, 1977), 172–8.

41 Alan C. Dessen, *Elizabethan Stage Conventions and Modern Interpreters* (Cambridge: Cambridge University Press, 1984), 68.

42 Hunter and Bevington, *Galatea: Midas*, 14–15.

43 Scragg, *Love's Metamorphosis*, 36.

44 Scragg, *Love's Metamorphosis*, 37.

45 Carolyn Ruth Swift, 'The allegory of wisdom in Lyly's *Endimion*', in Clifford Davidson, C. J. Gianakaris and John H. Stroupe (eds), *Drama in the Renaissance: Comparative and Critical Essays* (New York: AMS Press, 1986), 63.

46 James Wallace, '"That scull had a tongue in it, and could sing once": staging Shakespeare's contemporaries', in Christie Carson and Farah Karim-Cooper (eds), *Shakespeare's Globe: A Theatrical Experiment* (Cambridge: Cambridge University Press, 2008), 151.

47 Hunter and Bevington, *Campaspe: Sappho and Phao*, IV.ii.1.

48 On Cupid in early modern culture more generally, see Jane Kingsley-Smith's excellent *Cupid in Early Modern Literature and Culture* (Cambridge: Cambridge University Press, 2010).

49 Scragg, *Love's Metamorphosis*, 30.

50 Greg Walker, *Plays of Persuasion: Drama and Politics at the Court of Henry VIII* (Cambridge: Cambridge University Press, 1991), 137.

51 Scragg, *Love's Metamorphosis*, 30.

52 Louis Adrian Montrose, '"Shaping fantasies": figurations of gender and power in Elizabethan culture', *Representations* 2 (1983), 61–94 (76).

53 Susanne Scholz, *Body Narratives: Writing the Nation and Fashioning the Subject in Early Modern England* (London: Macmillan, 2000), 119–26.

54 Scragg, *Love's Metamorphosis*, V.iv.14, n.

55 Best, 'Lyly's static drama', 76 and 81.

56 Parnell, 'Moral allegory', 2.

57 John H. Astington, *English Court Theatre 1558–1642* (Cambridge: Cambridge University Press, 1999), 164.

58 Stern, 'Taking part', 47.

CHAPTER 4

'This is the first': creating a market for printed plays (1584–94)

A reader opening the 1591 quarto of Lyly's *Endymion* would first come upon the following letter, from 'The printer to the reader':

> Since the plays in Paul's were dissolved, there are certain comedies come to my hands by chance which were presented before Her Majesty at several times by the Children of Paul's. This is the first, and if, in any place it shall misplease, I will take more pains to perfect the next. [...] And if this may pass with thy good liking, I will then go forward to publish the rest.[1]

This letter is the only prefatory material ever included in a Lyly play quarto, and was presumably written by the play's publisher, Joan Brome, the first English woman to publish a play. Brome's husband William had published new editions of Lyly's first two plays in 1591 and died shortly afterwards. When Joan Brome wrote that *Endymion* 'is the first' of a sequence of plays, she referred to a collection of Lyly manuscripts that she knew had not been published before: *Endymion*, *Gallathea* and *Midas*. Neither Brome had published a play before 1591, and Joan would not publish another play after 1592.[2] Joan's letter testifies to her sense that she is engaged in something innovative and extraordinary.

The play's most recent editor, however, does not agree. Bevington notes, 'This was to be the only quarto of *Endymion*, in a clear sign of the dramatist's declining fortunes during the early 1590s'. In his other editions of Lyly plays, Bevington is equally convinced that the Bromes' publications were economic failures that demonstrate the increasing irrelevance of Lylian authorship to late Elizabethan culture. Thus the 1591 reprint of *Sapho and Phao* is a sign of 'the rapid eclipse of fortune that brought Lyly's career to an untimely halt'. In his edition of *Midas*, Bevington dismisses the fourth edition of *Campaspe*, the third of *Sapho and Phao* and the first editions of *Endymion*, *Gallathea* and *Endymion* as 'an attempt to capitalize on John Lyly's once-bright reputation' which 'did not greatly succeed; none of these plays seems to have required further printing in quarto'.[3] As we have seen, Bevington's recent editions of Lyly's work were strongly influenced by the insistence of his co-editor, Hunter, that Lyly was an irrelevance by the 1590s. Thus, where Brome expected to interest her readers in a sequence of plays, Bevington reads each individual edition as a sign of Lyly's 'eclipse'.

There is, of course, no reason why an Elizabethan publisher and a modern editor should agree in their assessment of the market importance of a publication. Nor can Brome's letter be taken as a neutral form of evidence. Since the 1591 edition of *Endymion* advertises Brome's forthcoming play publications, her letter has an obvious marketing function. However, the disparity between Brome and Bevington exposes a difference in their perception of the early modern print market. In particular, Brome refers to the series of plays she has in hand: 'the plays', 'certain comedies', 'This is the first', 'the rest'. By contrast to this series, the modern editor emphasises each play as an individual act of publication. Brome and Bevington read these editions from divergent perceptions of the print market.

This chapter assesses the publication of Lyly's plays from Brome's perspective of the print market. It considers recent debates about playbook popularity in relation to the 1580s and 1590s print market and shows ways in which the two nascent markets for prose fiction and drama intersected. In the latter discussion, particular emphasis is placed on the way prose fiction writers responded to changes in theatre culture – in particular, the predominance of a smaller number of theatre companies in London from 1583 – by incorporating characters from the stage within their prose stories. Thus this chapter builds on the earlier demonstration that Lyly began and became associated with the market for prose fiction in order to argue that Lylian authorship enabled literary and print innovation across the boundary between drama and prose fiction.

1594: 'suddenly things changed'[4]

In their recent article on the popularity of early modern playbooks, Farmer and Lesser mischievously note, 'The popularity of English Renaissance printed plays declined dramatically in 1997'. This is a reference to Blayney's highly influential work on 'The publication of playbooks', which showed that 'printed plays [...] were not the best-selling moneyspinners that so many commentators have evidently believed they *should* have been'.[5] Scholars before Blayney tended to assume, to use McKerrow's version of the idea, that plays were 'popular books of which a ready sale was expected'; scholars after Blayney tend to agree, in David Scott Kastan's words, that plays were 'risky business ventures'. In their revision of Blayney's work, Farmer and Lesser claimed that 'Plays not only repaid their publishers' investments more quickly than other books, but they also remained profitable far longer'. In the ensuing debate, Blayney, Farmer and Lesser have redefined concepts of market investment, profitability and popularity.[6]

Partly in response to these debates over the economics of play publication, Shakespeare scholars have begun to rethink the culture of publication during Shakespeare's lifetime. This has been an important change in focus, for previous scholarship had tended to privilege folio over quarto and plays over poems. Indeed, studies that situate Shakespeare within book history have begun to acknowledge, in Stallybrass and Chartier's words, that 'The "authorial" Shakespeare was above all Shakespeare the poet, not Shakespeare the dramatist'.[7] Andrew Murphy's investigation of 'the textual culture of Shakespeare's time' has prompted Massai to ask, '[W]hat prompted early modern publishers to take considerable financial risks in publishing the dramatic works of Shakespeare and his contemporaries?'[8] An interest in Shakespeare's role in the publication of his plays has been accompanied by a greater focus on the stationers who printed his work.

The slow process by which printed plays became equated to literature (almost always defined with reference to poetry) has received much discussion. Lukas Erne has been especially influential in arguing that

> When Shakespeare started working as a playwright, playtexts were not considered literary artifacts, written by an author, with a life on the stage *and* the page. Such a summary statement no longer applies half way through his career, however, and is even less true at the moment of his death.[9]

But in fact plays did have some kind of literary status from the very beginning of print publication, and this book demonstrates that their status was radically transformed by the new market for single-story books that Lyly helped to create and dominated from 1578. Lyly's authorship and the prose fiction phenomenon were therefore a formative part of the process that saw the theatrical scripts of the commercial theatres preserved by print publication, and he needs to be taken into account by wider studies of the period's publication and authorial culture.

Brome's 1591 letter prefacing *Endymion* shows a publisher reacting to the unusual position of owning play manuscripts and her proactive use of one play to promote the others. In this letter, Brome repeats many of the tricks of the trade familiar to modern scholars from studies of title pages: she mentions the play's original performance circumstances ('at Paul's'), its royal performance before the queen and the theatre company ('the Children of Paul's'), and she does nothing to prevent readers from speculating that the play contains matters that helped to bring about the company's suppression ('Since the plays in Paul's were dissolved'). The play's position in a sequence of publications is spelt out in Brome's assurance that 'This is the first' and that 'I will [...] go forward to publish the rest', situating *Endymion* in relation to a forthcoming series of Lyly plays. Just as Lyly's prose fiction had initiated a series of *Euphues* publications, his two old plays and *Endymion* are here being used to publicise a forthcoming series of new Lyly plays. Erne asks us to consider 'Shakespeare's attitude toward the emergent printed drama, the place his plays occupy within it, and the way in which it may have affected the composition of his plays'; Brome's example shows that printed drama emerged earlier and more conspicuously than Erne suggests, making his questions all the more urgent.[10]

The debate over the popularity of plays in print has thrown up an important problem in the histories of both the theatre and the book. Despite their differences, Blayney and Farmer and Lesser agree that there was a sudden change in the availability of plays in print. Blayney notes that from December 1593 to May 1595 twenty-seven plays were entered in the Stationers' Register, when previously no more than three plays had ever been entered in a single year.

> The cause [...] is not difficult to guess, but the myth of the reluctant players has tended to obscure the obvious. Even [Alfred] Pollard drew what appears to be the only plausible conclusion – that on each occasion the acting companies themselves offered an unusual number of manuscripts for publication – and suggested that the first peak period was connected with the closure of the playhouses during the plague of 1592–1593[.][11]

Looking instead at extant published play books, Farmer and Lesser similarly identified what they call

> an aberrant one-year increase in 1594, a 'boomlet' caused by a sudden flood of eighteen new plays. Blayney's explanation of this flood – that

> companies were advertising the reopening of the theaters after a period of plague – seems logical[.][12]

This argument implies a highly sophisticated use of the print market by the theatre companies that survived the plague intact: it suggests a use of play books as a kind of merchandise promoting awareness of the theatres. Neither Blayney nor Farmer and Lesser make this point explicit and therefore do not provide any evidence to support it, but Tiffany Stern has recently shown that books were indeed used in this way by the theatres.[13] But the fact that Farmer and Lesser refer back to Blayney referring back to Pollard using the conditional voice ('appears to be [...] plausible'; 'seems logical') should alert us to a possible problem here, and though this chain of reference proposes the plague as a convincing explanation (Erne makes the same tentative suggestion), none of these critics quite commit themselves to it.[14] None of them attempts further explanation of the period in which 'plays became available to the book trade in such quantities that the market was temporarily glutted'.[15] The cause behind the sudden increase in the number of published plays, a process which enabled the preservation of texts now central to the Western literary canon, remains only tentatively explained. Its importance to these debates makes it strange that it has received no further attention, but it is tempting to speculate that a lack of scholarly curiosity over the date 1594 as the start of a new play book market might stem from the fact that it coincides so neatly with Shakespeare's early career. In any case, it seems limited to explain the events of one year using only evidence from that year.

The foremost scholars of the printed play book market have therefore not offered an economic reason for the 1594 change in the market. Plague may or may not explain why theatre companies released plays for publication, but it doesn't seem to explain why stationers would suddenly want to buy play manuscripts. Certainly, Blayney's demonstration that plays were not automatically lucrative investments for publishers, even taken with Farmer and Lesser's caveats, means that plague cannot explain why an unusual number of publishers suddenly invested in play manuscripts. A bibliographic and economic explanation seems far more likely to situate publishers' decisions and readers' responses, to identify why publishers decided more frequently and in larger numbers that play manuscripts might return an investment. But for Erne, 'The previous age, the first generation, as it were, of the London commercial stage between, say, the opening of the Red Lion in 1567 and the end of the 1580s, has left isolated traces of plays', concluding that 'Things radically changed in the early 1590s'.[16] Lesser similarly points to the 'few professional plays' printed in the twenty years before 1594, and he notes, 'What is striking is how suddenly things changed'.[17]

There are other ways to explain the 1594 'boomlet'. Surprisingly, no critic has considered what Andrew Gurr calls 'The great divide of 1594': his suggestion that existing theatrical companies were reorganised into two bodies, the Admiral's and the Chamberlain's Men, implies that the new companies released an unprecedented number of plays for publication in order to publicise their existence.[18] Where the plague explanation privileges the reopening of the theatre buildings, this explanation attends to company rivalry and repertorial identity. The sudden appearance of play books that year – with title pages which advertise, of course, neither the reopening of the theatre nor an author's name but instead the theatre company which staged the production and could stage it again – may therefore be part of a consolidation and promotion of the new, or newly reorganised, theatre companies. But given that 1594 marks the first appearance of a wide variety of plays by a wide variety of (unmentioned) authors, once again, this second explanation can only be pertinent to the sudden supply of plays. They explain why theatre companies were prepared to sell manuscripts to publishers, but not why publishers perceived a demand for printed plays amongst bookshop customers.

There are many other reasons for the sudden expansion of this market. Massai has recently shown that the print market's relationship with theatrical scripts was in flux before 1594. Richard Jones's 1590 edition of Marlowe's two *Tamburlaine* plays presented the scripts to the reader as an academic, prestigious and Italianate text, in marked contrast to Jones's previous play edition, that of Robert Wilson's *The Three Lords and the Three Ladies of London*. A prefatory letter, scene and act divisions, centred stage directions and speech prefixes in the left margin all situate Marlowe's two plays within a 'complex [bibliographical] presentation'.[19] Marlowe's own self-promoting rhetoric in the stage prologue works remarkably well with the publisher's bibliographical decisions, for the preface's dismissive reference to 'fond and frivolous jestures [*sic*]' echoes and prefigures (since it comes after stage performance but is situated earlier in the book) Marlowe's rejection of 'jigging veins of rhyming mother-wits/ And such conceits as clownage keeps in pay'.[20] Jones's typographical layout therefore combined with a Marlovian assertion of a 'blank-verse revolution' to produce a newly authoritative play book.[21] With its unusually 'clean' layout, innovative verse form and the playwright's and publisher's promotion of the text's difference from earlier commercial stage plays, the publication of Marlowe's two *Tamburlaine* plays marked the first print edition of a commercial success for the new outdoor playhouses that subsequently became part of the early modern theatre canon. Marlowe wrote commercial plays that repudiated previous models of commercial drama, and Jones's play book reworks that repudiation in order to legitimise itself.

But the Marlowe publication was itself reworking a precedent set earlier in the decade, and one of the reasons 1594 looks like an unprecedented change to scholars of the play book market is that Lyly's play publications have been actively discounted from previous research. The publication of *Tamburlaine* shows that the print market's relationship to performance culture had already changed. The play book's exotic title, its title-page emphasis on narrative, the publisher's preface distinguishing between a printed and a performance text and Marlowe's innovative verse style all help to explain two of his plays' early transition into print. The publisher promoted his book to his customers on the premise that the play scripts had been rescued from their commercial auspices.

In effect, book scholars have not identified any other explanation for the 1594 'boomlet' because of an inverted version of this prejudicial binary between the commercial and non-commercial worlds. Farmer and Lesser consulted every entry in Greg's *Bibliography of the English Printed Drama* but then limited their evidence and arguments to what they define as 'professional' plays.[22] They confirm that they use that term to 'describe precisely the same categories as' the term 'commercial', and the data they employ make clear that both terms refer only to plays produced by the outdoor theatres.[23] Attempts to explain the sudden increase in play publication have therefore been limited to outdoor theatre scripts, misleadingly termed 'professional' or 'commercial'. This roofless use of the data stems from the scholarly tradition of calling outdoor theatre 'public'; indoor theatres may have been smaller and more expensive, but that hardly makes them less commercial enterprises.

In a culture as stratified and hierarchical as early modern England, the translation from theatre scripts into book contents was predicated on an association with the court. As we have seen, all of Lyly's work is marked by an ability to transcend any binary between elite and popular. As Edward Gieskes has recently demonstrated, the word 'professional' is a slippery (early) modern concept, and needs to be treated with care and scepticism. Jeanne McCarthy has, in any case, insisted that we should see all London theatre companies as commercial, emphasising 'The professionalization of the children's companies, marked by the acquisition of permanent playing spaces – at the Blackfriars and at St. Paul's – and regular performances before the public'.[24] In an effort to clarify print economics, critics have used a model for theatre economics that assumes that playwrights associated with the indoor theatres did not write in exchange for money or that audiences did not pay to see their plays. But Lyly certainly fulfils the criteria used to define the term *professional* by Wickham: theatre practitioners 'who reckoned to earn a living from presenting plays regularly to a public that paid cash to gain admission to see them'. In 2000, Whitfield White warned that John Lyly had become 'overlooked as relevant to the professional stage because he has been misleadingly labeled a "court playwright"'.[25] This misleading label has prevented scholars from taking account of other explanations for the sudden publication of plays in 1594.

By 1594, as we have seen, Lyly's authorship had already created and defined the bibliographical form, narrative content and rhetorical style of the rapidly growing market for prose fiction, whilst many of his highly experimental plays had been performed in the same churchyard that disseminated that fiction. Later in the period the proximity of the King's Men to the Blackfriars brought them close to the centre of the publishing world, and Lyly anticipated and perhaps discovered the importance of this association for the composition and dissemination of dramatic texts almost thirty years before. Lyly was the first Elizabethan writer to see a succession of his plays into print and the first English writer to see his plays reprinted in a single year. In three years before 1594, in 1584 and 1591–92, a total of ten Lyly play editions were published in quick succession: three editions of *Campaspe* and two of *Sapho and Phao* in 1584, and single editions of *Campaspe*, *Sapho and Phao*, *Endymion, Gallathea* and *Midas* in 1591–92. These events were discounted from the Farmer and Lesser data but are vital for situating the sudden publication of plays from 1594 onwards. The publication of Lyly's plays was a crucial part of the transformation of the market for printed plays.

This book has attempted to show that the old view of Lyly as a writer whose importance was eclipsed in the 1580s is a myth premised on pro-Shakespearean bias. On the contrary, Lyly's transformative impact on the prose fiction market was increasing by the end of the decade, and in the 1590s Lyly's stories continued to be reprinted at regular intervals. Lyly's two prose fictions continued to outsell all of their imitations, and in their rhetorical style, narrative technique and titles these imitations furthered contemporary interest in Lyly's authorship and long stories in short books. Despite claims by Lylian and non-Lylian scholars that the writer's impact on his contemporaries died out at the end of the 1580s, his central character Euphues appeared on title pages more often after 1587 than ever before. The use of Lyly's character on a range of title pages suggests a bookshop clientele willing to invest time and money in books associated with Lyly himself, as does the fact that none of his imitators was ever reprinted with the frequency of *Euphues* books with Lyly's name on the front.

Reprints of Lyly's work in 1592, 1595 and 1597 coincided with or were followed by reprints of Lodge's *Euphues* book, *Rosalind*, in 1592, 1596 and 1598. In the early seventeenth century Rosalind's name was dropped from the title page, the book being simply called *Euphues' Golden Legacy*, and in all these ways publishers can be seen to respond to a continuing interest in Euphues. Euphues continued to be the subject of controversy following Lyly's involvement in the Martin Marprelate controversy, and was much discussed by Harvey and Nashe in publications from 1587 to 1594. The significance of Lylian authorship for the new literary genre of the printed prose fiction was thus only beginning to be defined in the years leading up to 1594. Perhaps most importantly of all, prose fiction publications continued to be dominated by the single-story book format that Lyly had introduced to the print market, rather than by the miscellany structure that previously defined the genre. Printed plays are, amongst other things, single-story books.

In the same years, the man most associated with Euphues was also strongly associated with boy companies, performances at court and a new kind of dramaturgy. In 1589 Harvey warned his readers not to attack Lyly in print for fear he would 'make a Playe of you; and then is your credit quite un-done for ever, and ever: Such is the publique reputation of their Playes', offering further evidence for Lyly's association with influential (and disturbing) dramatic performance (II, 213). Hoskyns's manuscript *Directions for Speech and Style*, which refers to the 1590 edition of Sidney's *Arcadia* and was therefore in composition after that date, mentions Lyly as an important contemporary writer who had transcended the limitations of euphuistic rhetoric. His statement that 'Lyly himself hath outlived this style and breaks well from it' shows a contemporary interest in this particular kind of prose style *and* in Lyly's distinction and departure from it (16).[26] If we discount the possibilities that Hoskyns is referring to

Lyly's Martin Marprelate pamphlet, the anonymous and controversial *Pap with an Hatchet*, or to a non-extant composition, this description of Lyly's writing style must refer to his plays, which indeed attest to a loosening of euphuistic form.[27] Lyly was therefore closely associated with a new and widely imitated bibliographical form of prose fiction as well as indoor theatre companies which regularly appeared at court. Harvey and Hoskyns make clear that they assumed Lyly was a celebrated playwright, not just a writer of prose fiction, amongst their readers.

The plays Lyly wrote for the boy companies therefore offer an important explanation of the 1594 play publication 'boomlet'. His role in the history of the printed book has been overlooked by book historians, in favour of plays deemed to be 'commercial'. But Lyly scholars have equally overlooked his importance in this area, seeing the single editions of five Lyly plays as a sign of diminished returns in comparison to the reprint rates of his prose fiction. Thus Bevington relies upon the paradigm of Lyly as an outmoded writer when he writes that there 'was to be only quarto of *Endymion*, in a clear sign of the dramatist's declining fortunes during the early 1590s'.[28] On the contrary, the Bromes issued two reprinted and three new Lyly plays in the space of two years at a time when no other playwright saw a series of plays into print, making an unprecedented investment in his authorship. We therefore need to look with care at the process in which Lyly's plays came to be published.

In 1584, Lyly became the first English playwright to be reprinted in a single year, when his first play *Campaspe* and his second play *Sapho and Phao* were printed in three and two editions respectively. It would be sixteen years before a play was published in three editions in a single year again, and that play, *Every Man In His Humour*, was by a playwright famously invested in his own sense of authorship.[29] The Lyly editions conform to the elite bibliographical conventions that Massai shows Jones used in the publication of *Tamburlaine* six years later, and, since they are the first to do so, it looks as though the Lyly playbooks set the model for Jones's Marlowe publications. Just as Marlowe had rejected previous models of commercial dramaturgy in the prologue to his first *Tamburlaine* play, so the indoor theatre's use of candles had required Lyly to write plays around a five-act division, increasing his texts' association with classical precedent.[30] Scragg refers to the 'conspicuously orderly and consistent' layout of the Lyly plays, their 'careful planning' and their use of italics to distinguish stage directions, speech prefixes, direct address to the audience and technical terms.[31] This care is in sharp contrast with many of the plays that were later published: as Gurr notes, 'Almost all the plays printed up to the Restoration had to be based on what the theatre companies would have counted as secondary copies of the text', but Lyly's printed plays strongly suggest the author's involvement in their publication. Adam Cohen suggests that Jonson 'may have been one of the first authors to be so meticulous in the preparation of his printed texts', but Lyly was an obvious precedent for Jonson's care.[32]

Henry Marshe's edition of Peele's *Arraignment of Paris* appeared in the same year as *Campaspe* and *Sapho and Phao*, and it shares with the five Lyly editions the status of being the first English plays 'printed throughout in roman and italic type with no use of the habitual black letter'.[33] Since Cadman's Lyly editions were reprinted in the space of a single year, it seems likely that Marshe was emulating Cadman's successful example. As Kate Narveson notes, 'Early modern writers' (and, we might add, their publishers and readers)

> developed their literary consciousness in a period when the choice of medium [print or manuscript] carried significance and when typographical conventions were still in formation, especially for a type of writing whose social status was as unstable as was poetry's.[34]

Dramatic texts had an even less clear social status than poetry, and the typographical features employed in 1584 helped to legitimate the texts they represent, as do other bibliographical decisions. The Lyly and Peele plays all refer to court performance on their title page, still an unusual claim for commercial boy company plays before 1590.[35] Lyly's first two plays were published in the same year as their court debut, suggesting the anticipation of strong public interest in these new works from the famous prose fiction writer.

Although Lyly's earliest plays were printed in the same year as their court performance, his subsequent plays were not immediately printed, leading Hunter to speculate that the author and his publishers were considering an anthology of plays.[36] When William and Joan Brome did begin to publish their copies of Lyly's plays, however, they did so in rapid succession, beginning by reprinting *Campaspe* and *Sapho and Phao* in 1591 and then printing the first editions of *Endymion*, *Gallathea* and *Midas* from 1591 to 1592. Once again, Scragg finds the Bromes remarkable for their 'conspicuously orderly and consistent' layout', and the Bromes followed Cadman by promoting their plays via their appearances at court.[37] Taken individually, the evidence presented by the Cadman and the

Brome publications suggests Lyly's involvement in the publishing process, helping to develop this nascent market.

Along with the first edition of *Mother Bombie* in 1594, these plays constitute an immediate context for the 1594 play publication 'boomlet' identified by Farmer and Lesser. In 1584 and from 1591 to 1594, Lyly and his publishers demonstrated that play texts had a potential readership. The fact that plays only began to be regularly published from 1594 helps to explain much in Joan Brome's prefatory letter to her edition of *Endymion* in 1591. What is truly extraordinary about the Bromes' actions in 1591–92 was that they published this number of plays at all. Since Joan Brome gained ownership of all but one of the plays that would be included in Blount's 1632 *Six Court Comedies*, she plays an important part in the formation of the Lylian canon. The first female publisher of plays, she also helped to determine which plays would be central to Lyly's reception.

Farmer and Lesser are right to stress the importance of reprints, but single editions of plays published at the beginning of the growth in the market for play books are equally important evidence for the causes of that growth. Jowett notes that Blayney's work 'suggests that there was little money to be made out of a first edition, and that the publisher would depend on a reprint for making a significant gain'. Since only around 48 per cent of plays were ever reprinted, however, Jowett questions Blayney's findings, since publishers would not 'repeatedly have invested in plays if they stood a less than 50 per cent chance of making an acceptable profit'.[38] Jowett's revision of Blayney's position may bear further revision itself, for publishers might well have invested in a publishing genre with a less than 50 per cent chance of reprinting if the reprints that did occur were lucrative enough to support other publications. Both Lyly's publishing agents, Cadman and the Bromes, issued five play books in quick succession, making Lyly the first playwright to see so many of his plays go into print. Since the one thing that distinguishes these plays was not the theatre company or their court performance, which other plays shared, but their authorship, it appears to be Lyly's name, despite its absence from title pages, that explains the printing of these plays. As has been already noted, single editions of texts are often taken as a sign of that text's marketplace failure, and here we have an example of how misleading that can be: these may have been single editions but they had a cumulative importance.

The argument that an author's identity helped to sell plays even when that author was not named on the title page is obviously contentious. Lyly's name did not appear on a play title page until 1597, and it therefore does not seem to have occurred to his earlier publishers that it might have a marketing function. But perhaps it never occurred to his publishers that anyone could doubt the play's authorship. Lyly was, after all, the only writer in this early period to see a succession of plays into print, and several references to his authorship by Harvey and Hoskyns suggest that their readers were perfectly aware of the authorship of the plays. Martin Wiggins reminds us that early modern plays very rarely engaged with Greek stories, and the Greek titles of Lyly's plays, their court auspices and distinctive prose all linked them back to Lyly and his Greek protagonist Euphues.[39] Alfred Hart long ago suggested that:

> Up to the year 1600, two-thirds of all the printed plays written for the public theatres or acted between the years 1587 and 1600 did not have the authors' names on their title-pages, though the names of the authors of many of these plays were certainly known to the play-going, and perhaps to many of the play-reading public. Lyly, Peele, Greene, Kyd, Marlowe, Shakespeare, Heywood, Drayton and others contributed to the long list of nameless plays. It is correct to state that anonymity was the rule rather than the exception.[40]

As Hart suggests and the evidence accumulated above confirms, bibliographical anonymity does not represent cultural anonymity, and the absence of Lyly's name from the title pages of his plays did not prevent his authorship helping the plays into print.

In addition to these suggestions of a wide awareness of Lyly's authorship, the prose style of the plays links them closely to Lyly. If euphuism explains the sudden publication of single-story books in the 1580s and 1590s, as scholars of prose fiction have argued, then it also helps to situate Lyly's plays. Their euphuistic composition linked them to Lylian authorship for those bookshop customers who were ignorant of their provenance, and it related them to the newly dynamic market for prose stories. Although scholars tend to assume that an external factor, plague, offers the best explanation for the increase in play publication in 1594, earlier play publications show that printed drama was becoming both a more classical and a potentially lucrative bibliographical form. Printed drama offered a similar reading experience to bookshop customers to that they found in prose fiction: short, innovative and contemporary English texts, controversial stories and dynamic representations of human personalities, full of exemplary and unexpected dialogue and soliloquy, and a willingness to engage, however obliquely, in social, political or religious controversy. The publication of the outdoor theatre's highly successful two-play *Tamburlaine* shows that a series of plays was attractive to publishers and their customers, and both Cadman and the Bromes provided readers with a series of plays performed before the Queen. The one Marlowe and ten Lyly play publications therefore offer a book market explanation of events in 1594.

In their analysis of the print market, Farmer and Lesser divide the period between the opening of the Theatre to the closing of all the playhouses into six periods. All but one of Lyly's plays fall squarely into the first period, from 1576 to 1597, which they define as 'an initial period of low production (48 first editions, 11 second-plus editions)'. For Farmer and Lesser, this period is exceptionally quiet: 'for the first thirteen years after the building of the Theatre, there was essentially *no* market for printed professional plays'. But if anything helps to explain the 'boom followed by sustained high production', from 1598 to 1613, it is the succession of Lyly's plays (at a time when Farmer and Lesser claim there to have been, in effect, no market at all).[41] In this 'initial period of low production', seven of Lyly's plays were published, three of them going into multiple editions. At a time when an average of 2.2 first editions and 0.5 second-plus editions were published a year, there were five Lyly play publications in both 1584 and 1591–92, around half of which were reprints.[42]

Lesser and Farmer claim that of the forty new play books printed from 1589 to 1597, 'only three had been reprinted before 1598', and these are the two parts of *Tamburlaine*, *The Spanish Tragedy* and *The Taming of a Shrew*: in other words, formative parts of the modern Renaissance canon.[43] But three more plays need to be added to this list, and they are all by Lyly: *Campaspe* (reprinted twice), *Sapho and Phao* and *Mother Bombie*. Furthermore, for Lesser and Farmer, the watershed period of printed drama (1598 onwards) is marked by the fact that 'stationers apparently perceived enough demand that they were willing to invest in second and third editions of these plays – editions that, as Blayney demonstrates, involved lower production costs than a first edition and so yielded higher profits'.[44] Farmer and Lesser are of course right to point to this period as a new one in which multiple editions became far more common, but there were two brief earlier periods before it, when Lyly's work was reprinted first by Cadman (five editions in 1584) and then by the Bromes (two new reprints in 1591). Discounted from earlier histories of play publication because of their 'courtly' auspices, Lyly's plays demonstrated to publishers the potential market for first and subsequent editions of plays.

The exclusion of Lyly's work from the most innovative recent studies of the print market has tended to endorse familiar claims for Shakespeare's cultural centrality. Farmer and Lesser use their figures to claim that 'Shakespeare plays led the development of this market': 'Not only was Shakespeare England's first best-selling playwright, then, but the success of the printed editions of his plays also helped to establish the playbook market itself.'[45] Farmer and Lesser are right to point to Shakespeare's crucial importance in this period, but the two roles they ascribe to Shakespeare had both been taken by Lyly already. Lyly was the first Elizabethan best-selling playwright, achieving that distinction despite a much shorter and less prolific career than many of his successors. Similarly, Jowett claims that 'By 1600 Shakespeare had become the most regularly published dramatist'.[46] Jowett does not explain how he measured regular publication, but Lyly's earlier run of play publications represents a much greater share of the overall market than Shakespeare's in 1600, partly because Lyly's work was helping to create that market.

Farmer and Lesser set out the importance of this early period in the history of play publication:

> We tend to take the printing of plays for granted – after all, without such printing we would not have the texts of our greatest plays – but the market for playbooks had to be created, and there was nothing inevitable about this creation. Stage success did not guarantee print success, for theaters in London were thriving long before playbooks were selling in bookstalls in any real numbers.[47]

Farmer and Lesser's important assertion that a market for printed plays was – had to be – created in the 1590s has important implications for our understanding of printed drama, the movement between stage script and printed plays. Lyly's works, long overlooked by Shakespeare-affiliated scholars of all stripes, helped to create the market for printed plays and printed stories. Associated with the period's best-selling stories, a new bibliographical form for prose fiction and an innovative prose style, Lyly was also the most imitated contemporary writer, and in 1584 and in 1591–92 he became the first repeatedly published playwright, offering a further model for early modern authorship.

'This is the first': Tudor contexts for the publication of plays

The early Lyly and Marlowe publications demonstrate continuity with previous play publication practice. Despite the sudden increase in play publication in the 1590s, as Zachary Lesser has shown, plays had been published in England since the introduction of printing to the country.[48] Indeed, Carol Symes and Graham Runnals have argued that the idea of plays as a form of literature set apart from other kinds of texts developed in the late fifteenth century, and, though they don't make this observation, this development coincided with the development of the printed play book.[49] In the early sixteenth century, John and William Rastell collaborated in what Massai calls 'a deliberate publishing venture', in which the printing of playtexts 'was not regarded as a cheap, hasty, stopgap job, but as an important project, on a level with the other publications issues by John Rastell's press'.[50] As Greg Walker demonstrates, the typographical and bibliographical precedents established in the first decades of the sixteenth century were developed by later publishers.[51] The Rastells are remarkable for the textual accuracy of their publications, and Lyly's, and later Jonson's, plays continued this textual care.[52] The Rastell family publication business, with its close ties to Sir Thomas More, John Ponet and Lyly's grandfather William Lily, set the bibliographical standards for play publication that would be emulated when Elizabethan publishers became more willing to fund a wide number of printed plays. Plays were therefore a potentially prestigious part of an early publisher's output. John Rastell later gave his copy of Sir Thomas More's *A Dialogue of Comfort Against Tribulations* (an unpublished manuscript) to Richard Tottell, so that an early Henrician play publisher handed over work to the publisher who, as we have seen, did so much to create a market for poetry and literary miscellanies.

Early printed plays are presented to the reader as a script for future performance, and in the mid-century title pages promoted the book's content by promising the 'small size of the cast' needed to perform them. In contrast, late sixteenth-century plays, including Lyly's, are published with reference to their previous cast, the company that performed and owned the script. Walker warns against any simple assumptions that printers and publishers slowly became willing to print dramatic texts 'for sale [...] to a target market of acting companies and the producers of household entertainments'. He nevertheless concurs that mid-sixteenth-century play publications were 'aimed primarily at a market among actors', whilst increasingly being aimed at 'private readers who wished to buy "hard copies" of performances that they had witnessed – or wished that they had witnessed'.[53] This process was particularly important for Lyly's plays, which with their massed entries and multiple audience addresses are presented not as the basis for future performances but as records of previous production circumstances. If 1580s and 1590s book buyers were at all interested in the viewing pleasures of the queen, Lyly's publishers offered them the experience they desired, and made sure potential book buyers understood this from the title page. Readers were also reminded of the play's courtly provenance by the alternative audience addresses for the Blackfriars and the court, solving a problem with the scripted text for court plays that had been articulated as early as a manuscript edition of Heywood's *Witty and Witless*, in which an epilogue spoken to King Henry is accompanied by a marginal note that reads, 'in the / Kyngs absens are voyde'.[54]

Four dramatic texts had used Elizabeth's name as a form of title page marketing by the time Lyly's plays were published. John Daye had published *Gorbuduc* around 1570, and perhaps in emulation Richard Jones then published the following year *Damon and Pithias*, a play written by Richard Edwards, Lyly's predecessor at the Blackfriars company. Jones then published *The Princely Pleasures at the Courte of Kenelwoorth* (1576) and *Promos and Cassandra* (1578), and Janette Dillon has claimed *The Princely Pleasures* as a new form of publication 'of this kind of elite and private entertainment'. With their references to court performance, these publications target, Walker argues, not only 'a readership of scholars and gentlemen' but 'a market among private readers beyond the schools and universities', offering those 'who had not been present [...] a vicarious experience of the event through ownership of a copy of the playbook'.[55] This 1570s development together with his prestigious position at the front of Oxford's boys helped Lyly's plays into print and, since none of the Daye or Jones publications was immediately reprinted, the three editions of *Campaspe* and two of *Sapho and Phao* once more offer evidence that Lyly's authorship not only continues but transforms developments in the market. Further evidence for this process is provided by the sudden succession of plays following Lyly's example: Henry Marshe's printing of *Arraignment of Paris*; Thomas Hacket's *Fedele and Fortunia* (1584–85); Robert Robinson's *Misfortunes of Arthur* 'presented to her MAJESTIE by the Gentlemen of *Grayes-Inne* at her Highnesse Court in Greenewich'; Edward White's *Rare Triumph of Love and Fortune*, 'Plaide before the Queenes most excellent Majestie' (1589); and, of course, the Bromes' series of reprints and first printings of Lyly's plays (1591–92). Lyly's first publisher imitated his own example by publishing *The Queen's Entertainment at Woodstock* in 1585.

There were other kinds of play publication at this time, however.

The year 1584 saw the publication of one outdoor theatre play, Wilson's *Three Ladies of London*. The printer of Lyly's prose fiction, East, printed Maurice Kyffin's translation of Terence's *Andria* in 1588. Cadman's publications of Lyly's first two plays were therefore accompanied by other courtly publications, but also by Wilson's outdoor theatre script which demonstrated a potential market for other kinds of playtext. It is therefore unfortunate that Ian Munro claims that 'only two plays were published in the 1580s', a claim which seems inexplicable unless it is built upon the assumption that plays associated with court or indoor performance are not really plays at all.[56] Ostovich, Schott Syme and Griffin, the editors of a recent collection of essays on the Queen's Men, are unduly worried by the failure of Queen's Men plays to be reprinted by their publishers: in comparison to *Tamburlaine*, *Doctor Faustus* and *The Spanish Tragedy*, they explain that 'No similar success stories can be told of any of the Queen's Men's plays, which fizzled in book form once they entered the market *en masse* in 1594'. This is a version of the familiar critical worry that single editions must always represent commercial failure. But 1594 is the very year of the expansion in the market, when, to return to Blayney's phrase, 'the market was temporarily glutted': these plays weren't fizzling, they were setting a precedent.[57] At this time publishers clearly prioritised new plays over reprints and the sudden shift in the market may well have prompted a major rethink of the economic and other possibilities of printed plays. Perhaps more importantly, these editors perceive the Queen's Men plays as individual publications rather than seeing them as a series. It is therefore unhelpful to use three of the period's most reprinted plays as comparison points: none of them was first printed in the extraordinary year of 1594, or as part of a longer series of publications, and the place of Queen's Men plays in the print market may simply tell us more about that market than any 'decline paradigm' that the volume's editors fear the evidence reveals.[58]

It is a measure of the binary positions into which scholarship has fallen that the most interesting recent collections on 1580s literary culture, *Locating the Queen's Men* and Melnikoff and Gieskes's *Writing Robert Greene*, take contrary stances on this issue. For the Queen's Men editors, there is 'a necessary distinction' between theatre and print, which 'evolved in different ways', whilst Melnikoff and Gieskes warn us not to 'unduly stress the distinction between Greene's pamphlet writing and his playwriting' and instead suggest we 'imagine Greene's writing for the pamphlet market and the theatrical market as a continuum'.[59] Scholarship needs to acknowledge that these two media were at once radically different and mutually dependent. Thus Ostovich, Schott Syme and Griffin may overstate their case and miss much that is exciting in their evidence when they claim that 1580s plays 'were received as performances, not as a writer's works, and Greene spilt much ink lamenting his invisibility as an author in the theatre'.[60] The irony here is that Greene's spilt ink was widely read by bookshop customers, and so such complaints about authorial invisibility were themselves highly visible in print. Greene is extending the visibility of playwriting as a form of authorship by discussing it in these printed texts, playing across the media which the Queen's Men volume suggests were distinct.

The second phase of Lyly play publications began when Lyly's first two plays were reprinted in 1591 alongside *Endymion*. These Lyly texts were published in the same year as the anonymous royal *Entertainment at Elvetham* and Peele's civic pageant *Descensus Astraeae*. Brome's printer for *Campaspe* and *Sapho and Phao*, Thomas Orwin, also printed *2 The Troublesome Reign of King John* and the closet translation *Phillis and Amyntas* (as part of *The Countess of Pembroke's Ivychurch*) that year. Thomas Scarlet printed *The Entertainment at Cowdray* and the Inns of Court play *Tancred and Gismund* in 1591, which may have recommended him to Joan Brome and Cuthbert Burby when they came to publish *Midas* and *Mother Bombie* respectively. The Lyly plays published in 1592 (*Midas* and *Gallathea*) coexisted with three commercial plays published by Edward White: *Arden of Faversham*, *Solimon and Perseda* and *The Spanish Tragedy* (the latter published without permission). The year 1592 also saw academic and closet publications: in Oxford, Joseph Barnes printed William Gager's Latin play *Ulysses Redux*, and in London William Ponsonby published the play translation, *Antonius*.

Burby, meanwhile, was a major figure during the 1594 'boomlet', publishing not only Lyly's *Mother Bombie* but also *The Taming of a Shrew*, Greene's *Orlando Furioso* and Wilson's *The Cobbler's Prophecy*. When Burby published a second edition of *Mother Bombie* in 1598, he used the printer Creede, who had himself been a major part of the 1594 'boomlet', printing two plays associated with Greene (*A Looking Glass for London and England* and *1 Selimus*) and two associated with Shakespeare (*The First Part of the Contention of the Two Famous Houses of York and Lancaster* and *The True Tragedy of Richard the Third*). Creede may have had experience of Lyly's work long before *Mother Bombie*, for he was apprenticed to East until 7 October 1578, the year that East began printing Lyly's prose fiction.[61] Creede was intimately involved in the *Euphues* culture outlined in Chapter 2, reprinting Greene's *Mamillia* and *Gwydonius* in 1593, *Greene's Groatsworth of Wit* in 1596 and Emanuel Ford's *Parismus* in 1598. These associations provide further evidence of the ways prose fiction and printed plays intersected.

As further evidence of the imbrication of the prose fiction and printed play markets, the publisher William Jones, who began his career co-publishing Painter's *Palace of Pleasure* with Tottell in 1566, went on to publish Marlowe's *Edward II* as part of the 1594 boomlet. He printed works by other writers associated with Lyly (Nashe's *Terrors of the Night* in 1594 and Dickenson's *Greene in Conceipt* in 1598), and later became the first publisher to offer a play with Lyly's name on it, *The Woman in the Moon* in 1597. Thus four men who printed Lyly's plays and had links to one another, Thomas Scarlet, Cuthbert Burby, Thomas Creede and William Jones, were major players in the 1594 'boomlet', becoming some of the first publishers to publish new commercial plays. Between them they printed nine of the eighteen plays published that year.

Lyly's play publishers and their many imitators used techniques that Walker and Massai have shown were established by earlier play publishers. Their title pages presented the play books to customers as a form of access to court performance, just as Lauren Shohet has claimed that the publication of Stuart masques was treated by publishers and bookshop customers as a way to spread court news in print.[62] Lyly's Blackfriars and Paul's audiences had been made keenly aware of the plays' forthcoming court performances; Lyly's potential readers were encouraged to share that awareness. Cadman therefore followed the earlier trend identified by Walker in which play books circulated texts written for elite consumption amongst cultures beyond the elite boundary.[63] Just as the London indoor theatres justified their performances by officially designating them as public rehearsals of plays destined for court performance, the printing of Lyly's plays offered another simulacrum of court entertainment. As Best puts it, 'Much of the attraction of the First Blackfriars and the Paul's theatres must have been their reflection of the glamour of the Court'.[64] Walker found that mid-sixteenth-century play publications were presented as scripts for future performance; three decades later, plays were increasingly published as, to adapt Lucy Munro's words, post-theatrical events.[65] Lyly's post-theatrical publications took care to emphasise one element in the theatrical provenance of his performances: the court.

Similarly, Cadman's use of roman font set a standard for play publication that would slowly become the established font to represent dramatic texts. Until the 1580s, all playbooks were printed in black letter, 'the usual typeface for vernacular texts in the sixteenth century and a signifier of "Englishness"'.[66] Lesser demonstrates the importance of black letter in his study of a translation of Terence's *Andria* which had been printed around 1520, in which the black-letter English translation is contrasted with Latin marginalia printed in roman typeface. Black letter, as Lesser shows, distinguished English plays from classical publications.[67] But Lyly's publications accord with T. H. Howard-Hill's description of much earlier play publications in their classical layout of theatrical details: they are 'parsimonious with the features that identify the works as plays'.[68] To put it another way, they negotiate the problem that it is difficult to put a performance script in a book, and difficult to sell new kinds of book without relating them to earlier and authoritative bibliographical forms.

Plays and the prose fiction market

In their article on playbook popularity, Farmer and Lesser demonstrate that publishers treated play publications differently from sermons and other print forms. Unlike these other forms of print literature, they were willing to fund a second edition of a playtext both within a 'five-year window' following an initial edition and, unusually, after this five-year period. They add, 'We know of no other category of speculative, non-monopolistic book that can boast such a record'.[69] The present book cannot match Farmer and Lesser's specialised use of statistical analysis, but its dual focus on prose fiction and plays allows the proposal of another literary 'category' that Farmer and Lesser overlook. The work of Greene alone suggests that at least one other kind of book, the single-story prose fiction, shares the characteristic they identify, that publishers might produce a second edition either side of a five-year 'window'. Thus the 1587 first edition of *Penelopes web* was not reprinted until 1601; the 1587 *Euphues His Censure to Philautus* was reprinted in 1634; the 1591 *Greenes farewell to folly* was reprinted in 1617; the 1589 *Ciceronis Amor* was reprinted in 1597; the 1589 *Menaphon* was reprinted in 1599; and the 1590 *Greenes never too late* was reprinted in 1599.[70] All of these prose fiction books are published in a second edition more than five years after the first edition, demonstrating that prose fiction books, like play books, 'were just as likely to be first reprinted *after* five years as *within* five years' (the characteristic Farmer and Lesser suggest may be unique to plays).[71]

This raises the important possibility that prose fiction and play books shared a place on the print market. This chapter has demonstrated that the publication of Lyly's plays can be read within a context of wider play publication, but the reprints of *Campaspe* and *Sapho and Phao* and the series of Lyly plays issued by the Bromes cannot be explained adequately by this context. These publishing decisions make most sense when situated against the market for prose fiction, within which Lyly's name was famous and definitive, and it may be that books with the names 'Campaspe', 'Sapho' and 'Gallathea' were recognisable and attractive to people who had bought books with the names 'Euphues', 'Menaphon' and 'Zelauto'. If Lyly's authorship explains the publication of his plays in 1584 and 1591–94, then this suggests that the market for printed plays may have emerged out of the market for prose fiction. Wiggins reminds us that early modern plays were far more likely to use Latinate than Greek subject matter and titles, and that Greek history and myth were 'rarely dramatized outside the universities'.[72] But it was plays on Greek topics that dominated the early Elizabethan playbook market, just as Greek names were dominating the prose fiction market. Peele's *Arraignment of Paris*, the only other play published in 1584, shares this characteristic. Put simply, these play books looked remarkably like prose fiction publications to early bookshop customers.

Thus, just as Stallybrass and Chartier claim that Shakespeare's name appeared on the title pages of plays because of his association with 'bestselling, and non-anonymous poetry', so it seems that earlier plays were published because of their bibliographical association with the newly emergent genre of printed fiction.[73] Raven has recently noted that the early modern bookshop has not been an object of curiosity for modern scholars, and suggests that 'By gleaning more information about how people used the developing bookshops and how those shops operated, we start to learn more about reading practices and how ideas circulated and were discussed'.[74] It appears that the idea of play books was strongly related to the idea of the single-story prose narrative. As we have seen, Lyly's stories transformed the prose fiction market; previously organised around story-miscellanies, from 1578 it became dominated by single-story books. The popularity of prose fiction single-story books was then given an authoritative status with the publication of Sir Philip Sidney's *Arcadia* in 1590. The increase in play publication in 1594 therefore came at a time when publishers were looking for new short texts that told engaging stories in innovative literary styles. Charlotte Scott has insisted 'how important the book is to the evolution of the theatre', and the single-story book that characterised prose fiction from 1578 onwards may have been particularly important because in its size and its interest in narrative, characters and rhetoric, it offered a convincing business model for speculative play publishers.[75]

By 1584, John Lyly was the most reprinted contemporary English author and had begun fronting the country's most prestigious theatre company, invited to perform his two new plays before the Queen early that year. Twelve editions of his two prose works had been printed in the previous five years, and with the publication of Gosson's *Ephemerides*, Munday's *Zelauto*, Riche's *Don Simonides* and no less than six Greene stories, the culture of Lylian imitation studied in Chapter 2 was already well under way. The composition, performance and publication of Lyly's first play, *Campaspe*, can be read in the context of the prose fiction market. The play dramatises a confrontation between Alexander and Apelles, the two most regularly named figures in Lyly's *Euphues* books. Lyly had opened the *Anatomy* with reference to Alexander's inability to limit Apelles' powers of representation, and in *Campaspe* Alexander discovers in Apelles' workshop that he is unable to paint as well as his artist. Lyly conceived of his first play as a continuation of one of the most basic euphuistic reference points of his fiction.

The interaction between drama and prose fiction may be seen in the extent to which each medium quotes the other. Lyly's first two plays, of course, are written in the prose style that made him famous, but following their performance and publication their characters began to be mentioned by prose writers. In the year after *Campaspe* first appeared on stage, Greene referred several times to the love triangle between Alexander, Apelles and Campaspe, the latter an otherwise fairly obscure figure in early modern England. In *Arbasto: The Anatomy of Fortune* (1584), a work whose subtitle registers the impact of Lyly's *Anatomy,* Greene refers to the fact 'that Alexander should crouch, and *Campaspe* bee coy', a phrase he repeated almost verbatim in *Alcida* (1588) four years later: '*Alexander* must crouch and *Campaspe* looke coy' (Grosart, III, 212; IX, 37). Again in 1584, in *Morando*, Greene referred to Campaspe no fewer than four times, including the prefatory letter to the Earl of Arundel where Lyly's story serves as a model of patronage:

> Apelles *(right Honourable) presented* Alexander *with the counterfaite of* Campaspe, *the face not fully finished, because hee liked the picture: and I offer this pamphlet unto your Lordship, not well furnished, because you are a lover of learning.* (Grosart, III, 48)

Later in the story Lacena asks Peratio, 'did not *Campaspe* preferre poore *Apelles* before mightie *Alexander*?' (Grosat, III, 73) Peratio says that '*Appelles* must be sad as long as *Campaspe* is coye', to which Silvestro replies, 'No doubt [...] the painter [was] passing pleasant before he sawe *Campaspe*' (Grosart, III, 82–3). These prose characters are discussing the Blackfriars Theatre's latest play characters.

Greene's references to the title characters of *Sapho and Phao* are even more extensive and offer more convincing evidence, since the story of Sappho and Phaon was relatively obscure in early modern England.[76] It is mentioned neither in Lyly's *Euphues* books nor elsewhere in prose fiction before 1584. In his play, Lyly became the first writer to call the boy 'Phao'. Abraham Fleming's 1576 translation of Aelian and George Turberville's 1567 translation of Ovid call him Phaon, the original classical form, and only Ovid links Phaon to Sappho before Lyly. After Lyly's play was performed in 1583–84 and printed in 1584, Greene started to use the boy in his writing, relating him to Sappho and using Lyly's version of his name.

Before this happened, Greene refers to Sappho only as a poet, without reference to a boy lover. Thus in his two-part *Mamillia*, published in 1583 and therefore written before Greene could have seen or read Lyly's play, the poet is simply an archetype for female immorality. Only fools could consider 'every seemely *Sappho*, to be a civill *Salona*, every *Lais* to bee a loyall *Lucreece*', here linking Sappho to Lais, a courtezan who appears in *Campaspe* (Grosart, II, 35). In 1584, in another reference to Sappho which appears to be unmediated by Lyly, the prefatory letter to *Gwydonius* notes that 'none sued to Sappho but poets'.[77] None of these references registers an awareness of Lyly's play: before *Sapho and Phao*, Greene thinks of Sappho as an aristocratic poet guilty of lechery.

Lyly's portrayal of Sapho on stage as a virginal princess with no literary ambition utterly transforms Greene's image of her. In *Arbasto* (1584), Myrania is advised to 'strive not with *Sapho* against Venus', which looks strongly like a direct reference to Lyly's plot (Grosart, III, 197). In the second part of Greene's *Mamillia*, published in 1584, a letter from Clarinda to Pharicles explains: '*Sappho* (*Pharicles*) was both learned, wise, and vertuous, and yet the fire of fancie so scorched and scalded her modest minde, as she was forced to let slip the raynes of silence to crave a salve of *Phaon* to cure her intollerable malady' (Grosart, II, 197). This is the first time Phaon is linked to Sappho in Greene's work, and the spelling may suggest Greene had seen the Lyly play rather than reading it. Later references to the boy employ the Lyly spelling. In *Alcida*, Telegonus laments: 'Tush *Telegonus*, enter not into these doubts: *Sapho* a Queene loved *Phao* a Ferri-man; she beautiful and wise, he poore and servile: she holding a scepter, hee an Oare; the one to governe, the other to labour' (Grosart, IX, 33). This appears to be a reworking of the first speech in Lyly's play, in which Phao tells himself: 'As much doth it delight thee to rule thine oar in a calm stream as it doth Sappho to sway the sceptre in her brave court' (I.i.7–9).

Greene continued to explore Lyly's stage characters in his fiction. *Menaphon* (1589) engages in a particularly complex manner with Lyly's work, when the story's two lovers use both his plays and fiction to flirt with one another:

> Menaphon, half nipped in the pate with this reply, yet like a tall soldier stood to his tackling, and made this answer:
>
> 'Suppose, gentle Samela, that a man of mean estate, whom disdainful fortune had abased, intending to make her power prodigal in his misfortunes, being feathered with Cupid's bolt, were snared in the beauty of a queen, should he rather die than discover his amours?'
>
> 'If queens,' quoth she, 'were of my mind, I had rather die than perish in baser fortunes'.
>
> 'Venus loved Vulcan,' replied Menaphon.
>
> 'Truth', quote Samela, 'but though he was polt-footed, yet he was a god'.
>
> 'Phao enjoyed Sappho, he a ferryman that lived by his hands' thrift, she a princess that fate invested with a diadem'.
>
> 'The more fortunate', quoth Samela, 'was he in his honours, and she the less famous in her honesty'.[78] (Cantar, 115)

Lyly had referred to Vulcan's polt foot as early as the first prefatory epistle to the *Anatomy*, and the reference to *Sapho and Phao* is nothing short of a review of Sapho's sexual status in the play. In *Ciceronis Amor* (1589), a year after *Endymion*'s court debut, Terentia 'blusht more than *Cynthia* did when shee wantond it with hir faire faced shepheard', and is told by her suitor Cicero:

> *Aeneas* was a stragling *Trojan*, an exile perjured and banisht even from the ruines of *Troy*, yet *Dydo*, the famous *Carthage* queene made him hir paramour [...]. *Phao* a ferryman, a slave, yet favoured by *Sapho*. [...] Think not *Terentia* but love as hee hath roses so hee hath nettles, as he hath perfumes so hath hee hemblocke[.] (Grosart, VII, 194–5)

Here Lyly's *Sapho and Phao* is linked to the same author's *Endymion* and, possibly, another boy company play, Marlowe's *Dido Queen of Carthage*, and the reference to love's nettles is a paraphrase from Lyly's earlier play ('you shall be stripped from top to toe, and whipped with nettles, not roses', V.ii.79–81). In 'The host's tale' in *Francesco's Fortune*, Eurymachus falls in love with Mirimida, 'which was the means that wrought him into a prejudicial labyrinth' (suggestive of the *Sapho and Phao* epilogue and its 'labyrinth of conceits', l. 10), and he writes a 'fancy' comparing himself to Lyly's hero: 'As Phao, so a ferryman I was, / The country lasses said I was too fair, / With easy toil I laboured at mine oar.' Greene's work alone demonstrates that Lyly's plays had transformed his contemporaries' view of the characters he dramatised.

Greene's *Menaphon* also suggests that Lyly's plays were read in the context of his prose fiction, giving further proof that Lyly's readers knew – and cared about – the identity of the author of his plays. As Melicertus and Samela speak to one another, they both begin to affect a style of speech associated with Lyly's fiction, which the narrator explains thus:

> Samela made this reply because she heard him [Melicertus] so superfine, as if Ephebus [the ideal schoolboy Euphues describes in Lyly's *Anatomy*] had learned him to refine his mother tongue, wherefore [she] thought he had done it of an ink-horn desire to be eloquent. And Melicertus, thinking that Samela had learned with Lucilla in Athens to anatomize wit and speak none but similes, imagined she smoothed her talk to be thought like Sappho, Phaon's[79] paramour. (Cantar, 130)

In other words, one studies Lyly's prose fiction, the *Anatomy*, in order to talk like Lyly's theatrical heroine, Sapho. Jowett has suggested that 'The early history of publication tells us much about "Shakespeare" as an institutionalized authorial figure in its earliest manifestations'.[80] In 1589, it was clear to Greene, and, Greene thought, to his readers, that *Sapho and Phao* had been written by Lyly. Lyly's authorship of the *Anatomy* and *Sapho and Phao* was considered as a kind of continuum. These two works may have been written for two entertainment media now generally treated separately by literary critics, but they were related for Greene by the unifying presence of their author. Barbara Mowat has argued for 'the obvious dependence of the theater on nondramatic literary culture', but the evidence suggests that this dependence worked in both directions.[81] This gives further evidence that Brome's 'anonymous' publications were only bibliographically anonymous: certainly Greene assumed his readers had read Lyly's plays with reference to their authorship. Eleven years after Lyly's first prose fiction appeared, six years after

Sapho and Phao debuted at the Blackfriars, Greene continued to conceive of his own writing in terms of Lyly's print and performance legacy. At least one of Lyly's contemporaries considers (and expected his readers to consider) Lyly's plays in terms of their role in the print market and their impact on the way Lyly's readers spoke to one another.

This chapter offers part of an answer to Massai's question, 'What prompted early modern publishers to take considerable financial risks in publishing the dramatic works of Shakespeare and his contemporaries?' These 'considerable financial risks' were taken 'within a network', to quote Raven, 'of low-price and narrow-margin parameters, but also of high volume production'.[82] Brome was herself responding to the problem Massai raises, and she fulfils Squires's definitions of a reactive and a proactive publisher. She reacted to what was presumably some sort of profit made by her late husband's reprints of Lyly's old plays, and she proactively ensures that her first new play, *Endymion*, is prefaced by a letter that advertises future publications. Brome made full use of her prefatory material as, in Voss's words, 'space outside the text proper, for excuses and explanations, publicity and promotion'.[83] Just as Lyly's prose fiction had initiated a series of *Euphues* publications, his two old plays and *Endymion* were used to publicise a forthcoming series of new plays.

Because none of the plays published by the Bromes from 1591 to 1592 was reprinted until Blount's *Six Court Comedies*, they have been read as evidence that Lyly was no longer a famous writer. It is certainly true that the fact that they were not reprinted offers a compelling contrast to Lyly's first two plays (printed in quarto four and three times, respectively), and an even more compelling contrast to Lyly's prose fiction (nine and eight editions respectively by 1592). But in the context of the early 1590s these publications are extraordinary for being issued at all. At a time when very few plays made it into print, ten editions of Lyly plays were printed in 1584 and 1591–92. These years are therefore as important as 1597, the year Massai celebrates as the time when 'a London stationer started to invest consistently in the publication of [Shakespeare's] dramatic works', and the year Lyly's name is first advertised in a play book.[84]

The fact that Lyly's plays were being published despite their title-page anonymity suggests that an anonymous book may not be the same as an anonymous text: there is plenty of evidence to demonstrate that the authorship of these 'anonymous' publications was notorious. Joad Raymond has proposed a typology of anonymity, and bibliographical anonymity needs to be added to this list.[85] Moreover, the apparent, bibliographical anonymity of these play books only serves to underline the fact that it is Lyly's plays which are being successively (and, sometimes, recurrently) printed in the 1580s and early 1590s. Other playwrights with successes on the stage did not see their work go quickly into print in such numbers, even when, as with Marlowe, Peele, Lodge or Munday, they wrote for one of Lyly's theatre companies. Greene's prose fiction suggests Lyly was associated with his plays by Greene and his readers, suggesting the need to rethink the implications of bibliographical anonymity.

Bevington employs Hunter's model of Lyly as 'victim of fashion' to explain the single editions of Lyly's plays in the early 1590s: 'After 1591, to be sure, *Sappho and Phao* shared with other Lyly plays the rapid eclipse of fortune that brought Lyly's career to an untimely halt', just as Ostovich, Syme and Griffin assume that the single editions of early Queen's Men plays suggest that they were not 'success stories'.[86] But the significant fact is that these plays were published at all. A single edition of a work does not necessarily indicate failure: in this context, these texts may simply have merited a single (and still highly unusual) edition. Thus where the authors argue that 'the company might have been doomed to fail on the page', we could equally argue that the printed Queen's Men plays helped to open up the print market to play scripts.[87] After all, in 1609 a book called *Shakespeares Sonnets* was printed, a book that was not reprinted for over thirty years.[88] The fact that Shakespeare's sonnets were not immediately reprinted has never been used to argue for Shakespeare's cultural irrelevance. If the single editions of Lyly's plays are evidence of Lyly's dwindling cultural importance, this seems to have major implications for the seventeen Shakespeare plays that were never printed in single editions at all. The fame of *The Comedy of Errors*, *The Taming of the Shrew*, *Julius Caesar*, *Twelfth Night*, *As You Like It*, *Macbeth*, *Measure for Measure*, *All's Well That Ends Well*, *Cymbeline*, *Antony and Cleopatra*, *The Tempest* and *The Winter's Tale*, to list only a few of the Shakespeare plays never published in quarto, rests on the sole decision to print the First Folio. We therefore need to be cautious about the implications of a text which is published 'only' once.

The cumulative evidence of the reprinting of Lyly's work demonstrates his importance for the history of the printed book, and his early place in the history of printed drama demonstrates his formative place in the process by which plays became more likely to be printed, preserved and perceived as literature. Given the rate with which Lyly's work was reprinted, recent research by Blayney and Jowett showing that London bookshops stocked works printed in the previous two or three years suggests that Lyly's work was permanently available to prospective London book-buyers for over sixty years.[89] In 1592, for example, a browse through Paul's bookshops might have included the first editions of *Gallathea* and *Midas* and the eighth reprint of *Euphues and His England*, together with stock from the previous year's publication of *Endymion*, the third reprint of *Sapho and Phao* and the fourth of *Campaspe*. It is not surprising, in this context, that Lyly's authorship was as visible and as useful to contemporaries as the evidence suggests.

Printed plays are, Jowett tells us,

> both misrepresentations and the privileged and essential representations of the lost manuscripts on which they are based. They are secondary forms of publication that put the text into an entirely different form of circulation from the performance of plays on the stage, yet they are the very locus of the text as we apprehend it.[90]

Yet 'printed texts' are also books in their own right, and represent for their printers and publishers commodities to be sold. They may be, for us, then, 'misrepresentations' of 'lost manuscripts', but that is not necessarily how they appeared to the bookseller or purchaser. Printed texts are 'secondary forms of publication' only with respect to time: the early modern reader's and audience member's reception of their respective medium of publication need not operate within the hierarchical representation that a modern bibliographer perceives. This may be a particularly pertinent point in relation to Lyly, whose non-extant manuscripts apparently blurred the difference between authorial and theatrical copy.[91] Lyly's theatrical manuscripts, in other words, may have been laid out in a manner modern scholars would describe as classical and 'literary', only taking theatrical form when divided into parts for individual actors and spoken on the stage.

Conclusion

The central section of this book has traced what Michael Bristol calls the 'chronic tension between a more exclusive culture of the book and a more popular culture of performance'.[92] This chapter has argued that the publication of Lyly's plays was founded upon his authorship, even though the play books were usually anonymous. Certainly their publication cannot be explained by Blayney's or Erne's contention that theatre companies released plays to publishers in order to promote the theatres. In 1584 and 1591–92, when Lyly's plays were published, both his theatre companies had recently been suppressed. Lyly's authorship therefore seems to have helped to sell these books to customers, many of whom shopped near Lyly's theatres. His authorship helped to inaugurate an Elizabethan market in successive play publications. Its associations with the thoroughly print phenomenon of prose fiction, with a newly celebrated and innovative prose style, and with court performance created the conditions in which publishers, starting with Thomas Cadman and the Bromes, funded multiple play editions. This in turn implies that scholars need to rethink the context in which all printed plays were read.

Lyly wrote at a time when, as Jowett puts it, 'Anonymity, collaboration, and the absence of authorial rights were the typical circumstances of dramatic writing'.[93] The best recent scholarship has attempted to understand how this culture changed, how collaborative and previously anonymous writers of plots, dialogues and scenes came to be understood as distinct and definitive kinds of authors marketed as though they were independently responsible for entire playscripts. Lyly's marginalisation has prevented scholars from appreciating his unusual 'status', in Hunter's terms, as the head of his theatre company and the owner of the performance text, with 'the power to release it to be printed'. Wells has claimed Lyly as the only writer for whom there is no evidence that he wrote in collaboration.[94] Lyly's editors are in agreement that Lyly probably worked with his publishers to produce the printed text.[95] Lyly's authorial fame, moreover, has been established in the first part of this book: in the 1580s and 1590s his authorship was closely identified with a bibliographical form, the single-story book, characters with Greek names, a literary style, euphuism, and with juvenile theatrical troupes.

Lyly's work therefore offers a site from which to interrogate Jowett's three defining features of early modern dramatic writing: 'Anonymity, collaboration, and the absence of authorial rights'. Lyly was famous and exercised an unprecedented degree of control over the composition, the performance and the publication of his playtexts. His authorship is therefore a vital part of the growing marketability of playscripts in early modern England, a marketability that ensured the survival of texts now considered to form the centre of the English literary canon. Having opened up a new market for single-story fiction books in the late 1570s, Lyly's authorship then helped to open up the market for play books in the 1580s and early 1590s. With their title-page references to the queen and their use of pseudo-classical typography, Lyly's playbooks helped to legitimate printed dramatic scripts, a process that enabled the printing of many of the works now central to the English literary canon. If, as Lesser argues, 'the emergence into print of the plays of Marlowe, Shakespeare, Jonson and their contemporaries was by no means inevitable', this chapter has shown how the survival of these plays became a little more likely.[96] The next and final chapter explores how Lyly's vital place in early modern culture has come to be forgotten.

Notes

1 John Lyly, *Endymion*, ed. David Bevington (Manchester: Manchester University Press, 1996), 74.
2 See Massai, *Rise of the Editor,* 99–100.
3 Bevington, *Endymion,* 1–2; Hunter and Bevington, *Campaspe: Sappho and Phao*, 190; Hunter and Bevington, *Galatea: Midas*, 111.
4 Lesser, 'Playbooks', 525.
5 Farmer and Lesser, 'Popularity', 1; Peter Blayney, 'The publication of playbooks', in John D. Cox and David Scott Kastan (eds), *A New History of Early English Drama* (New York: Columbia University Press, 1997), 416 (his emphasis).
6 McKerrow, *Introduction to Bibliography,* 134; David Scott Kastan, *Shakespeare After Theory* (London: Routledge, 1999), 35; Farmer and Lesser, 'Popularity', 24; see also Blayney, 'Alleged popularity', and Farmer and Lesser, 'Structures of popularity'.
7 Peter Stallybrass and Roger Chartier, 'Reading and authorship: the circulation of Shakespeare 1590–1619', in Andrew Murphy (ed.), *A Concise Companion to Shakespeare and the Text* (Oxford: Blackwell, 2007), 39.
8 Andrew Murphy, 'Introduction: what happens in *Hamlet*?', in Murphy, *Concise Companion,* 14; Sonia Massai, [review of Andrew Murphy, *Shakespeare in Print*], *Library* 7th ser. 6:2 (June 2005), 196–8 (198).
9 Lukas Erne, *Shakespeare as Literary Dramatist* (Cambridge: Cambridge University Press, 2003), 33 (his emphasis).
10 Erne, *Literary Dramatist, 10.*
11 Blayney, 'Publication', 386.
12 Farmer and Lesser, 'Popularity', 7.
13 Tiffany Stern, 'Watching as reading: the audience and written text in the early modern playhouse', in Laurie Maguire (ed.), *How To Do Things With Shakespeare* (Oxford: Blackwell, 2007), 139.
14 For Erne's view, see *Literary Dramatist*, 90.
15 Blayney, 'Publication', 386.
16 Erne, *Literary Dramatist*, 14–15.
17 Lesser, 'Playbooks', 525.
18 Andrew Gurr, 'The great divide of 1594', in Brian Boyd (ed.), *Words that Count: Early Modern Authorship: Essays in Honor of MacDonald P. Jackson* (Newark: University of Delaware Press, 2004); see also Gurr, *Shakespeare's Opposites: The Admiral's Company 1594–1625*

(Cambridge: Cambridge University Press, 2009), esp. 1, and Gurr, *The Shakespeare Company, 1594–1642* (Cambridge: Cambridge University Press, 2004), 1–40.
19 Massai, *Rise of the Editor*, 84.
20 Christopher Marlowe, *Tamburlaine the Great*, ed. J. S. Cunningham (Manchester: Manchester University Press, 1981), 'To the gentlemen readers', l. 9, and 'Prologue', ll. 1–2.
21 McMillin and MacLean, *Queen's Men*, 166.
22 See Farmer and Lesser, 'Popularity', 6.
23 Farmer and Lesser, 'Vile arts', 111.
24 Edward Gieskes, *Representing the Professions: Administration, Law and Theater in Early Modern England* (Newark: University of Delaware Press, 2006), esp. 41–5; Jeanne H. McCarthy, 'The Queen's "unfledged minions": an alternate account of the origins of Blackfriars and of the boy company phenomenon', in Paul Menzer (ed.), *Inside Shakespeare: Essays on the Blackfriars Stage* (Selinsgrove: Susquehanna University Press, 2006), 94.
25 Glynne Wickham, *Early English Stages 1300 to 1660*, 2 vols (London: Routledge and Kegan Paul, 1959–1972), II, 158; Whitfield White, 'Playing companies', 266–7.
26 For discussions of this passage, see Peter Mack, *Elizabethan Rhetoric: Theory and Practice* (Cambridge: Cambridge University Press, 2002), 149, and Howell, *Logic and Rhetoric*, 330–2.
27 Barish, 'Prose style', 27.
28 Bevington, *Endymion*, 1–2.
29 See W. David Kay, 'The shaping of Ben Jonson's career: a reexamination of facts and problems', *MP* 67:3 (February 1970), 224–37 (225).
30 See Jowett, *Shakespeare and Text*, 41, for an account of this process in relation to the second Blackfriars theatre.
31 Scragg, *Sapho and Phao*, vii–viii.
32 Gurr, 'Did Shakespeare own his own playbooks?', *Review of English Studies*, n.s., 60:244 (2009), 206–29 (206); Adam Max Cohen, *Technology and the Early Modern Self* (New York: Palgrave Macmillan, 2009), 93.
33 Scragg, *Sapho and Phao*, xix.
34 Kate Narveson, 'The *Ars longa* trope in a sublunary world', in Jeanne Shami (ed.), *Renaissance Tropologies: The Cultural Imagination of Early Modern England* (Pittsburgh: Duquesne University Press, 2008), 261.
35 See Scragg, *Sapho and Phao*, viii, and Farmer and Lesser, 'Vile arts', 87 and 106.
36 G. K. Hunter, 'Lyly, John', *Oxford Dictonary of National Biography* (Oxford: Oxford University Press, 2004) (www.oxforddnb.com, accessed 23.10.12).
37 Scragg, *Gallathea*, vi.
38 Jowett, *Shakespeare and Text*, 53.
39 Wiggins, *Shakespeare and the Drama of His Time*, 22.
40 Alfred Hart, *Stolne and Surreptitious Copies: A Comparative Study of Shakespeare's Bad Quartos* (Melbourne: Melbourne University Press, 1942), 6.
41 Farmer and Lesser, 'Popularity', 7 (their emphasis).

42 For these average figures, see Farmer and Lesser, 'Popularity', 9.
43 Farmer and Lesser, 'Popularity', 10.
44 Farmer and Lesser, 'Popularity', 10; Blayney, 'Publication', 410–13.
45 Farmer and Lesser, 'Popularity', 11.
46 Jowett, *Shakespeare and Text*, 8.
47 Farmer and Lesser, 'Popularity', 10.
48 See Lesser, 'Playbooks', 520–5.
49 Carol Symes, 'The appearance of early vernacular plays: forms, functions and the future of medieval theater', *Speculum* 77 (2002), 778–831; Graham Runnals, 'The catalogue of the Tours bookseller and late medieval French drama', *Le moyen français* 11 (1982), 112–28.
50 Massai, *Rise of the Editor*, 42 and 59.
51 Greg Walker, *The Politics of Performance in Early Renaissance Drama* (Cambridge: Cambridge University Press, 1998), 20.
52 On Jonson, compare Massai, *Rise of the Editor*, 67–8, and Walker, *Politics of Performance, 9.*
53 Walker, *Politics of Performance,* 22–5 and 39–40.
54 *The Plays of John Heywood*, ed. Richard Axton and Peter Happé (Cambridge: D. S. Brewer, 1991), ll. 675.1–2.
55 Dillon, *The Language of Space*, 51; Walker, *Politics of Performance*, 29–30.
56 Ian Munro, 'Page wit and puppet-like wealth: orality and print in *Three Lords and Three Ladies of London*', in Ostovich et al., *Locating the Queen's Men*, 115.
57 Ostovich et al., *Locating the Queen's Men,* 8–9; Blayney, 'Publication', 386.
58 Ostovich et al., *Locating the Queen's Men*, 8.
59 Ostovich et al., *Locating the Queen's Men*, 9; Melnikoff and Gieskes, *Writing Robert Greene, 5.*
60 Ostovich et al., *Locating the Queen's Men, 4;* compare Melnikoff and Gieskes, *Writing Robert Greene*, 5–6.
61 David L. Gants, 'Creede, Thomas', *Oxford Dictionary of National Biography* (Oxford: Oxford University Press, 2004) (www.oxforddnb.com, accessed 23.10.12).
62 Lauren Shohet, *Reading Masques: The English Masque and Public Culture in the Seventeenth Century* (Oxford: Oxford University Press, 2007), 2.
63 Walker, *Politics of Performance*, 34.
64 Best, 'Staging and production', 104.
65 Walker, *Politics of Performance*, 22; Lucy Munro, 'Reading printed comedy: Edward Sharpham's *The Fleer*', in Marta Straznicky (ed.), *The Book of the Play: Playwrights, Stationers and Readers in Early Modern England* (Amherst and Boston: University of Massachusetts Press, 2006), 40.
66 Lesser, 'Playbooks', 521.
67 See Lesser, 'Typographic nostalgia', 285.
68 T. H. Howard-Hill, 'The evolution of the form of plays in English during the Renaissance', *Renaissance Quarterly* 43 (1990), 112–45 (133).
69 Farmer and Lesser, 'Popularity', 22.
70 Melnikoff and Gieskes, *Writing Robert Greene*, 227–33.

71 Farmer and Lesser, 'Popularity', 22 (their emphasis).
72 Wiggins, *Shakespeare and the Drama of His Time*, 22.
73 Stallybrass and Chartier, 'Reading and authorship', 39.
74 Raven, *Business of Books*, 379; compare Kevin Sharpe, *Reading Revolutions: The Politics of Reading in Early Modern England* (New Haven: Yale University Press, 2000), 45–6.
75 Charlotte Scott, *Shakespeare and the Idea of the Book* (Oxford: Oxford University Press, 2007), 187.
76 Hunter and Bevington, *Campaspe: Sappho and Phao, 152.*
77 Robert Greene, *Gwydonius, or The Card of Fancy*, ed. Carmine di Biase (Ottawa: Dovehouse Editions, 2001), 79.
78 Robert Greene, *Menaphon: Camilla's Alarm to Slumbering Euphues*, ed. Brenda Cantar (Ottawa, Canada: Dovehouse Editions, 1996), 115. The character is called Phaon in Sampson Clarke's 1589 edition, but Phao in John Smethwick's 1599 edition.
79 In the 1589 edition, this is spelt 'Phao'.
80 Jowett, *Shakespeare and Text*, 11.
81 Barbara A. Mowat, 'The theater and literary culture', in John D. Cox and David Scott Kastan, *A New History of Early English Drama* (New York: Columbia University Press, 1997), 218.
82 Raven, *Business of Books*, 5.
83 Voss, 'Books for sale', 735.
84 Massai, *Rise of the Editor*, 91.
85 Raymond, *Pamphlets and Pamphleteering*, 64–5.
86 Hunter and Bevington, *Campaspe: Sappho and Phao*, 190; Ostovich et al, *Locating the Queen's Men, 8–9.*
87 Ostovich et al., *Locating the Queen's Men*, 10.
88 Andrew Murphy, *Shakespeare in Print: A History and Chronology of Shakespearean Publishing* (Cambridge: Cambridge University Press, 2003), 20–1.
89 Jowett, *Shakespeare and Text*, 11.
90 Jowett, *Shakespeare and Text*, 4.
91 Scragg, *Gallathea*, vii.
92 Michael Bristol, *Big-time Shakespeare* (London: Routledge, 1996), x.
93 Jowett, *Shakespeare and Text*, 8.
94 Hunter and Bevington, *Campaspe: Sappho and Phao,* 2–3; Wells, *Shakespeare and Co.*, 250.
95 Bevington, *Sappho and Phao*, 141; Scragg, *Love's Metamorphosis, 2.*
96 Lesser, 'Playbooks', 525.

PART III

Euphuism and reception

CHAPTER 5

A hopeless Romantic? Lyly, euphuism and a history of non-reading (1632–1905)

Sonic booms, Saddam Hussein and golf: euphuism without Lyly

In his poem 'Pleasures of a technological university', Edwin Morgan set out those pleasures in the form of a list of strange academic jargon. The poem consists of short lines composed from unusual terminology emanating from the academy, with scientific terms juxtaposed to literary ones: 'retro-rockets and peripeteia', 'hubris and helium', 'anti-hero and anti-matter', 'H_2O and 8vo', 'sonic booms and euphuism'.[1] Like many of the words in the poem, 'euphuism' is a word that some readers will recognise and others will see for the first time, a part-familiar, part-disorientating piece of jargon.

But two recent *Spectator* articles suggest that the word 'euphuism' can be used beyond the university system. Philip Hensher's review of Don DeLillo's celebrated 1997 novel *Underworld* complained of the novel's diction, 'so removed was it from any notion of the speaking voice' that 'His narrators [...] couldn't quite talk normally': 'the mangling of the syntax has amounted to euphuism'. Despite Morgan's suggestion that 'euphuism' is caught up in the academic domain, Hensher suggests the word might have a modern meaning, describing a prose style that is not 'deeply rooted in the vernacular', that is unreal, abnormal and self-consciously literary: 'An exercise in non-speak', as the title of Hensher's review has it.[2]

Writing in the same magazine five years later, Rod Liddle also employed the word 'euphuism'. Liddle, the former editor of Radio Four's *Today* programme, relates a story in which he broadcast an English translation of 'an especially bloodthirsty speech by Saddam

Hussein'. As is conventional in news broadcasts, the Arabic speech was played quietly beneath the English translation. But Liddle later discovered that this Arabic speech had not, in fact, been Saddam Hussein advocating international war, and he had instead mistakenly broadcast 'the Arabic commentary to a golf tournament'. Defending this 'glorious misconception', Liddle claimed that 'even if we had run the correct clips, there would still have been a question about interpretation: the euphuism and hyperbole of Arab satraps is just that: hyperbole and euphuism. It is not meant to be taken literally.'[3] Here euphuism is such a self-evidently straightforward word that it can be defined within a tautology: 'euphuism [...] is just that: [...] euphuism'. Once again, it describes inappropriately florid language, but there is an added dimension to the deviancy inherent in the term since it is being used to describe aggressive political hyperbole by an almost paradigmatic 'Orientalist' Arab speaker, Saddam Hussein. Across Hensher's and Liddle's usages, euphuism is exotic and suspect, non-literal and aggressive, and so worthless as to be replaceable.

Early modern scholars define euphuism in terms of its formal properties, as when Bevington breaks the style down into isocolon, paramoion, parison, alliteration, *similiter cadens*, word-repetition, polyptoton, natural and other analogies.[4] But that is clearly not how the word is being used by these modern writers. All three suggest that, whatever self-evident meaning euphuism has, it has nothing to do with the sixteenth century in general or with John Lyly in particular. None of the above quotations exhibits an awareness of the writer who gave the style its name.

How did a word relating to Lyly's prose fiction, *Euphues: The Anatomy of Wit* and *Euphues and His England*, become detached from Lyly's writing to the point that it could be applied to sonic booms, American experimental novels and Iraqi dictators? Might the changes in the meaning of *euphuism* tell us something about the cultural discourse in which it features, as Jean Aitchison suggests of all language change?[5] And what consequence did the use and meaning of the word *euphuism* have for the reception of John Lyly's works? This chapter examines the extremely brief early modern history of the word euphuism and its far more extensive afterlife in the eighteenth century and beyond. By becoming detached from Lyly himself, the word has accrued associations of its own, but these associations have subsequently affected the way scholars perceive Lyly and his writing.

In recent years Shakespeare's reception history has become a major critical field. As Taylor claims, 'Observing the changes in Shakespeare's image from the mid-seventeenth to the late twentieth century alters your perspective on the progress, geography, and substance of criticism'.[6] Linda Rozmovits argues that Shakespeare's reception does not so much alter as create cultural perception: 'The relationship between history, the literary text, and the way it is read, thought about, and endlessly reproduced [... does] not reflect history but actively constitute[s] it'.[7] Kathryn Prince therefore recommends that we avoid perceiving Shakespeare scholarship as 'evolving towards an inevitable conclusion in the present while a colourful selection of tangents and blind alleys provide some interesting historical context'.[8] Given these problems with the history of Shakespeare's reception, it may be strangely comforting to reflect on the far smaller task awaiting the Lylian critic, but it is certainly hard to find 'incontrovertible progress' in the history that this chapter maps out. In contrast to work on Shakespeare's reception history, this chapter essentially charts a history of non-reading, in which Lyly is ignored in favour of his contemporaries or dismissed because of his presupposed euphuism.

For that reason, the chapter presents a reading of Lyly's reception history that is not comprehensive. Because comparatively little has been written about Lyly, particular strands in what little there was have had a disproportionate impact. This chapter therefore focuses on the fractious evidence for the meaning of the word 'euphuism' amongst Lyly's own contemporaries before showing how Blount's use of the word was understood and redefined in Robert Walter Dodsley's 1744 *Old Plays*. Dodsley in turn determined Walter Scott's presentation of euphuism in his 1820 *Monastery*, and a peculiar fusion of Blount, Dodsley and Scott has since defined Lyly's subsequent reception, standing in place of the writer himself. One way to think about Lyly's reception history, then, is the way it has been determined by a dynamic relationship between the terms of Blount's 1632 prefatory material and their changing, shifting subsequent meanings. Taylor writes that 'The issue of the value accorded to Shakespeare's works cannot be disentangled from the values that people have found within those works'.[9] Precisely the opposite is true of Lyly: the value accorded to Lyly's works has actively prevented people from reading it. Studies of the reception of Elizabethan writers demonstrate, as Thomas Dabbs puts it, 'the lasting influence of certain modes of critical thinking that came into being during the past century'.[10] The eighteenth- and nineteenth-century constructions of *Lyly* and *euphuism* continue to determine our understanding of those terms today.

The more important – and more widely used – of these two words is *euphuism*, not *Lyly*, and this chapter traces that word rather than the scholarly reception of Lyly himself. The word is used only twice before the Civil War, by Harvey and Blount, with very different meanings, and the first part of this chapter examines these two uses to demonstrate that, from its coining, the word's meaning was contested. By focusing on the first reprint of a Lyly play in 1744, this chapter then shows how this edition began a tradition of dismissing Lyly because of his supposedly unnatural, corrupting rhetoric, though not yet in the name of euphuism. The third part of the chapter shows how an 1820 novel helped euphuism to displace Lyly himself, to stand for the writer whilst also encompassing something much bigger. The final section examines the association of Walter Pater and Oscar Wilde with euphuism at the end of the nineteenth century and shows how the meaning of euphuism became further dislocated from Lyly himself, whilst simultaneously influencing Lyly's own reception. By moving from Edward Blount to John Addington Symonds, this chapter moves from a Lyly for whose euphuism 'Our nation are in his debt' to a Lyly whose euphuism spread a 'universal disease'.[11] This reception process continues to shape the way Lyly and euphuism are understood, whether we think of a student's violent response to Lyly in 2005 or the RSC's 2007 depiction of Lyly as a feminine flirt.

Naming euphuism: Harvey, Nashe and Blount

In 1820, as we shall see, Sir Walter Scott included a character in his novel *The Monastery* who was a self-described and enthusiastic euphuist. Referring to his own mode of speech, this character says, 'while we call it by its own name of Euphuism, we bestow on it its richest panegyric'.[12] But, just as we saw with Liddle, it is by no means clear what exactly 'it' is, nor why it should be called 'Euphuism'. The word *euphuism* is formed from the word Euphues, the title character in Lyly's two prose fictions. But Euphues was from his first beginnings protean and unfixed, and Lyly emphasised his two prose fictions as discontinuous and different. Describing his sequel as 'another face to Euphues', Lyly's narrator worried that 'So may it be that had I not named Euphues, few would have thought it had been Euphues' (155–7). To add to this complexity, Lyly is here discussing both the character and the title of his book, a combination that the modern editor is unable to represent typographically. As we have seen, Lyly's style in these books is also discontinuous. In the first prefatory letter to the *Anatomy*, Lyly employs many classical references which are now thought to be part of the constitutive features of the euphuistic style; but in his second prefatory letter he avoids all such references entirely. Even in the opening letters to the first '*Euphues*', then, Lyly's writing style evades the rhetorical consistency (or tediousness) associated with euphuism. Attached to two books which may or may not be two parts to the same story, attached to a character with an inconsistent biography and identity, and describing a protean style, the term 'euphuism' has uncertainty and instability built into it.

The term, moreover, may not be an early modern term at all, at least in the sense that modern scholars use it. Its first usage does not coincide with the publication of Lyly's two *Euphues* books in 1578 and 1580. Nor did the word appear during Cawood's serial republications of Lyly's fiction in unbroken runs from 1578 to 1582 and 1585 to 1588. From 1580 until 1594, a variety of authors also published new *Euphues* books, but it was not until quite late into this period, 1592, that the word 'euphuism' was first used, when Harvey and Nashe argued over the term. The word was not used again until Blount's *Six Court Comedies* preface forty years later. There is evidence that it was in oral use in Middleton's *The Nightingale and the Ant* (1604), where the possibility that a speaker might 'Euphuize' is rejected as something 'which once was rare / And of all English phrase the life and blood', but would now be a form of borrowing.[13] Apart from this instance, and although we now use the word as part of the jargon of early modern criticism, it does not seem to have been part of the semantics of early modern literary culture. And the two instances of its use, between Harvey and Nashe and then Blount, are highly ambiguous: there is no evidence whatsoever that they use the word with the meaning that modern literary critics now ascribe to it, that of a particular prose style incorporating certain stylistic features.

The emergence of the word 'euphuism' in the year 1592 is itself suggestive. Its relatively late emergence, indeed, offers further evidence against Hunter's influential belief that interest in Lyly had faded with the 1580s. In 1592, an eighth edition of *Euphues and His England* appeared, and 1591–92 was also the second period of Lylian play publication, in which his *Campaspe* became the first English play to go into a fourth edition. By 1592, all but one of the *Euphues* books had been written and published: Lodge's *Euphues Shadow* appeared that year, and Dickenson's *Arisbas* followed two years later. When the word 'euphuism' was either first coined or first printed, Lyly's print authorship was still being established in prose, in drama and in the imitative use of his protagonist on other peoples' title pages.

The term also comes into being at a time when the meaning of authorship was itself changing rapidly. Prose fiction authorship became more visible in the 1570s and 1580s, as can be seen in the transition from Gascoigne's *Hundreth Sundrie Flowres* (published anonymously as though it were a co-authored collection) to the use of authors' names as part of their titles (Pettie's *Petite Palace of Pleasure,* Riche's *Riche His Farewell to Military Profession*) and the marked difference in reprint rates between Lyly's *Euphues* books and such books which lacked Lyly's name. In the late 1580s and early 1590s literary authorship became more visible still, as at least three literary events foregrounded authorial identity. The Martin Marprelate controversy played with and thus fetishised interest in (otherwise anonymous) authorial identity, whilst the deaths of Greene and Marlowe continued the cult of the dead celebrity author that had begun with Sidney.[14] The infamous pamphlet war between Harvey and Nashe emerged out of these debates and focused ever more on each other's distinctive writing styles, in effect reifying authorial identity as represented by prose style. It was out of this latter controversy that the word *euphuism* emerged, when Harvey accused Nashe of writing 'with a little Euphuisme, and Greenesse enough'.

This passage is, to put it mildly, difficult to interpret satisfactorily. Whereas scholars tend to assume Harvey is referring to Lyly and Greene respectively, it is not clear whether the two terms, 'Euphuisme, and Greenesse', are used to describe two different styles or are two ways to describe the same thing. By 1592, of course, many different writers had imitated Lyly's writing style, and many different writers had produced *Euphues* books. When Richard Braithwait came to write of Euphues in 1640, for example, his reference to '*Euphuus* [*sic*] golden slumber' suggests that the character was defined by an odd fusion of Lodge's *Euphues' Golden Legacy* (as it was called after 1612) and Greene's *Menaphon: Camilla's Alarum to Slumbering Euphues* rather than Lyly's *Anatomy of Wit.*[15] The very dissemination of the culture of *Euphues* and the extent to which Lyly's style had become an object of emulation means that a word formed from the title of *Euphues* should not be automatically presupposed to refer exclusively or specifically to Lyly. An association with Lyly is certainly made more likely by the unparalleled print run of those *Euphues* texts which had Lyly's name on the title page, but the sheer scope of authors involved in *Euphues* compositions should make us wary of associating Harvey's term *euphuism* simply or exclusively with Lyly. Rooted in this multi-authored culture, and coined to describe Nashe, not Lyly, the word 'euphuism' from its inception bespeaks a multi-authored and multivalent writing style.

Harvey's reference to 'a little Euphuisme, and Greenesse enough' does not make clear whether 'Euphuisme' and 'Greenesse' are intended to be in opposition or apposition, whether Harvey is describing a single style with two adjectives, or two different styles of writing. Since Harvey had described Greene in the same pamphlet as 'the Ape of Euphues', the term 'Greenesse' itself might be taken as a subdivision of a thing called euphuism. Though Harvey does not describe the style he refers to as euphuism, he clearly means it to represent a kind of style identified with Nashe, but it is not clear what relation Nashe's style has either to Lyly's authorship or to Greene's.

In his response, Nashe does not clear up the meaning of either euphuism or 'Greenesse'. He asks 'Wherein haue I borrowed from *Greene* [. . .?] Is my stile like *Greene* [. . .]? Do I talke of any counterfeit birds, or hearbs, or stones[?]' He thus associates a rhetorical device often thought characteristic of euphuism (animal, mineral and lapidary references) with Greene rather than 'Euphuisme'. Nashe then moves on to the charge that he writes with 'Euphuisme', and, though he clearly associates this word with Lyly and not with Greene, he does not associate Lyly with references to 'counterfeit birds, or hearbs, or stones'. He read Harvey's 'little Euphuisme, and Greenesse enough', in other words, in opposition, not apposition:

> *Euphues* I readd when I was a little ape in Cambridge, and then I thought it was *Ipse ille*: it may be excellent good still, for ought I know, for I lookt not on it this ten yeare: but to imitate it I abhorre, otherwise than it imitates *Plutarch*, *Ovid*, and the choisest Latine Authors.[16]

If Nashe last read '*Euphues*' around 1582, this situates his reading of Lyly's work at the end of its first unbroken print run, when Cawood was printing a total of twelve editions from 1578 to 1582, suggesting that many other readers also thought the work was *ipse ille* (roughly, unique). Echoing Harvey's phrase, 'Ape of Euphues', Nashe concedes himself to have admired *Euphues* 'when I was a little ape', but his references to Plutarch, Ovid and other Latin writers fail to clarify the relationship between euphuism, Lyly and Greene.

The consequences of this debate between Harvey and Nashe for our understanding of the word euphuism seem fundamental. None of the meanings now ascribed to euphuism makes any sense of either

Harvey or Nashe's understanding of the term, and indeed Nashe distinguishes 'euphuism' from a writing style that makes references to the natural world. There is nothing to link their use of the word with the meaning now ascribed to it. It is not possible to separate the words 'Euphuisme' and 'Greenesse' in Harvey's usage, and, although it is possible to separate them in Nashe's response, it appears that Nashe associates learned references to the natural world with Greene rather than with euphuism. Nashe instead equates Harvey's word 'euphuism' with a book he read at university, rather than a 'stile' that employs nature similes. In so doing, Nashe anticipates modern critics who associate 'euphuism' with Lyly, but he apparently understands the word to refer to something other than a writing practice organised around nature similes. This suggests, then, that Nashe read Lyly's work – or remembered reading Lyly's work – without any sense of the modern understanding of euphuism.

The second and final early modern use of the word euphuism comes in Blount's preface to *Six Court Comedies*. It appears that Blount used the term independently of Harvey, since for Blount it is a term of praise:

> Our nation are in his debt for a new English which he taught them. *Euphues and his England* began first that language. All our ladies were then his scholars, and that beauty in court which could not parley Euphuism was as little regarded as she which now there speaks not French. (A5v)

Here at least we have clearer signals of the meaning of the word. Blount unequivocally associates it with Lyly himself, although he does claim that it was a style that became co-opted by Lyly's admirers. Blount intends the word to designate what looks like a style: it is 'a new English', 'a new [...] language' which could be learnt and imitated ('parley Euphuism') much as one learns a foreign language. Blount's interest in 'new English' came at a time characterised by, in Derek Hirst's words, 'the intensely polemical nature of effusions of Englishness'.[17] This may explain why Blount refers to Lyly's second prose fiction, not the first, the title *Euphues and His England* perhaps working to endorse the claim for Lyly's 'new English'.

Blount had been publishing contemporary English literature for five decades. As we have seen, Taylor claims Blount 'had an unparalleled gift for recognizing new works that would eventually become classics'.[18] The Lyly publication was Blount's retirement act, and, in Lyly's case, Blount's endorsement failed to ensure the work became a modern classic. However, Blount does set the terms for future discussion of Lyly's work, even though the meaning of those terms, particularly his reference to Lyly's associations with the court, with women and French, changed radically in later cultures. One of the reasons for Blount's major impact on Lyly's reception is the fact that his publication is an anthology. As Stallybrass and Chartier observe, early published Shakespearean playtexts 'appeared only in the perishable and disposable form of pamphlets', but in contrast: 'The 1623 First Folio of Shakespeare's plays has had such a powerful impact upon the construction of Shakespeare's authorship because it marketed Shakespeare in bound volumes in which he was *bound with himself*.'[19] Blount's Lyly edition appeared in the same year as the second edition of the Shakespeare First Folio; the Lyly volume was not reprinted, and it would be over thirty years before the third edition of the Shakespeare Folio would appear.[20] The 1630s mark the end of the extraordinary print run of Lyly's works, with the final early modern editions of both plays and prose fiction. Lyly was in good company when he lost public interest just before the 1640s, a fate shared by Shakespeare's poetry and Marlowe's plays, for example.[21] When John Benson published *Poems Written by Wil. Shakespeare. Gent* in 1640, he promised his readers 'such gentle straines as shall recreate and not perplexe your braine, no intricate or cloudy stuffe to puzzell intellect'.[22] His terms demonstrate further evidence of the profound discursive shift in the language of literature since Lyly's work was first published.

It is Blount's euphuism, not Harvey's, that has come down to us. Harvey and Nashe allow us to historicise the word's early modern meaning, and underline how little and ambiguously the word was used in the early modern period. Blount's concept of a literary style which was 'new', foreign and influential at court and amongst ladies came to dominate later understandings of Lyly. A self-consciously literary style of language, an influence that might be compared to the French language, female titillation and courtly influence were not neutral ideas after a Civil War that had broken out over the power and prerogative of the monarch and the influence of his Catholic French queen, and in a country that rapidly came to define its imperial power in opposition to France. Readers and especially cultural commentators came to look for solidly, reassuringly English and masculine literary archetypes, not for men who apparently won over courtly beauties with Gallic affectation.[23]

From Blount to Dodsley: Lyly from 1650 to 1750

In the century before the next edition of a Lyly work, occasional publications show publishers trying to recommodify Lyly for a new age and in very different cultures. At no point do any of these editions mention euphuism. Lyly's prose fiction was published one further time in early modern London, in a joint edition in 1636, and a Dutch translation by John Grindal of the narrative section of the *Anatomy* was published in Rotterdam in 1668 and 1671 and Amsterdam in 1682.[24] Lyly's work appeared amongst a dozen translations of English prose fiction texts printed from 1667 to the end of the century, but, in a study of Anglo-Dutch translations, Cornelis Schoneveld describes the three editions of Lyly's work as particularly unusual, suggesting that 'it must have had quite an appeal'. The Lyly publications contain no preface to provide a clue to the decision to translate Lyly into Dutch, but Lyly's work followed Sidney's *Arcadia* and a number of Arcadian imitations. As Schoneveld notes, the translator Grindal had tackled not only Lyly's prose but that of John Donne, Joseph Hall, Henry Hammond and Sir Thomas Browne, choices which demonstrate a particular focus on innovative prose style. Whereas Sidney was still the subject of discussion amongst Grindal's English contemporaries, the same was not true of Lyly, and Schoneveld speculates that Grindal came across the last *Euphues* edition (1636) during his schooling at the Atheneum Illustre. What is clear is that Lyly's work formed part of a late-seventeenth-century Dutch interest in an English brand of Protestant prose fiction. Schoneveld suggests, for example, that Grindal had become interested in 'the pure Englishness of [Lyly's] word choice' and sought to emulate this semantic range in Dutch.[25]

These Dutch translations coincided with the first English discussions of Lyly since Blount, all of which emphasise Lyly as a writer who was for an age, not for all time. Thus in 1675 Edward Phillips, in the first Restoration reference to Lyly, describes 'a Writer of several old fashion'd Comedies and Tragedies, which [...] might perhaps when time was, be in very good request'; twelve years later William Winstanley spoke of 'a famous Poet for the State [*sic*, for 'Stage'] in his time'; and four year later still Gerard Langbaine spoke simply of 'An Ancient Writer'.[26] Lyly's apparent 'oldness' need not surprise us. As early as 1623, a Revels office record (now lost) referred to a performance of 'an olde playe called *Winters Tale*', at a time when Shakespeare's play was barely a decade old.[27] As Carter Daniel has pointed out in an unpublished survey of Lylian criticism, none of these writers exhibits any knowledge that this dramatist also wrote the best-selling prose narratives of the age, and their failure to mention *Euphues* or euphuism suggests their dependence on single-play quartos, rather than on Blount's edition.[28] But most of the literary figures of the age fail to show any knowledge of Lyly's existence, and Shakespeare's early editors, Rowe, Pope and Theobald, though aware of traditionally minor works such as Preston's *Cambises,* do not mention Lyly.

In 1716 the first new edition of Lyly's work since 1636 appeared, an abridged (and therefore much cheaper) version of the narrative section of the *Anatomy*, published as *Euphues and Lucilla: The False Friend and the Inconstant Mistress*. This publication appeared in the same year as Rowe's Shakespeare edition and may have capitalised on the suddenly lucrative market for English Renaissance literature, though its updated, contemporary title meant that it was not likely to appeal to professional antiquarians. A 1718 reprint, retitled *The False Friend and the Inconstant Mistress, an Instructive Novel, to Which is Added 'Love's Diversion'*, removed Euphues' name, and thus any sign of Renaissance humanism from the title, and, as Daniel notes, assimilated the work to the current vogue for French '*nouvelle*' romance.[29] In the middle of what Ros Ballaster calls 'the "pre-novelistic" period of fiction from 1684 to 1740', a 'period of intense generic confusion and disturbance', Lyly was moving ever closer to the French, and becoming assimilated into a literary genre associated with women.[30] This would give a new dimension to Blount's 1632 association of Lyly with his female readership, a phrase which would soon be not only much cited but also serve to stand for and replace Lyly's writing itself.

J. J. Richetti observes that Ian Watt's influential *The Rise of the Novel* has profoundly summarised and perpetuated our distance from sixteenth- and seventeenth-century prose fiction. Richetti argues that the book performs 'a gratuitous imposition of the social and philosophical norms (summed up in such terms as bourgeois democracy and pragmatism) and the narrative effects (summed up in the term realism) we value most upon a body of writing which was at least partly unaware of, if not hostile to, them'. Richetti here articulates a whole series of concerns which have contributed to an alienation from Lyly's narrative style and Tudor fiction more generally.[31] Ballaster notes that Elaine Showalter's *A Literature of Their Own*, an early ground-breaking feminist study of women's fiction, was 'as trapped in realist teleologies as its masculinist counterpart'.[32] For Jennie Batchelor, 'a gendered division of labour [...]

cast politics and business as the preserve of men, while women were expected to perform the cultural work of domesticity itself', and this shift directly inaugurated the meaning of the literary as, in Jane Spencer's words, 'a special category supposedly outside the political arena, with an influence on the world as indirect as women's was supposed to be'.[33] These associations served to heighten – and politicise – Blount's praise for Lyly as a writer who appealed to women, particularly women within the political domain of the court.

In February 1731, an adaptation of Lyly's *Campaspe* was performed in London as *Cynic; or, The Force of Virtue*. Lyly's work was once again retitled to align it with a currently lucrative genre, this time sentimental drama, and it was performed in a season in which Lyly may have been rather lost amongst 'sixty-seven Shakespearean performances and fifteen performances of works by Marlowe, Jonson, and Beaumont and Fletcher'.[34] In contrast to the title pages of the *Euphues* narratives, which had always included Lyly's name, his dramatic quartos had most often been published without his name, and the anonymous 1731 performance of *Campaspe* may therefore suggest that the adaptation was based on a 1584 or 1591 quarto, rather than Blount's collected edition, which names and celebrates the author. If this is the case, this lone performance was unlikely to impact on Lyly's eighteenth-century status, since it was neither given in his name nor based on an edition that provided five more of his plays. The adaptation called for a significantly smaller cast which reduced the number of philosophers, captive women and soldiers and eradicated the citizens and performing boys.[35] An emphasis was therefore presumably thrown on to Diogenes' railing and the play's love triangle, an emphasis certainly made by the new title. This would have downplayed the alternating points of view upon which Lyly's counterbalancing dramaturgy depends, but brought the play into line with current controversies about George II's court as a place of political decision-making.[36] These alterations are further confirmations of the contemporary alienation from Lyly's dramaturgical procedures, although this alienation affected all Renaissance plays performed at this time.

The one-hundred-year period between Blount's and Dodsley's prefaces, then, was characterised by a small number of Lylian adaptations: a late seventeenth-century translation of the *Anatomy* into Dutch, its early eighteenth-century adaptation into a cheap, abridged *nouvelle* version, and an anonymous and shortened adaptation of *Campaspe* in a season with eighty-two other plays. By the end of the seventeenth century Lyly had attracted the attention of three antiquarians, who all viewed him as an 'old fashioned' or 'Ancient' writer. And the *nouvelle* adaptation of his work, in particular, brought Lyly into a genre associated with Gallic culture and a female readership. In the following years, as Shakespeare began to be canonised as the archetypal national, masculine literary figure, none of the above was likely to please his few readers, and certainly helped to create the majority of people who were proud not to have read his work.[37]

'Unnatural, affected [and] infected': Dodsley, Lyly and the canonisation of Shakespeare

The gathering interest in Shakespeare in this period became gradually self-sustaining. Colin Franklin has shown that 'it was common for an editor [of Shakespeare] to use the most recent text, if only to oppose and replace it'.[38] Each new edition therefore provoked a newer one, creating an unbroken conversation about Shakespeare. Lyly and many of his contemporaries were at the periphery of this conversation. In 1738 two works published in two different countries represented Lyly as a poet. Johann Heinrich Zedler's *Grosses Vollständiges Universal Lexicon* labelled Lyly '[a good English poet]',[39] whilst Thomas Hayward's 'Thoughts Moral, Natural, and Sublime' anthologised excerpts from Blount's edition of the plays, presenting Lyly's prose as if it was blank verse. This is not the last example in which Lyly's prose writing has been presented as poetry; indeed, modern scholars often lay out Lyly's writing in this manner because, in Lanham's words, 'Prose like this stands at the typographical interface between prose and poetry'.[40] Here is another way in which Lyly confounds eighteenth-century and current literary expectations, by defying the unwritten laws that divide prose from poetry.

Despite these small signs of a positive response to Lyly's writing, in 1744 Dodsley included *Campaspe* in his collection of *Old English Plays*, and his negative assessment of Lyly's achievement was to have a lasting and negative effect on his subsequent reception. Dabbs has described Dodsley's series as 'perhaps the single most important event in the critical rediscovery of Renaissance drama', which 'greatly influenced editors of old drama for nearly 150 years after its appearance'.[41] In Lyly's case, Dodsley's influence lasted even longer, his assessment continuing to influence modern scholarship.

Dodsley's preface to *Campaspe* is in part a redaction of Blount's 1632 preface, but, as we have seen, much of the information Blount offered as praise for Lyly – his position at court, his influence over women, his association with French and his creation of a new kind of language – now looked highly suspicious in early eighteenth-century literary culture. As Dabbs demonstrates, Dodsley's edition was an attempt to 'establis[h] the superiority of English dramatic efforts over the dramatic legacies of the French' and therefore was determined by 'Dodsley's bias toward the accomplishments of indigenous dramatists'.[42] In this light, Blount's reference to French did Lyly no favours. Moreover, E. J. Clery claims the late 1720s and 1730s as the 'time when the political culture of misogyny was at its height', and, whilst Blount could praise Lyly's 'new English' and its influence over courtly ladies, the discursive context of Lyly's work had now completely shifted.[43] Dodsley found himself confronted with

> *John Lillie*, famous in his time for Wit, and for having greatly improved the *English* Language, in a Romance which he wrote, entitled, *Euphues and his England*, or *the Anatomy of Wit*; of which it is said by the Publisher of his Plays, 'Our Nation are in his Debt for a new *English* [...] as she which now there speaks not *French*'. This extraordinary Romance, so famous for its Wit, so fashionable in the Court of Queen *Elizabeth*, and which is said to have introduced so remarkable a Change in our Language, I have seen and read. It is an unnatural affected jargon, in which the perpetual Use of Metaphors, Allusions, Allegories, and Analogies, is to pass for Wit; and stiff Bombast for Language. And with this Nonsense the court of Queen *Elizabeth* (whose times afforded better Models for Stile and Composition, than almost any since) became miserably infected, and greatly helped to let in all the vile Pedantry of Language in the following Reign. So much Mischief the most ridiculous Instrument may do, when he proposes to improve upon the Simplicity of Nature.[44]

Whereas Blount had celebrated the nation's 'debt' to Lyly, Dodsley perceived only an infection: Lyly's style was a kind of infectious illness. As Richard Turley insists, both 'Romantic and neoclassical literary values' believed 'that "good" language gave rise to, and was thought to guarantee, "good" culture'. This meant that Lyly's work was received – when it was received at all – by readers invested in the moral functions of language use. Turley explains the 'ferocity' with which neoclassical and Romantic writers attacked transgressive or non-normative writing by claiming that 'the thought that the literary and political status quo might be vulnerable to rogue theories of diction was supremely disquieting', rooting this Romantic fear in its eighteenth-century origins.[45] It was in this context that Dodsley's repudiation of Lyly was made and received. Reprinted by Theophilus Cibber in 1753 and by Isaac Reed in 1825, this judgement of Lyly's work was more available to readers in this period than Lyly's work itself.

'More perhaps than any single writer', George Justice claims, Dodsley was

> responsible for the consolidation of an aesthetic public sphere in the eighteenth century [...]. It has even been suggested that critics might call the mid-eighteenth century the 'Age of Dodsley' as accurately as they have termed it the 'Age of Johnson'.[46]

Nicholas Hudson's work on the language of nature in this period shows how 'many European scholars increasingly valued "nature" over human ingenuity, [...] as represented by the purity and directness of "living speech", along with a dislike of what is human-made'.[47] Dodsley's edition of *Old Plays* 'remained a standard work throughout the nineteenth century', determined the terms of Lylian criticism for the next century and a half and continues to influence the way we now think of the writer.[48] In 1748, four years after Dodsley's edition, Peter Whalley complained of Elizabethan writings 'over-run with unnatural and far-fetched Sentiments' and, in particular, Lyly's 'perfect Magazine of Affectation and Conceit'; Whalley similarly complained in 1756 that Lyly was 'extremely affected'.[49] Whalley repeats Dodsley's key terms, 'unnatural' and 'affected' and 'corrupt': their Lyly committed an affront against the natural integrity of English writing.

This terminology abounds in later criticism. In an undated marginal note in William Oldys's copy of Langbaine's *Account of the English Dramatick Poets*, Oldys wrote a defence of Lyly as 'a man of great reading, good memory, ready faculty of application and uncommon eloquence', but criticised his 'vast excess of allusion' (which was 'not true in nature'), his 'affectation of sententiousness' and 'artificial cadence'.[50] By 1839 Henry Hallam was merely rehearsing the conventional view when he wrote that 'the style which obtained celebrity [...] is sententious to affection'.[51]

Dodsley's highly influential attack on Lyly's 'unnatural, affected jargon', 'miserable infection' and 'vile pedantry' is an important effect of Shakespeare's early eighteenth-century canonisation. Although Dodsley himself does not draw the comparison, he writes of Lyly at exactly the same time that Shakespeare was being canonised in the opposite terms. From the 1740s onwards, Lyly became one of Shakespeare's many Others. Pope's first sentence in his preface to Shakespeare's works insists that the playwright represents an opportunity 'to form the Judgment and Taste of our Nation', and Dodsley's preface to Lyly shows that he might offer the negative side to this opportunity.[52] Indeed, William Tooke in his 1798 *New and General Biographical Dictionary* made this particularly clear when he complained:

> If indeed what has been said [by Blount] with regard to his reformation of the English language had been true, he certainly would have had a claim to the highest honours from his countrymen; but those eulogiums are far from well founded, since his injudicious attempts at improvement produced only the most ridiculous affectation. The style of his Euphues exhibits only the absurdest excess of pedantry, to which nothing but the most deplorable bad taste could have given even a temporary approbation.[53]

Just as Pope advanced Shakespeare as an opportunity to establish the 'Taste of our Nation', Tooke used Lyly to assert his own 'good taste'.

Lyly and his increasingly more famous identity as a corrupt prose stylist were caught up in the canonisation of Shakespeare. Dodsley's 1744 *Old Plays* therefore needs to be set in the context of the process in which 'Shakespeare's works were, by and large, successfully appropriated to fit what became the dominant, nationalist ideology of mid-eighteenth century England', which Dobson traces through the middle of the eighteenth century.[54] Dodsley's 1744 collection of *Old Plays* was another indication of Shakespeare's increasing cultural prestige, helping to establish his unique originality by opposing it to and denigrating his contemporaries. Ian Donaldson shows that the eighteenth-century response to Shakespeare and Jonson was to divorce Shakespeare from his age, 'idealized to a transcendental role', and to 'relegat[e Jonson] to the age in which he lived, seen as its product, its chronicler, and ultimately its victim'.[55] The same process can be seen in Dodsley's preface to Lyly's *Campaspe.*

These core decades of imperial expansion witnessed the editorial and dramatic adaptation of a newly national, patriotic, heroic and familial Shakespeare. For Jean Marsden, 'In the period between 1740 and the publication of Samuel Johnson's edition in 1765, literary critics began to establish a new iconography of Shakespeare', making him 'a model of liberty'.[56] Lyly had been associated by Blount with women, with monarchical tyranny and with the French, and associated by Dodsley with a pedantic affectation that infected nature. At a time in which 'the politics of masculinity' had become the 'prerequisite for true manliness in politics and letters', Lyly became a figure who had to be either overlooked or demonised.[57]

Indeed, some commentators tried to do both. In 1753, and with a direct reference back to 'the author of the British Theatre', Dodsley, Theophilus Cibber wrote: 'This extraordinary Romance ["*Euphues*"]

I acknowledge I have not read, so cannot from myself give it a character, but I have some reason to believe, that it was a miserable performance.'[58] Twenty-five years later, in his 1777 *Biographia Literaria*, John Berkenhout wrote in much the same vein in relation to Lyly's plays: 'As to Lilly's dramatic pieces, I have not seen any of them; but from the style of this romance, I have no doubt but they are wretched performances.'[59] It is striking how both writers are proudly and automatically prejudiced ('I have some reason to believe'; 'I have no doubt'). Blount's praise for Lyly had passed through Dodsley's hostile redaction and was now inflecting the way the writer was – and was not – read. Nearly a century later, Charles Kingsley would rebuke Lyly's detractors, writing, 'if they shall quote against me with a sneer Lilly's Euphues itself, I shall only answer by asking – Have they ever read it? For if they have done, I pity them if they have not found it, in spite of occasional tediousness and pedantry, as brave, righteous, and pious a book as man need look into'.[60] Bate notes that 'no English poets of the late eighteenth or early nineteenth century could be without a sense of Shakespeare's superiority', a superiority over current and earlier writers.[61] The same writers were strongly discouraged from reading Lyly whilst being reassured they already knew what his writing entailed. All of this had happened in the absence of the word 'euphuism'. In effect it had not yet been invented in its modern form. As we shall see in the next section, whilst Lyly's work was repudiated in general, the word 'euphuism' began to develop a reception history of its own which then reinforced and reinflected Lyly's unfortunate reputation.

'"I hate your gentlemanly speakers"': euphuism and nineteenth-century novelistic discourse[62]

It was in the nineteenth century that euphuism became a term at once independent from and definitive of Lyly. By the start of the century, only *Campaspe* had been printed within living memory, in Dodsley's 1744 collection and its 1780 reprint, and Bishop Thomas Percy had included a song from *Campaspe* in his anthology of *Reliques of Ancient Poetry*, published in 1765 and reprinted in 1767, 1775 and 1790. Though we tend to think of him as a prose stylist, Lyly was also represented to many readers and students as a song lyricist, which is how my own grandmother encountered him at school in 1920s South Africa. Overall, however, there were few opportunities to encounter Lyly's works, and it took a hardy specialist like William Hazlitt to read *Mother Bombie*, *Midas* and *Endymion*. Hazlitt did not enjoy *Mother Bombie*, but in *Midas* 'the dialogue (to my fancy) glides and sparkles like a clear stream from the Muses' spring'. And *Endymion* shows that Lyly could elicit positive responses from later readers, and might have had a very different nineteenth-century reception history: 'Happy Endymion! Faithful Eumenides! Divine Cynthia! [...] There is something in this story which has taken a strange hold of my fancy'.[63]

As Hazlitt wrote, Lyly's work was becoming more widely available. Sir Walter Scott had himself reprinted *Campaspe* from Dodsley's edition in his *Ancient British Drama* (1810), and Charles Wentworth Dilke included *Midas*, *Mother Bombie* and *Endymion*, the very plays that incited Hazlitt's response, in his *Old English Plays* (1814–16). Half of Lyly's dramatic work was now in print. But, despite the fact that he was publishing the plays, Dilke's preface concentrated on Lyly's prose fiction, and he used the familiar terms to complain that it was 'deformed by affectation and a perpetual pursuit of brilliance'.[64] Hazlitt may well have had Dilke's comments in mind when he wrote: 'It is singular that the style of this author, which is extremely sweet and flowing, should have been the butt of ridicule to his contemporaries' (54).

In 1820, something happened to make Lyly, and one aspect of his authorship in particular, far more widely known. Sir Walter Scott included in his novel *The Monastery* a self-conscious and self-defined euphuist who comes from the Elizabethan court and corrupts the simple, 'natural' Scottish countryfolk with his strange syntactical affectations. This figure rejoices in the doubly phallic name of Sir Piercie Shafton and is particularly influential over women, testifying to contemporary concepts of euphuism in the following speech glorifying Lyly's work:

> Ah that I had with me my Anatomy of Wit – that all-to-be-unparalleled volume – that quintessence of human wit – that treasury of quaint invention – that exquisitely-pleasant-to-read, and inevitably-necessary-to-be-remembered manual of all that is worthy to be known – which indoctrines the rude in civility, the dull in intellectuality, the heavy in jocosity, the blunt in gentility, the vulgar in nobility, and all of them in that unutterable perfection of human utterance, that eloquence which no other eloquence is sufficient to praise, that art which, while we call it by its own name of Euphuism, we bestow on it its richest panegyric. (136)

Scott seems to understand euphuism to mean the unnecessary elongation and elaboration of a thought or even a sentence across tortuous and tautologous phrases, a language of hyperbolic excess. It thus accords closely to eighteenth-century definitions of Lyly's writing, but nevertheless bears few formal rhetorical similarities to Lyly's style or to euphuism as currently defined by scholarship. There are here few carefully balanced parisonal or isocolic phrases, little alliteration or rhyme, and none of the citations of medieval encyclopedias, classical history or proverbial knowledge. *The Anatomy of Wit* reworked the early modern sentence with its concise cola and its succinct reorganisation of the early modern phrase, and several critics have noted that Lyly helped to shorten the English sentence. But the long passage quoted above is all one sentence. Scott was, Graham Tulloch suggests, 'as much an Augustan as a Romantic', and he transmitted Augustan views of Lyly's writing into the nineteenth century. Scott owned the Blount edition that had prompted Dodsley's attack on Lyly, and had copies of Lyly's prose fiction (early modern editions since the texts were not reprinted until 1868). He also owned Dodsley's edition with its *Campaspe* preface.[65]

The characterisation of Scott's Euphuist also brings him into line with Blount's association of Lyly with women and France, which so worried later commentators (it may not be correct to call them readers). Shafton is a Catholic refugee from France, and women are 'the sex, for whose sake he cultivated his oratorical talents' (143): Shafton is able to drop the stylistic silliness when in the company of men. His very name seems to identify and mock him as a sexual threat.

As Lori Humphrey Newcomb has shown, the preface to Samuel Richardson's *Clarissa* (1747–48) included several attacks on earlier prose fiction, and the novel itself banishes other forms of prose fiction with a scene which demonstrates the dangers posed, at least to female readers, by *Dorastus and Fawnia*, a later version of Robert Greene's *Pandosto*.[66] Modern concepts of the novel are thus founded on a repudiation of the prose fiction genre that Lyly helped to create, even though novels continue Lyly's model of the single-story book. Seventy years after Richardson's novel, Scott's *Monastery* also attacks contemporary book culture, in particular the 'half-bound trashy novel', alongside its hostile adaptation of euphuism, and this condemnation of trash and euphuistic speech helped to define Scott's own novelistic project (7).

Scott's reliance upon Blount rather than upon Lyly can be seen not only in his reference to Blount but also in the fact that he claims Shafton to be based on 'that singularly coxcomical work, called *Euphues and His England*', rather than on *The Anatomy of Wit* (134). It was Blount who claimed that '*Euphues and His England*, began first that language', but it would be clear to anyone who had read Lyly's two *Euphues* books which was the earlier book. Scott was equally influenced by his editorial predecessor, Dodsley, his praise for Lyly tempered by Dodsley's influential terminology: 'Lylly was really a man of wit and imagination, though both were doomed by the most unnatural affectation that ever disgraced a printed page.'[67] But as we have seen, Scott's imitation is far removed from Lyly's own prose. Instead, Scott's 'euphuism' is simply a nineteenth-century fulfilment of Dodsley's eighteenth-century criteria: it is affected, circumlocutious and bombastic. Dodsley had offered these terms to antiquarians in 1744 in Lyly's name; Scott offered them to the early nineteenth-century novel-reading public in the name of the Euphuist. The word 'euphuism' now passed into a surprisingly general usage.

This can be seen most clearly in the use of the word in a number of British and American novels between 1832 and 1885 amongst a generation of writers who had grown up reading Scott. As Mark Twain was later to complain (in terms which curiously resemble Dodsley's attack on Lyly), Scott

> did measureless harm; more real and lasting harm, perhaps, than any other individual that ever wrote. [...] Not so forcefully as half a generation ago, perhaps, but still forcefully. There, the genuine and wholesome civilization of the nineteenth century is curiously confused and commingled with the Walter Scott Middle-Age sham civilization[.][68]

Scott's influence can be seen in the breadth of novelists who use the word 'euphuism', the period in which they do so and the particular meaning with which the word becomes invested. Most significantly, none of these writers or their characters and narrators use the word with any sign of associating it with Lyly: Scott had created an autonomous nineteenth-century word.

In John Pendleton Kennedy's *Swallow Barn* (1832), the lover Ned Hazard worries that he 'committed a thousand trespasses upon [his lover's] notions of decorum' whilst drunk, for 'he had certainly ventured into her presence, and had said a great many things to her in very hyperbolical language'; these are almost immediately labelled 'the euphuism of your speech'.[69] Euphuism stands, via Scott (who is himself reliant on Blount via Dodsley), for an inappropriate kind of speech, and once again it has been inappropriately aimed at a lady. Though some nineteenth-century uses of the term appear to be a synonym for 'euphemism' (as with Dickens and Eliot below), here it means almost the opposite: bombast rather than demure circumlocution. Lyly was affected by the same process that Elizabeth Eger describes banishing women poets from anthologies, 'at a moment of cultural conservatism, designed to appeal to a respectable readership in the conservative and reactionary aftermath of the French Revolution. By the end of a century in which a strong public sense of a national canon of literature was forged, women [. . .] were excluded from their nation's major monument to cultural posterity.'[70] Lyly's association with women and the French made constructions of euphuism seem increasingly threatening through the nineteenth century.

For both George Eliot and Charles Dickens, meanwhile, euphuism is the preserve of those with middle-class social pretension, bringing the word ever closer to a synonym for euphemism. In Eliot's *Scenes of Clerical Life* (1858), the workhouse is 'euphuistically called the "College"'. This circumlocution is repeated in Dickens's *Edwin Drood* (1870), in which the schoolroom is 'euphuistically, not to say roundaboutedly, denominated "the apartment allotted to study"'.[71] In *Current English Usage* (1962), Frederick Wood quotes H. G. Wells, who wrote, in 1903, 'You commited the sin of euphuism: you called it, not fat, but weight'. Wood explains to his readers that the accused 'had not commited the sin of euphuism, but of *euphemism* (if that is a sin)'.[72] But if euphuism is being confused with euphemism in Eliot, Dickens and Wells, it carries with it an additional taint of ridicule, pretension and, should we wish to draw implications from Wood's conditional exoneration of euphemism from sin, just a little evil.

These concepts are rooted in gender by a number of other novels from the period. William Gilmore Simms employed the word a number of times in two works, *The Scout* (1841) and *Beauchampe* (1842). In the former, another satire of American provincial life, a 'dandy' speaks with 'euphuism', a style of speech as inappropriate as his 'dress and wardrobe' (305). In the same year as Eliot's *Clerical Life* appeared, Anthony Trollope's *Doctor Thorne* (1858) features Mr Oriel, 'not an enterprising man', who attempts to broach the subject of matrimony but 'always softened down' into another topic, always 'failed' to speak properly. These attempts to come to the point are described as spoken 'with a soft, euphuistic self-complacency' which verges on the 'silly'.[73] This is a novel rooted in the signs of appropriate masculinity: its central male character is explicitly not a 'dandy' (168), in contrast to the 'dapper', 'simpered' Moffat with his 'pretty, mincing voice' (163). Euphuism's identification as an unmanly and failed discourse would come to define Lyly's critical reputation towards the end of the century.[74] This helps to explain some of the odder ways he has been described in modern criticism, as the 'dainty', 'passive' or 'beautiful' early modern writer we saw in the introduction.

In George Meredith's *Evan Harrington* (1861), a novel much concerned with the definition of gentlemanly behaviour, a character is once again defined in terms of 'her affectedness, her euphuism, and her vulgarity'. This is the countess, a woman who 'has made a capital selection of her vocabulary from Johnson, and does not work it badly'. The narrator writes sardonically that 'Euphuism in "woman" is the popular ideal of a Duchess', revealing that women too were expected to avoid euphuistic expression.[75] Elizabeth Gaskell's *Wives and Daughters* (1866) makes this all the clearer. Set in the 1820s, just after euphuism had been introduced to novelistic discourse by Scott, the novel contrasts the home-grown Molly to Cynthia, who has been raised in France. Elsewhere the novel challenges automatic 'hatred of the French, both collectively and individually', but Cynthia epitomises the dangers of a French education, speaking 'ostentatiously' with 'affectation and false sentiment':

> 'At any rate, sir', said Cynthia, turning towards [Mr Gibson] with graceful frankness, 'I am glad you should know it. You have always been a most kind friend to me, and I daresay I should have told you myself, but I did not want it named [. . .]. In fact, it is hardly an engagement – he' (she blushed and sparkled a little at the euphuism, which implied that there was but one 'he' in her thoughts at the moment) 'would not allow me to bind myself by any promise until his return!'[76]

Gaskell's negotiation of the term and its relationship to the hated French auspices of its speaker can be seen in the difficult phrase, 'graceful frankness', since one quality clearly prevents a full expression of the other. At the end of the same chapter, she fears something might '"go wrong, you know", [. . .] using a euphuism for death, as most people do', and Cynthia's engagement with euphuism is not only a characteristic of her upbringing but also a repercussion of a wider debate about suitable linguistic styles of conversation as well as of literature (459). In the same year Eliot came at the same issue from a different perspective in *Felix Holt* (1866), where 'euphuism' is used with Gaskell's sense of tactful circumlocution, but this time by a character who is angered by it. Felix complains of 'niceties', of saying 'something else such a long way off the fact that nobody is obliged to think of it': 'Those are your roundabout euphuisms that dress up swindling till it looks as well as honesty [. . .]. I hate your gentlemanly speakers.'[77] By the second half of the nineteenth century, euphuism came to be something that could arouse hate and anger.

In 1870, Bret Harte's short story 'The idyl of Red Gulch' shows that euphuism could mean not so much circumlocution or tact as 'metaphor', in an extension of the meanings given it by Eliot and Dickens: 'As the long, dry summer withered to its roots, the school term of Red Gulch – to use a local euphuism – "dried up" also.'[78] In Richard Jefferies's *After London* (1885), the word 'servant' is employed in place of the word 'slave', a 'euphuism used instead of the hateful word, which not even the most degraded can endure to hear'.[79] In Edward Eggleston's *The End of the World* (1872), a character is accused of speaking 'somewhat periphrastically and euphuistically, and – he'll pardon me – but he speaks a little ambiguously'.[80] Originally coined by Harvey to describe Nashe, and used independently by Blount to celebrate Lyly, euphuism was affected by Dodsley's description of Lyly's unnatural affectation and then used by Scott to describe pretension and unnecessary volubility. By the end of the nineteenth century, it represented either a poisonous, disingenuous mode of speech or simply a synonym for euphemism. For all of the above novelists, euphuism meant these things independently of Lyly: it was a nineteenth-century style of speech or writing that had nothing to do with an Elizabethan writer.

The use of the word 'euphuism' within these novels is significant. It is a term most often used by the narrator, and less often used by one character to describe another, suggesting the word was not quite quotidian, and still possessed the aura of literary specialisation. This is in stark contrast to Shakespeare in the eighteenth-century novel, whom Kate Rumbold discovers 'quoted by the widest range of characters', and rarely by narrators themselves. 'Literary quotations in the eighteenth-century novel are usually difficult to miss', Rumbold explains, but conversely it seems that few readers have noticed anything unusual or surprising about the use of the word euphuism in the nineteenth-century novel.[81] Such a usage, it seems, does not count as quotation at all, which emphasises even more strongly that the word was no longer part of sixteenth-century literary jargon – and of course it may never have been.

In addition to his use of the word in *Edwin Drood*, Dickens's biography affords two further uses of the word euphuism. On holiday in Broadstairs in 1840, Dickens was described by Eleanor Christian as flirting with two ladies 'in the old English style of euphuism'.[82] Valerie L. Gager has studied Dickens's use of Shakespearean quotation whilst on this holiday, and demonstrates that Christian simply means pseudo-Elizabethan English.[83] This style apparently included one-liners such as 'Wilt tread a measure with me, sweet lady?' (we are not informed whether this line worked the desired effect), and, although the style has no real affinity with Lyly's work, it is striking that the word is, once again, associated with a man trying to win over ladies. In a short story about the notorious prose stylist and poisoner Thomas Griffiths Wainewright, Dickens describes the 'insufferable fop' as he 'pens the following sublime bit of euphuism', writing, not incidentally, by the light of 'a new elegantly gilt French lamp'. Once again, Wainewright's 'bit of euphuism' bears no relation whatsoever with Lyly's work: 'Fast and faster came the tingling impetus, and this running like quicksilver from our sensorium to our pen.'[84] This sounds exhausting, but it doesn't sound like Lyly.

Dickens provides a particularly rich example of the new meanings euphuism had been given. In *Edwin Drood*, the word stood for social pretension. For Eleanor Christian, Dickens's own attempts to impress ladies with his mastery of 'old' English phrases came across as euphuism. But it is his description of Wainewright that most indicates the position euphuism had come to take in literary discourse. Dodsley had called Lyly's writing an infection, Whalley had called it a corruption, and in 1884 J. A. Symonds would describe it as a disease. Lyly and euphuism had repeatedly been associated with something infecting and poisonous. But in Dickens's description of Wainewright, the association is made in reverse: a poisonous man is described as a euphuist. As the final section of this chapter demonstrates, the link between euphuism and poisonous illness took on a powerful meaning at the end of the nineteenth century.

'Let modern Euphuists be warned': late nineteenth-century style and its perversion

Although Lyly and, more importantly, euphuism, were becoming more well-known in this period, they did not share in the nineteenth-century process in which 'Shakespeare became part of popular culture largely through the unprecedented attention accorded to him in the periodical press'.[85] Lyly was still a form of specialised knowledge for the Victorians, at a time when Shakespeare was 'all around them, on stage and on posters, in paintings and print and cartoons, in the air they breathed, on the china they ate off'.[86] For fifty years, eleven novels and one short story employed the word *euphuism* and its cognates with various meanings, none of them relating to Lyly and his prose fiction. Scott influenced critics and antiquarians too, for in the nineteenth century academic discourse was likely to associate Lyly with many of the qualities attributed to euphuism in these novels: silliness, circumlocution, social pretension, biographical failure and a sense of latent threat posed by inappropriate linguistic style. Indeed, although all of the above novels after Scott employ the word euphuism without reference to Lyly, in academic discourse Lyly and euphuism were becoming increasingly aligned. Since the two terms continue to this day to be used interchangeably and in conjunction ('Lyly's prose style' meaning, for the most part, 'euphuism', and vice versa), it is worth repeating the fact that before Scott the word 'euphuism' was not an essential term for discussing Lyly or anything else. The word became part of Victorian novelistic discourse at a time when Shakespeare was involved in 'a complex interaction of cultural and political exigencies and literary desires, of contemporary practical concerns and the Victorians' obsession with their self-location within the terms of an appropriately configured past, of both national and international identities'.[87] Now, by definition, Lyly could not be a part of this appropriate configuration.

This all occurred whilst critics continued to employ and rehearse Dodsley's terminology. In 1839 Henry Hallam described Lyly's style as 'sententious to affectation', and complained of 'the perpetual effort with no adequate success rendering the book equally disagreeable and ridiculous' (II, 408). Hallam's language chimes with novelistic references to 'euphuism', such as Kennedy's 'supremely ridiculous' euphuistic speaker and Trollope's 'failed' Euphuist. Hallam's image of a Lyly whose 'perpetual effort' brought 'no adequate success' was supported by these novelistic definitions of euphuism, and survived into twentieth-century constructions of Lyly as Hunter's failed humanist-courtier.

The first post-Scott critical elision of Lyly and euphuism came in 1858, when Fairholt published the first collected edition of Lyly's plays, some years after Lyly's contemporaries had been similarly edited (for example, Alexander Dyce's Peele in 1829 and Greene in 1831). This fresh chance to assess Lyly's dramatic achievement was published not only in Lyly's name but in the name of the euphuist. *The Dramatic Works of John Lilly (the Euphuist)* bears a title that anticipates that euphuism was more recognisable to readers than Lyly's name alone. Fairholt successfully rehabilitated interest in Lyly, since new articles followed in his wake discussing Lyly and euphuism, and in the next thirty years at least twelve such articles appeared.[88] Interest in this topic was great enough to encourage the publication of two books on the subject, and the fact that the first book related to euphuism and Shakespeare demonstrates how much this new critical discourse on euphuism operated within late nineteenth-century attempts to define Shakespeare's originality.[89]

But euphuism also operated as part of a contemporary debate about literary and conversational style. Lene Østermark-Johansen has shown how late nineteenth-century debate over euphuism was related to 'the new poetical prose which emerged in the 1860s in the critical writings of Swinburne and Pater' and demonstrated 'a keen critical attempt to declare the death of Euphuism'.[90] Following the impact of Scott's novel, the term euphuism had become a useful way to describe new kinds of rhetoric precisely because its many meanings (pretentious circumlocution, exotic diction, experimental syntax, poisonous corruption and a foreign, unmanly sensibility) had long been divorced from an association with any one writer.

At the end of the nineteenth century, as Østermark-Johansen shows, 'foreignness, effeminacy, and [...] a false focus on manner rather than matter' became particularly pressing questions.[91] The impact of this discourse can be seen in modern criticism, for example when Best refers to 'the accepted image of Lyly as a gentle and rather effete dramatist', and this book's introduction provides many more examples of critical images of Lyly as the unimportant pretty boy of early modern culture.[92] Already in 1885, Walter Pater defended euphuism, by which he meant any writing style that reminded him or others of his own. This reveals the need to fight against an embattled and entrenched prejudice against the term. Attacking those who claimed that ''Tis art's function to conceal itself', Pater suggested that this was 'a saying, which, exaggerated by inexact quotation, has perhaps been oftenest and most confidently quoted by those who have had little literary or other art to conceal'.[93]

Pater's essay refers to 'the Euphuism of the Elizabethan age' (without mentioning any particular Elizabethan), but it also refers to 'the Euphuism of the days of Marcus Aurelius' and indeed to contemporary euphuism, testifying to the fact that nineteenth-century euphuism had very little, perhaps nothing to do with Lyly's writing (72–3). And Pater's own writing style, which he associates with euphuism, was characterised by a combination of word play on Latin etymology and the use of neologisms. Neither of these is particularly characteristic of Lyly's writing. Once again, the term 'euphuism' has less relevance to Lyly's style than might be presumed, but it would come to colour the way Lyly was viewed for subsequent generations.

In his review of Fairholt's edition of the Euphuist's plays, Henry Morley made clear the uses to which Lyly and the euphuist might be put. After expressing conventional horror for Lyly's affectations, unnatural vices and social flourishes, Morley admonishes his contemporaries:

> By the fate, then, of the writers who have flattered fashion and are read no more, let modern Euphuists be warned. Nothing is lasting that is feigned. John Lyly censured, as we have seen, the men who desired 'to eat finer bread than is made of wheat', while he himself yielded to the taste of his day for affected writing; and the end is, that, with all its wit and worthiness of purpose, 'Euphues' is dead.[94]

As Østermark-Johanen notes, Morley's attack on euphuism is an attack upon modern literary style, 'thus suggesting that perhaps Euphuism was not quite as dead as he would have liked it to be'.[95]

J. A. Symonds makes clear why Morley might have wished euphuism dead. In his book on *Shakespeare's Predecessors* (1884), Symonds described euphuism as

> the English type of an all but universal disease. There would have been Euphuism, in some form or other, without Euphues; just as the so-called aesthetic movement of to-day might have dispensed with its Bunthorne [a character in a contemporary comic opera satirising aestheticism], and yet have flourished.[96]

Symonds's reference to euphuism as a 'disease' recalls Dodsley's reference to Lyly's 'miserable infecti[on]' of the Elizabethan court, Whalley's reference to Lyly's 'corrupt[ion of] the Judgment of the Age', and Gifford's reference to his 'mischief', vice and corruption of the court. Tom Lockwood makes clear that William Gifford's edition of Ben Jonson had a 'massive influence' over its readers, and scholars lacked a 'complete alternative' to his edition until 1952.[97] This repetition and heightening of the language of illness is particularly significant at the end of the nineteenth century, especially coming from Symonds, whose groundbreaking work on sexuality constructed Marlowe as an early example of Symonds's notion of the assertive homosexual.[98] An anonymous article in 1886 had lamented the influence of 'euphuism' over contemporary writing, citing it as the reason that 'manliness is not just at this moment the capital distinction of our literature': 'The modern style is, indeed, the modern man', and that man, it seems, was not manly enough.[99] At the same time, Richard Le Gallienne's obituary of Pater suggested that critics of euphuism were motivated by the anxious wish to define and defend masculinity. Mimicking and mocking Pater's detractors, Le Gallienne wrote:

> Mr Pater was not a 'simple' writer. Indeed – dreadful thought! – was he not a 'euphuist'? Was he not mannered and very sugary? Was he, indeed, quite 'manly'? I cannot resist asking by what literary council has it been

> decided, as an absolute law, that writing must be always simple, unmannered, unadorned, or, indeed, so-called 'manly'?[100]

Thus when Lionel Johnson insisted of Pater that 'his Euphuism, if that be not too suspect a word, was no dreamy toying with rich and strange expressions', he acknowledged that for many of his readers euphuism was indeed thought to be something rich, strange and inappropriate.[101] Euphuism was something suspect, a world away from Sir Arthur Quiller-Couch's 1925 celebration of the prose style of 'Our fathers [...], dignified as Latin, masculine, yet free of Teutonic guttural'.[102]

This process was heightened in the first monograph on Lyly, Dover Wilson's undergraduate essay published in 1905. Dover Wilson wrote his essay in the wake of Oscar Wilde's trial, imprisonment and death, and his book on Lyly suggests that Wilde had a major impact upon this young undergraduate's conceptualistion of literary authorship.[103] Indeed, Wilde becomes a surrogate Lyly for Dover Wilson, and vice versa. Perhaps most obviously, Dover Wilson appears to be a little in love with Lyly: 'though the stylist's mask he wears is uncouth and rigid, it cannot always conceal the twinkle of his eyes'. Dover Wilson writes repeatedly of 'the man Lyly himself', for 'the personality of an author is always more fascinating to me than his writings'. Bond's edition had encouraged exactly this kind of approach to Lyly. 'We can picture him', Dover Wilson assured his readers, 'stepping daintily about the ante-chambers [at court], shrewd and humorous [...]; now enjoying a brisk passage of arms with some sprightly maid of honour'.[104] Dover Wilson found this image of Lyly almost too 'familiar', but this familiarity, this easy picturing of him, is based entirely on nineteenth-century novelistic accretions rather than on early modern sources, and these pictures were to have a claustrophobic and delimiting effect on Lylian scholarship, as every critic began with the assumption that they already 'knew' their subject matter. This appears to be a more positive version of Cibber and Berkenhout's eighteenth-century certain critical opinions about a writer they proudly claim never to have read.

But for Dover Wilson, this 'irresponsible madcap' seemed to be 'familiar' in another way, for his description of him resembles a rather more infamous, rather more recent 'euphuist' at 'the centre of a pleasure-seeking circle of friends, despising the persons and ideas of their elders, eager to adopt the latest fashion whether in dress or in thought, and intolerant alike of regulations and of duty'.[105] 'Dover

Wilson writes here with the confidence of a man who feels he knows Lyly's social world, and the final section of his book makes clear where this confidence comes from: 'it would not be altogether fanciful, I think, to say that *The Importance of being Earnest* finishes the process that *Campaspe* started; and to view that process as a circle begun in euphuism, and completed in aestheticism'.[106] Oscar Wilde, also of Magdalen College, Oxford, haunts and permeates Dover Wilson's conception of Lyly, and his death in 1900 had a hitherto unacknowledged influence over the first twentieth-century monograph on Lyly. Wilde, tutored by the archetypal and self-confessed euphuist Pater, confirmed many of the negative stereotypes of euphuism: effeminacy and a delight in performance and aesthetic flourishes for their own sake. Lyly's name might have encouraged this association: Wilde's favourite flower was famously the lily.[107] Dover Wilson's descriptions of Lyly, the man who is too familiar, grow increasingly anachronistic, as he writes that Lyly's 'Variation of costume [his stylistic experimentations] cannot conceal the identity of his personality – the personality of the fop of culture'. Soon Dover Wilson comes to write of 'a modern euphuist' who 'has taught us, of all poses the natural pose is the most irritating'.[108] Wilde's trial and death may well have had previously unrecognised consequences for the representation of authorship more generally, affecting both past and future authorial careers, and it certainly did so for Lyly.

Dover Wilson summarised nineteenth-century associations of euphuism with effeminacy, decadence and corruption and fed them directly into academic discourse. The implications for modern scholarship are evident in Edwin Haviland Miller's description of Lyly's prose fiction as 'a middle-class *Courtier* [...] stylistically embellished like women's clothes' and 'decorative rather than intrinsic'.[109] The *OED* lists affectation in dress as a possible meaning of *euphuism*, and the *Encyclopaedia Britannica* declares that 'for a comprehension of the nature of Euphuism it is necessary to remember that the object of its invention was to attract and to disarm ladies'.[110] Lyly may have represented a heterosexual camp, but its heterosexuality was still threatening and perverted. By the time Matthew Arnold came to formulate a theory of literature as a cultural medicine, at a time when 'the creative and sympathetic powers of the imagination' and 'organic unity' had become key terms in post-Romantic culture, Lyly had been fairly systematically trapped within a discourse of infection, corruption, vice and unnatural affectation.[111] The scene was set for the dainty, sexually ambiguous and insignificant figure charted in critical discourse in the introduction to this book, a figure who continues to haunt Shakespearian and early modern scholarship.

Rozmovits tells us that 'While World War I is often used by historians to symbolize the end of neo-Victorian thinking and the irrevocable shift to the modern world, [...] it did little to dispel Victorian idealism about Shakespeare'.[112] The academic institution of literary criticism was itself a post-Romantic, perhaps even modernist phenomenon. 'Shakespeare was central to the modernist project', Cary DiPietro claims, 'because, as a cultural formation in conflict with its own self-constituting systems, he was demonstrative of modernity and the subsequent crisis of modernity'.[113] Lyly continued into the modern era as a diminutive, uninteresting and sometimes even dangerous literary figure, defined by a pretentious, ridiculous and unmanly style called euphuism.

Conclusion

Subsequent Lylian scholars, from R. Warwick Bond in 1902, the Earl of Crawford in 1924 and Leah Scragg in recent years, have worked hard to rethink his reputation. William Hazlitt and Charles Kingsley both show that Lyly might have had a very different reception history, as do brief references by Virginia Woolf, in *The Voyage Out* to 'Euphues' as 'The germ of the English novel' and in 'Donne after three centuries' to Spenser, Sidney, Lyly, Marlowe and Shakespeare as the primary early modern writers.[114] But despite these glimpses of a different response to Lyly's work, the accretions associated with the word euphuism traced by this chapter have increased the difficulties of Lylian scholarship. This explains why Violet Jeffrey found in 1928 that 'the present state of criticism of Lyly's works reveals curious contradictions'. Half a century later Scragg complained of 'the curiously crab-like progress of twentieth-century Shakespeare-Lylian scholarship which has been distinguished, to a large extent, by its rejections and regressions rather than its orderly advance'.[115] The introduction to this book makes clear that Lyly remains a problematic figure in early modern scholarship, whether he is being taught to undergraduates as an inconvenient precursor to Shakespeare or dismissed because of his supposed surface beauty or awkward, reductive attempts at flattery. As this chapter shows, such representations of Lyly's work date from Enlightenment and nineteenth-century thinking, not from the early modern period itself. In his essay, 'What is an author?', Foucault answered his own question: 'the author is the principle of thrift in the proliferation of meaning'.[116]

But critical thrift in the interpretation of Lylian authorship has ensured a thrifty reading of Lyly's works, and a prejudicial limitation of what they might mean, because it has been geared towards liberating meanings for Shakespearean authorship. The thrifty meanings of Lylian authorship studied in this chapter have therefore aided the proliferation of Shakespearean meaning.

But Shakespeare's freedom was bought at the price of a restricted and distorted view of his contemporaries. Despite the uncertain early modern meaning of *euphuism*, it has come to be defined as a rhetorical style that is unsuitable, both aesthetically suspect and anti-social. Enlightenment concepts of subjectivity and authorship have militated against a writer who is routinely evasive, playful and protean, in preference for writers supposed to offer direct thought, seriousness and psychological coherence. Romantic notions of natural talent then exacerbated Lyly's growing reputation for artifice and rhetorical fussiness. Lyly helped to define, even to create, Elizabethan print literature, but the general obscurity of all such literature in the mid- to late seventeenth century followed by the denigration of Lyly's work in the eighteenth and nineteenth centuries has been an important part of the modern formation of an Elizabethan canon. His suppression has enabled the veneration of his contemporaries by making their achievements seem unique. Lyly is neither canonical nor completely forgotten, but sits uncomfortably in between: there is then a Lyly border around the edges of the early modern canon.

Notes

1 Edwin Morgan, *From Glasgow to Saturn* (Cheadle: Carcanet Press, 1973), ll. 4, 7, 12, 14 and 33.

2 Philip Hensher, 'An exercise in non-speak', *The Spectator*, 10 February 2001, consulted at www.spectator.co.uk (30.07.09).

3 Rod Liddle, 'A big thank you to Guy Goma: the wrong man in the right place', *The Spectator*, 17 May 2006, 20.

4 For this list, see Hunter and Bevington, *Campaspe: Sappho and Phao*, 176.

5 Jean Aitchison, *Language Change: Progress or Decay?*, 3rd ed. (1981; Cambridge: Cambridge University Press, 2001), 17.

6 Gary Taylor, *Reinventing Shakespeare: A Cultural History from the Restoration to the Present* (Oxford: Oxford University Press, 1989), 5.

7 Linda Rozmovits, *Shakespeare and the Politics of Culture in Late Victorian England* (London: Johns Hopkins University Press, 1998), 7–8.

8 Kathryn Prince, *Shakespeare in the Victorian Periodicals* (London: Routledge, 2008), 1.

9 Taylor, *Reinventing Shakespeare*, 6.

10 Thomas Dabbs, *Reforming Marlowe: The Nineteenth-Century Canonization of a Renaissance Dramatist* (London: Associated University Presses, 1991), 13.
11 John Addington Symonds, *Shakespeare's Predecessors in the English Drama* (London: Smith, Elder and Co., 1967), 505.
12 Walter Scott, *The Monastery*, ed. Penny Fielding (Edinburgh: Edinburgh University Press, 2000), 136.
13 *'The Nightingale and the Ant' and 'Father Hubburd's Tales'*, ed. Adrian Weiss, in Gary Taylor and John Lavagnino, (gen. eds) *The Collected Works of Thomas Middleton* (Oxford: Oxford University Press, 2007), 156.
14 Mike Rodman Jones, *Radical Pastoral, 1381–1594: Appropriation and the Writing of Religious Controversy* (Aldershot: Ashgate, 2010), 140; Alexander, *Writing After Sidney*, 56–75; Melnikoff and Gieskes, *Writing Robert Greene*, 22–4.
15 Gariel Harvey, *Foure Letters, and Certaine Sonnets*, in *The Works of Gabriel Harvey*, ed. Alexander Grosart, 3 vols (1884; New York: AMS Press, 1966), 1, 202; Richard Braithwait, *The Two Lancashire Lovers* (London: R. Best, 1640), 139.
16 *The Works of Thomas Nashe*, ed. Ronald B. McKerrow, rev. F. P. Wilson, 5 vols (Oxford: Basil Blackwell, 1958), I, 319.
17 Derek Hirst, 'Text, time and the pursuit of "British identities"', in David J. Baker and Willy Maley (eds), *British Identities and English Renaissance Literature* (Cambridge: Cambridge University Press, 2002), 256.
18 Taylor, 'Blount, Edward'.
19 Stallybrass and Chartier, 'Reading and authorship', 42 (their emphasis).
20 Anthony James West, 'The life of the First Folio in the seventeenth and eighteenth centuries', in Andrew Murphy (ed.), *A Concise Companion to Shakespeare and the Text* (Oxford: Blackwell, 2007), 76.
21 Murphy, *Shakespeare in Print*, 19; John T. Shawcross, 'Signs of the times: Christopher Marlowe's decline in the seventeenth century', in Kenneth Friedenreich, Roma Gill and Constance B. Kuriyama (eds), *'A Poet & a filthy Play-maker': New Essays on Christopher Marlowe* (New York: AMS Press, 1988).
22 *Poems: written by Wil. Shake-speare* (London: John Benson, 1640), 2v.
23 Compare Jean I. Marsden, *The Re-Imagined Text: Shakespeare, Adaptation, & Eighteenth-Century Literary Theory* (Lexington: University Press of Kentucky, 1995), 3.
24 For a brief context of prose translations into Dutch, see J. L. Price, *Dutch Culture in the Golden Age* (London: Reaktion Books, 2011), 152–3.
25 Cornelis W. Schoneveld, *Intertraffic of the Mind: Studies in Seventeenth-Century Anglo-Dutch Translation With a Checklist of Books Translated from English into Dutch, 1600–1700* (Leiden: E. J. Brill and Leiden University Press, 1984), 127, 103, 76, 96 and 101.
26 Edward Phillips, *Theatrum Poetarum* (London: Charles Smith, 1675), xxii; William Winstanley, *The Lives of the most Famous English Poets, or the Honour of Parnassus* (1687), ed. William Riley Parker (Gainesville, FL: Scholars' Facsimiles & Reprints, 1963), 97; Gerard

Langbaine, *An Account of the English Dramatick Poets* (1691; Menston, Yorkshire: Scolar Press, 1971), 327.

27 William Shakespeare, *The Winter's Tale*, ed. J. H. P. Pafford (New York: Routledge, 1963), xvi.

28 Carter A. Daniel, 'John Lyly's critical reputation to the mid-twentieth century', paper given at the John Lyly Symposium, University of Birmingham 24.03.07, 7. I am indebted to Daniel's work in much of the following discussion.

29 Daniel, 'Reputation', 11.

30 Ros Ballaster, *Seductive Forms: Women's Amatory Fiction from 1684 to 1740* (Oxford: Oxford University Press, 1998), 11 and 21.

31 J. J. Richetti, *Popular Fiction Before Richardson: Narrative Patterns 1700–39* (Oxford: Clarendon Press, 1969), 4.

32 Ballaster, *Seductive Forms*, 20.

33 Jennie Batchelor, *Women's Work: Labour, Gender, Authorship, 1750–1830* (Manchester: Manchester University Press, 2010), 12; Jane Spencer, *The Rise of the Woman Novelist: From Aphra Behn to Jane Austen* (Oxford: Blackwell, 1986), xi.

34 Daniel, 'Reputation', 12.

35 Daniel, 'Reputation', 12–13.

36 Henry Fielding, *Plays*, ed. Tom Lockwood, 3 vols (Oxford: Oxford University Press, 2004–11), II, 6.

37 See Marsden, *Re-Imagined Text, 6.*

38 Colin Franklin, *Shakespeare Domesticated: The Eighteenth-Century Editions* (Aldershot: Scolar Press, 1991), 3.

39 Johann Heinrich Zedler, *Grosses Vollständiges Universal Lexicon*, 68 vols (Leipzig: Johann Heinrich Zedler, 1738), XVIII, 1504. I am grateful to Conny Loder for confirming my otherwise amateur translation of this text.

40 Lanham, *Analyzing Prose, 130.*

41 Dabbs, *Reforming Marlowe*, 25–6.

42 Dabbs, *Reforming Marlowe*, 25 and 44.

43 E. J. Clery, *The Feminization Debate in Eighteenth-Century England: Literature, Commerce and Luxury* (Basingstoke: Palgrave Macmillan, 2004), 2.

44 Robert Dodsley (ed.), *Select Collection of Old English Plays* (London: Robert Dodsley, 1744), xvii–xix.

45 Richard Marggraf Turley, *The Politics of Language in Romantic Literature* (Basingstoke: Palgrave Macmillan, 2002), 2.

46 George L. Justice, *The Manufacturers of Literature: Writing and the Literary Marketplace in Eighteenth-Century England* (London: Associated University Presses, 2002), 26 and 116.

47 Nicholas Hudson, *Writing and European Thought 1600–1830* (Cambridge: Cambridge University Press, 1994), 92.

48 Justice, *Manufacturers of Literature*, 116.

49 Peter Whalley, *An Inquiry into the Learning of Shakespeare* (London: T. Waller, 1748), 38; *The Dramatic Works of Ben Jonson, and Beaumont and Fletcher: The First Printed from the Text, and with the Notes of Peter Whalley; the Latter, from the Text, and with the Notes of the Late George Colman*, 4 vols (London: John Stockdale, 1811), I, 94.

50 Oldys, manuscript note, quoted from John Lyly, *'Euphues. The Anatomy of Wit.' Editio princeps. 1579. 'Euphues and His England.' Editio princeps. 1580.*, ed. Edward Arber (1868; London: Alex Murry & Son, 1919), 19.
51 Henry Hallam, *Introduction to the Literature of Europe in the Fifteenth, Sixteenth, and Seventeenth Centuries*, 4 vols (London: John Murray, 1837–39), II, 408.
52 Alexander Pope, 'Preface to Edition of Shakespeare', in D. Nichol Smith (ed.), *Eighteenth Century Essays on Shakespeare* (Glasgow: MacLehose and Sons, 1903), 47.
53 William Tooke, *A New and General Biographical Dictionary*, 15 vols (London: G. G. et al., 1798), X, 88.
54 Dobson, *National Poet*, 12.
55 Ian Donaldson, *Jonson's Magic Houses: Essays in Interpretation* (Oxford: Clarendon Press, 1997), 184.
56 Marsden, *The Re-Imagined Text*, 103.
57 Tim Fulford, *Romanticism and Masculinity: Gender, Politics and Poetics in the Writing of Burke, Coleridge, Cobbett, Wordsworth, De Quincey and Hazlitt* (Basingstoke: Macmillan, 1999), 12.
58 Theophilus Cibber, *The Lives of the Poets of Great Britain and Ireland*, 5 vols (London: R. Griffiths, 1753), I, 121–2.
59 Berkenhout, *Biographia Literaria*, in Arber, *Euphues*, 19–20.
60 Charles Kingsley, *Westward Ho!* (Cambridge: Macmillan, 1855), I, 276.
61 Jonathan Bate, *Shakespeare and the English Romantic Imagination*, 2nd ed. (Oxford: Clarendon Press, 1986; 1989), 1.
62 George Eliot, *Felix Holt, The Radical*, ed. Lynda Mugglestone (London: Penguin, 1995), I, 103.
63 William Hazlitt, *Lectures on the Dramatic Literature of the Age of Elizabeth; Delivered at the Surrey Institution*, 2nd ed. (London: John Warren, 1821), 50–1.
64 Charles Wentworth Dilke (ed.), *Old English Plays; Being a Selection from the Early Dramatic Writers: Vol. 1* (London: John Martin, 1814), 200.
65 J. G. Cochrane, *Catalogue of the Library at Abbotsford* (Edinburgh: [n.pb.], 1838), 102, 208 and 217.
66 Newcomb, *Reading Popular Romance*, 230–2.
67 Arber, *Euphues*, ix.
68 Mark Twain, *Life on the Mississippi* (New York: Collier, 1917), 375–6.
69 John Pendleton Kennedy, *Swallow Barn*, ed. Lucina H. MacKethan (Baton Rouge: Louisiana State University Press, 1986), 351–3.
70 Elizabeth Eger, 'Fashioning a female canon: eighteenth-century women poets and the politics of the anthology', in Isobel Armstrong and Virginia Blain (eds), *Women's Poetry of the Enlightenment: The Making of a Canon, 1730–1820* (Basingstoke: Palgrave Macmillan, 1999), 207.
71 George Eliot, *Scenes of Clerical Life*, 2 vols, Works of George Eliot (London: Virtue, [n.d.]), I, 32; Charles Dickens, *The Mystery of Edwin Drood* (London: Oxford University Press, 1966), 82–3.
72 Frederick T. Wood, *Current English Usage* (London: Macmillan, 1962), 86.
73 Anthony Trollope, *Doctor Thorne* (London: J. M. Dent, 1908), 472.
74 For central studies of masculinity in this period, see Philip Carter, *Men*

and the Emergence of Polite Society: Britain 1660–1800 (London: Longman, 2001); Michèle Cohen, *Fashioning Masculinity: National Identity and Language in the Eighteenth Century* (London: Routledge, 1996); and Cohen, 'Manliness, effeminacy and the French: gender and the construction of national character in eighteenth-century England', in T. Hitchcock and M. Cohen (eds), *English Masculinities 1660–1800* (London: Longman, 1999).

75 George Meredith, *Evan Harrington* (London: Constable, 1910), II, 188.

76 Elizabeth Gaskell, *Wives and Daughters* (Harmondsworth: Penguin, 1969), 299, 442–3 and 432.

77 Eliot, *Felix Holt, The Radical*, I, 103.

78 Bret Harte, *The Luck of Roaring Camp* (New York: P. F. Collier, 1892), 50.

79 Richard Jefferies, *After London* (Oxford: Oxford University Press, 1980), 156.

80 Edward Eggleston, *The End of the World: A Love Story* (London: Routledge, 1872), 110.

81 Kate Rumbold, '"Alas, poor YORICK": quoting Shakespeare in the mid-eighteenth-century novel', *Borrowers and Lenders: The Journal of Shakespeare and Appropriation* 2:2 (Winter 2006), accessed at www.borrowers.uga.edu (03.08.09).

82 *The Letters of Charles Dickens II: 1840–1841*, gen. ed. Madeline House, Graham Storey and Kathleen Tillotson (Oxford: Clarendon Press, 1969), 120.

83 Valerie L. Gager, *Shakespeare and Dickens: The Dynamics of Influence* (Cambridge: Cambridge University Press, 1996), 44–6.

84 Charles Dickens, 'Thomas Griffiths Wainewright (Janus Weathercock)', in Robert Shelton Mackenzie, *The Life of Charles Dickens* (Philadelphia: T. B. Peterson, [1870]), 345.

85 Prince, *Shakespeare in the Victorian Periodicals*, vii.

86 Adrian Poole, *Shakespeare and the Victorians* (London: Arden Shakespeare, 2004), 1.

87 Gail Marshall, 'Introduction', in Gail Marshall and Adrian Poole (eds), with a foreword by Stanley Wells, *Victorian Shakespeare, Vol. 1: Theatre, Drama and Performance* (Basingstoke: Palgrave Macmillan, 2003), 4.

88 Henry Morley, 'Euphuism', *Quarterly Review* 109 (April 1861), 350–83; J. A. Symonds, 'Euphuism', *Pall Mall Gazette* 8 (1868), 12; Anon., 'Lyly's *Euphues*', *Saturday Review* 27 (May 1869), 722–4; Richard F. Weymouth, 'On euphuism', *Philological Society Transactions 1870–72*, Part III, 1–17; George Saintsbury, 'Modern English prose', *Fortnightly Review* 25 (1876), 243–59; F. Landmann, 'Shakespeare and euphuism: *Euphues* an adaptation from Guevara', *New Shakespeare Society Transactions* 3 (1880–82), 241–76; Walter Pater, *Marius the Epicurean: His Sensations and Ideas*, 2 vols (London: Macmillan, 1885); Anon., 'An Alexandrian age', *Macmillan's Magazine* 55 (November 1886), 27–35; Pater, 'Style', *Fortnightly Review* 50 (December 1888), 728–43; J. A. Symonds, 'Notes on style', in *Essays Speculative and Suggestive*, 2 vols (London: Chapman & Hall, 1890); Anon., 'Lyly and the euphuists', *Chambers's Journal* (October 1891),

667–9; J. M. Robertson, 'Concerning preciosity', *Yellow Book* 13 (April 1897), 79–106.

89 William Lowes Rushton, *Shakespeare's Euphuism* (London: Longman's, Green & Co., 1871); Clarence Griffin Child, *John Lyly and Euphuism* (Leipzig: G. Böhme, 1894).

90 Lene Østermark-Johansen, 'The death of Euphues: Euphuism and decadence in late-Victorian literature', *English Literature in Transition (1880–1920)* 45:1 (2002), 4–25 (4–5).

91 Østermark-Johansen, 'The death of Euphues', 5.

92 Best, 'Lyly's static drama', 86.

93 Pater, *Marius the Epicurean*, 72.

94 Henry Morley, 'Euphuism', *Quarterly Review* 109 (April 1861), 350–83 (383).

95 Østermark-Johansen, 'The death of Euphues', 6.

96 John Addington Symonds, *Shakespeare's Predecessors in the English Drama* (1884; New York: Cooper Square, 1967), 505.

97 Lockwood, *Ben Jonson*, 221–2.

98 Dabbs, *Reforming Marlowe*, 123–7.

99 Anon., 'An Alexandrian age', 31.

100 Richard Le Gallienne, *Retrospective Reviews: A Literary Log*, 2 vols (London: Bodley Head and Dodd Mead & Co., 1896), II, 138–9.

101 Lionel Johnson, Obituary notice, *Fortnightly Review* 62 (1894), 363–4.

102 Sir Arthur Quiller-Couch (ed.), *The Oxford Book of English Prose* (Oxford: Clarendon Press, 1925), xvii.

103 For an account of the impact of Wilde's trial more generally, see Alan Sinfield, *The Wilde Century: Effeminacy, Oscar Wilde and the Queer Moment* (London: Cassell, 1994).

104 Dover Wilson, *John Lyly*, 21 and v–vi.

105 Dover Wilson, *John Lyly*, 5–6.

106 Dover Wilson, *John Lyly*, 131.

107 Richard Ellmann, *Oscar Wilde* (Harmondsworth: Penguin, 1988), 267.

108 Dover Wilson, *John Lyly*, 63 and 58.

109 Edwin Haviland Miller, *The Professional Writer in Elizabethan England: A Study of Nondramatic Literature* (Cambridge, MA: Harvard University Press, 1959), 7 and 62.

110 *OED*; *Encyclopaedia Britannica*, 9th ed. (London: Encyclopaedia Britannica, [1956]), VIII, 819.

111 Younglim Han, *Romantic Shakespeare: From Stage to Page* (London: Associated University Presses, 2001), 14.

112 Rozmovits, *Shakespeare and the Politics of Culture, 8.*

113 Cary DiPietro, *Shakespeare and Modernism* (Cambridge: Cambridge University Press, 2006), 2.

114 Virginia Woolf, *The Voyage Out* (1915; London: Vintage, 2004), 269; 'Donne after three centuries' (1932) in Andrew McNeillie (ed.), *The Common Reader Vol. 2* (London: Vintage, 2003) 23. I am grateful to Derek Ryan for pointing out these references to me.

115 Violet M. Jeffery, *John Lyly and the Italian Renaissance* (1928; New York: Russell & Russell, 1969), 5; Scragg, *Metamorphosis*, 1.

116 Foucault, 'What is an author?', 118.

CONCLUSION: GO DARE

I like to start any seminar discussion of playtexts with a simple question: 'who here has bought a film script in the last week?' This question rarely meets an affirmative response, even when I open it out: 'how about the last two weeks? month? year? decade?' Despite addressing this question to a wide variety of people – English literature students, history students, even theatregoers, actors and drama students – most people regard my question as somehow peculiar, unexpected, odd. Which raises the obvious question: why did people begin to buy play scripts in the late sixteenth century?[1] Many modern readers, theatregoers and actors take the existence of *King Lear* for granted, but what is *King Lear*: is it a book or a performance, a production or a playscript? why would you sit down and read it? what would you think you were doing as you did so? and which of its various versions should we take to be 'it'? John Lyly offers the chance to rethink these various problems.

In recent years, scholars have started to worry away at the meaning of texts in books and on stage in early modern England. The catalyst to this discussion has been Shakespeare, now the period's most famous and contentious writer, and the challenge he poses to modern editors. Nothing of Shakespeare's original drafts or completed texts survives, and our sole witness to these papers is therefore the printed versions of the plays. Print preserves plays, then, but a printed book is also not a play: the bibliographic form of a book cannot capture a live and real-time performance by a group of people in front of an audience. John Jowett captures this central paradox when he tells us that printed plays are 'secondary forms of publication that put the text into an entirely different form of circulation from the performance of plays on the stage, yet they are the very locus of the text as we first apprehend it'.[2] Jowett warns us here to beware of assuming that words in a book can satisfactorily preserve words spoken on a stage ('the text as initially produced and [...] originally transmitted', as Jowett puts it).[3] Yet Tiffany Stern warns us that it is equally misleading to think of a theatre 'text' in the first place. Instead of a single, stable and non-negotiable script, theatrical scripts always existed in the early modern theatre as 'a series of large and small fragments'.[4] We therefore need to ask how and which of these disparate kinds of document came together on stage and made their way into the printing house. Jowett shows us the contingent nature of texts-in-books, and Stern does the same for texts-on-stage.

Stern's work asks us to think about the materiality of the text in the playhouse, where a script was only ever a series of optional and interchangeable items. Once a theatre company began to use certain versions of these items during a performance, however, yet further choices needed to be made by the actors. Robert Weimann's work on the role of a script during performance puts further strain on our notion of 'text', emphasising the way that fictional worlds overlap with the real world of the theatre, with productive and anarchic results. For Weimann the new commercial theatres of the late sixteenth century placed text into an entirely new relationship with performance.[5] As a result, actors and their audiences had to make sudden decisions about the way they should or could relate themselves to bits of text on stage. When the actor playing Rosalind walked on to the early modern stage and said, 'So this is the forest of Arden', this bit of text challenged him and his audience to make a series of decisions about where and what 'this' was.

The printed text retains much of this theatrical friction between action and gesture, adding its own questions about source text, correction and variation which the modern editor tries to solve. Sonia Massai has recently demonstrated that the printed script was presented to the early modern reader as an incomplete and contingent text. For her, 'the early modern printed text was understood as a process, as opposed to a finite and definitive state *anterior* or *imminent* to the material witness itself': 'the text preserved in early modern printed playbooks was in fact regarded as positively fluid and always in the process of being perfected'.[6] Readers of early modern texts, then, were and are confronted with unstable and unfinished words that attempt to represent lost manuscripts and unrecorded performances which themselves incorporated unfinished decisions, unstable suggestions. Between them, these scholars challenge notions of a stable text in the theatre or in the book.

It is easy to think of these issues as early modern problems, with purely scholarly implications, but they have very modern consequences for modern actors and audiences. In his study of early twenty-first-century productions of Shakespeare, *Popular Shakespeare*, Stephen Purcell identifies the challenge posed by modern performance. Referring to Vesturport's production of *Romeo and Juliet*, hosted by the Young Vic in 2003, with its 'elements of circus, stand-up, song, parody, and occasionally seriousness', Purcell writes:

> Extratextual interpolation in Shakespearean performance not only raises questions about the perceived sanctity of Shakespeare's script, but also

> forces an examination of what it is, exactly, that we mean by 'Shakespeare' in the first place[.][7]

Later in the same study Purcell suggests that

> when actual improvisation starts to become a feature of performances, the argument that it is performing merely a 'textual' function – faithful, in [Peter] Davison's phrase, 'to the spirit of the plays' – becomes more difficult to sustain. Clearly an improvisation will always provide a 'metatext' of sorts.[8]

But perhaps it would be better to say that improvisation provides another performance text amongst the many texts that make up the fragmented and contingent words spoken on stage, some of which survive into print.

Throughout his book, Purcell explores how modern theatre practitioners contest the notion of a fixed and ready Shakespeare text. Thus, in Kneehigh Theatre's *Cymbeline* (2006), for example, 'much of the production's drama resided in the confrontation it staged between the discourses of official "Shakespeare" and the company's own unofficial metanarrative', so that 'An element of unsanctioned performance lay in the production's challenge to the institutionalisation of Shakespeare'. Responses to the production, 'whether sympathetic or hostile, [. . .] position[ed] the text as the absolute and ideal original by which Kneehigh's production must be judged'; Purcell records audience members complaining that 'It's too far from the original Shakespeare' and, on one occasion, physically threatening theatre staff and actors.[9] And yet these responses, with their concerns for 'the original Shakespeare', radically overestimate our access to Shakespeare's originality, in every meaning of that term: Shakespeare's writing papers, his performance scripts and the printed witnesses of his work all existed as temporary, in-progress versions.

When Hamlet utters the most famous line in English literature, 'To be or not to be, that is the question', we encounter a moment which raises problems for the actor, the reader, the editor, the critic and the audience member. An early modern actor needed to decide how to address the audience with this question which is also a statement. This decision rests on the actor's understanding of Hamlet's thoughts at this moment, his sense of whom he is talking to (himself? all of the audience? certain sections of the audience?) and whether Hamlet knows that other characters in the play can hear him, something different versions of the play present differently. The line encourages immediate audience interaction, posing a problem for the audience in the same way that a lawyer might challenge a jury to make a decision.

It thus combines the real world of the actor and the fictional world of the character in the ways Weimann suggests.

But although this probingly self-conscious question has now become almost self-evidently famous, the first edition of *Hamlet* sees the character pose a slightly different problem: 'To be, or not to be, I there's the point'.[10] For Jowett, the two different versions of this speech must raise questions about error and the reconciliation of variants: which version should an editor print? From Stern's point of view, these versions underline the contingency of dramatic script both in the theatre and in the printing house, confirming her argument that playscripts always existed in optional and replaceable fragments. Weimann suggests that 'for Hamlet to say, "I there's the point," is to address spectators rather than his own interior state of mind', though, as I've argued above, the now-famous version of this speech also asks the actor to address spectators.[11] For Massai, Hamlet's different speeches provide further evidence of the contingency of the printing process. Scholars continue to debate the meaning of words in books, with arguments by Peter Blayney, Lukas Erne, Zachary Lesser and Alan Farmer only the most influential in an ongoing debate over the popularity of printed plays and the creation of a market for books containing plays. Hamlet's most famous line is a question about existence, and itself exists in textual forms that question our sense of textual stability. Scholars, practitioners and audiences continue to battle over their sense of 'text' because that is the question (or there's the point) that early modern textuality poses about states of existence.

Lyly was the most famous writer of the period, during the period itself. He created a kind of prose fiction that was not only new but came to define the shape the future novel was to take. He was the first professional Elizabethan playwright to see a succession of plays into print. He created characters, phrases and literary forms that dominated contemporary writing. He deserves more space in these debates than he has so far been given. Early modern literary culture was defined to a large degree by printers, publishers and bookshop customers, working within a much more established manuscript culture. The miscegenation of literary form that can be observed in Gascoigne's *Hundreth Sundrie Flowres* articulates the relationships between manuscript, print and speech that animates any early modern book. When Gascoigne's reader finishes with his play *Jocasta* and turns over the page, they move from a Greek tragedy to a contemporary fiction, 'The Adventures of Master F.J.', from Jocasta's 'twelve Gentlemen very bravely apparelled, following after hir eight Gentlewomen' at whose entrance 'the Trumpettes sounded', to a tale of furtive English flirtation carried out without the assistance of trumpets and set in 'August last' (61, 141). *Hundreth Sundrie Flowres* mixes two literary forms, drama and prose fiction, and two worlds often contrasted as elite and popular, for the same target readership, but four hundred years of critical tradition has seen them splintered into different directions.

When literary scholars read, teach or write about *The Faerie Queene*, *Tamburlaine* or *Euphues*, we generally do so with a sure sense of generic identity: this is a poem, play or prose fiction. But that is not the label affixed to these books by their publishers. Instead, each book is defined in relation to a central and marketable character. It may therefore be time to reassess disciplinary boundaries in light of the miscegenation of literary form prompted and promoted by manuscript composition and the bibliographical effect wrought on literature by its consumption in books. The same is true of dramatic genres: Blount's title *Six Court Comedies* has been extremely influential, but its only uncontentious word is 'six'.

As we have seen, Lyly's role as a court writer has been much misunderstood, not least in Hunter's *Humanist as Courtier*, and Lyly has shared with Beaumont and Fletcher critical distaste for their supposedly distinctive association with monarchical entertainment.[12] We should be equally wary of Lyly's reputation as a writer of comedies. Stuart definitions of the genre, as seen in Blount's Shakespeare First Folio as well as in his Lyly publication, have little resemblance to 1580s usages. Despite the certainty with which the three genres, comedies, histories and tragedies, are listed on the Shakespeare title page, that book contains a play, *The Taming of the Shrew*, in which Christopher Sly is baffled by the word *comedy* and is told it is 'a kind of history'. Written at a time when comedy lacked generic definition, Lyly's plays were in any case published without generic label: the one exception, *Campaspe*, is described in its running titles as 'A tragicall Comedie'. His plays regularly end in failed courtship, and his only unproblematic romantic conclusion is in *Gallathea*, which sends two girls off to get married in church. We should celebrate this ending, but not for its conformity to traditional definitions of romantic comedy.

This book puts Lyly forward as a vital and overlooked part of this history of the different kinds and fragments of text performed on stage and printed in books. Lyly's work helped to redefine what could be put in books. His prose fiction defined a new model of storytelling but his plays also seeped into the discourse of printed books, so that Greene's *Menaphon* and Lodge's *Rosalind* engage with both sides of his authorship. Whereas Painter presents his work as a 'goodly document' and Gascoigne's G.T. puts himself forward as an editor who has reduced his material to good order, Lyly's discursive intrusion produced a new form of authorship, so that Munday could ask his readers to 'like that *Lilly*' and 'favour his freend', Greene could sell his books as a gift from 'authenticall' Euphues and Riche could promise that his new character 'Simonides is now he whome Euphues was once'. As we have seen, Lyly has come to be seen as someone gentle, conservative and a little irrelevant, but his writing spoke to his contemporaries in a much more vital, astonishing and aggressive manner than scholars suggest. It therefore seems fitting to conclude with his religious pamphlet, *Pap with an Hatchet*, where Lyly presents his writing as something physically painful, divisive and combative:

> Room for a roister; so, that's well said, itch a little further for a good fellow. [. . .] I'll make such a splinter run into your wits as shall make them rankle till you become fools. Nay, if you shoot books like fools' bolts, I'll be so bold as to make your judgements quiver with my thunderbolts.[13]

From the late 1570s to the mid-1630s, Lyly itched a little further in the early modern marketplace, making possible new forms of expression, creativity and commerce. Although we tend to see the 1580s and 1590s as the time of Spenser, Marlowe, Sidney and Shakespeare, this book has shown that Lyly and Euphues were at least as central as these now much more famous figures. It will be exciting to see how Lyly contributes to ongoing debates about early modern literary culture.

Notes

1 Compare Neil Rhodes, 'Shakespeare's popularity and the origins of the canon', in Andy Kesson and Emma Smith (eds), *The Elizabethan Top Ten: Defining Print Popularity in Early Modern England* (Aldershot: Ashgate, 2013).
2 Jowett, *Shakespeare and Text*, 4.
3 Jowett, *Shakespeare and Text*, 5.
4 Tiffany Stern, *Documents of Performance in Early Modern England* (Cambridge: Cambridge University Press, 2009), 7.
5 Weimann, *Author's Pen and Actor's Voice*, 8.
6 Massai, *Rise of the Editor*, 204 (her emphasis).
7 Purcell, *Popular Shakespeare*, 54.
8 Purcell, *Popular Shakespeare*, 92.
9 Purcell, *Popular Shakespeare*, 131–2.
10 William Shakespeare, *The tragicall historie of Hamlet* (London: Nicholas

Ling and John Trundell, 1603), D4v.
11 Weimann, *Author's Pen and Actor's Voice*, 21.
12 Clark, *The Plays of Beaumont and Fletcher*, 4.
13 John Lyly, *Pap with an Hatchet*, in *The Complete Works of John Lyly*, ed. R. Warwick Bond, 3 vols (Oxford: Clarendon Press, 1902), III, 394.

BIBLIOGRAPHY

Aitchison, Jean, *Language Change: Progress or Decay?*, 3rd edn (1981; Cambridge: Cambridge University Press, 2001)

Alexander, Gavin, *Writing After Sidney: The Literary Response to Sir Philip Sidney 1586–1640* (Oxford: Oxford University Press, 2006)

Alfreds, Mike, *A Shared Experience: The Actor as Story-Teller* (Dartington: Dartington College of Arts, 1979)

Allain, Paul, *The Art of Stillness: The Theater Practice of Tadashi Suzuki* (Basingstoke: Palgrave Macmillan, 2002)

Altman, Joel B., *The Tudor Play of Mind: Rhetorical Inquiry and the Development of Elizabethan Drama* (London: University of California Press, 1978)

Andreadis, Harriette, *Sappho in Early Modern England: Female Same-Sex Literary Erotics 1550–1714* (London: University of Chicago Press, 2001)

Anon., 'An Alexandrian age', *Macmillan's Magazine* 55 (November 1886), 27–35

Anon., 'Lyly and the euphuists', *Chambers's Journal* (October 1891), 667–9

Anon., 'Lyly's *Euphues*', *Saturday Review* 27 (May 1869), 722–4

Ascham, Roger, *The Scholemaster* (London: printed by John Day, 1570)

Astington, John H., *English Court Theatre 1558–1642* (Cambridge: Cambridge University Press, 1999)

Austen, Gillian, *George Gascoigne* (Cambridge: D. S. Brewer, 2008)

Baker, Ernest A., *The History of the English Novel*, 10 vols (London: Witherby, 1924–39)

Bal, Mieke, *Narratology: Introduction to the Theory of Narrative*, 2nd edn (1985; Toronto: University of Toronto Press, 1997)

Baldwin, William, *Beware the Cat: The First English Novel*, ed. William A. Ringler and Michael Flachmann (San Marino: Huntington Library, 1988)

Ballaster, Ros, *Seductive Forms: Women's Amatory Fiction from 1684 to 1740* (Oxford: Oxford University Press, 1998)

Barbour, Reid, *Deciphering Elizabethan Fiction* (Newark: University of Delaware Press, 1993)

Barish, Jonas, 'The prose style of John Lyly', *English Literary History* 23:1 (March 1956), 14–35

Barker, Francis, *The Tremulous Private Body: Essays on Subjection* (London: Methuen, 1984)

Barthes, Roland, 'The death of the author' (1967), in *Image Music Text*, ed. and tr. Stephen Heath (London: Fontana Press, 1977)

Batchelor, Jennie, *Women's Work: Labour, Gender, Authorship, 1750–1830* (Manchester: Manchester University Press, 2010)

Bate, Jonathan, *Shakespeare and the English Romantic Imagination*, 2nd edn (1986; Oxford: Clarendon Press, 1989)

Bates, Catherine, '"A large occasion of discourse": John Lyly and the art of civil conversation', *Review of English Studies* n.s. 42 (1991), 469–86

Bates, Catherine, *The Rhetoric of Courtship in Elizabethan Language and Literature* (Cambridge: Cambridge University Press, 1992)

Beaumont, Francis, *The Knight of the Burning Pestle*, ed. J. W. Lever (London: Longmans, 1962)

Beaumont, Francis, *The Knight of the Burning Pestle*, ed. Sheldon P. Zitner (Manchester: Manchester University Press, 2004)

Beecher, Donald (ed.), *Critical Approaches to English Prose Fiction 1520–1640* (Ottawa: Dovehouse Editions, 1998)

Belsey, Catherine, 'Literature, history, politics', *Literature and History* 9 (1983), 17–26, rpt in Richard Wilson and Richard Dutton (eds), *New Historicism and Renaissance Drama* (London: Longman, 1992)

Benedetti, Robert, *The Actor at Work: An Introduction to the Skills of Acting* (1970; Englewood Cliffs, NJ: Prentice-Hall, 1998)

Bennett, Susan, *Theatre Audiences: A Theory of Production and Reception*, 2nd edn (1997; London: Routledge, 2005)

Berry, Philippa, *Of Chastity and Power: Elizabethan Literature and the Unmarried Queen* (London: Routledge, 1989)

Best, Michael R., 'Lyly's static drama', *Renaissance Drama* n.s. 1 (1968), 75–86

Best, Michael R., 'The staging and production of the plays of John Lyly', *Theatre Research, Recherches Theatrales* 9:2 (1968), 104–17

Bevington, David, 'The first edition of John Lyly's *Sappho and Phao* (1584)', *Studies in Bibliography* 42 (1989), 187–99

Blake, N. F., *A Grammar of Shakespeare's Language* (Basingstoke: Palgrave Macmillan, 2002)

Blayney, Peter, 'The alleged popularity of playbooks', *Shakespeare Quarterly* 56.1 (Spring 2005), 33–50

Blayney, Peter, *The First Folio of Shakespeare* (Washington, DC: Folger Library Publications, 1991)

Blayney, Peter, 'The publication of playbooks', in John D. Cox and David Scott Kastan (eds), *A New History of Early English Drama* (New York: Columbia University Press, 1997)

Blayney, Peter W. M., *The Bookshops in Paul's Cross Churchyard* (London: Bibliographical Society, 1990)

Bourdieu, Pierre, *Distinction: A Social Critique of the Judgment of Taste*, tr. Richard Nice (London: Routledge & Kegan Paul, 1984)

Bowers, Terence N., 'The production and communication of knowledge in William Baldwin's *Beware the Cat*: toward a typographic culture', *Criticism* 33 (1991), 1–29

Braithwait, Richard, *The Two Lancashire Lovers* (London: R. Best, 1640)

Bristol, Michael D., *Big-time Shakespeare* (London: Routledge, 1996)

Brome, Richard, *A Critical Old-Spelling Edition of Richard Brome's 'A Mad Couple Well Match'd'* (1653), ed. Steen H. Spove (London: Garland Publishing, 1979)

Brooker, Will, *Batman Unmasked: Analyzing a Cultural Icon* (London: Continuum Books, 2001)

Brooks, Douglas A., *From Playhouse to Printing House: Drama and Authorship in Early Modern England* (Cambridge: Cambridge University Press, 2000)

Bruster, Douglas, *Drama and the Market in the Age of Shakespeare* (Cambridge: Cambridge University Press, 1992)

Bruster, Douglas, 'The structural transformation of print in late Elizabethan England', in Arthur F. Marotti and Michael D. Bristol (eds), *Print, Manuscript, Performance: The Changing Relations of the Media in Early*

Modern England (Columbus: Ohio State University Press, 2000)
Burns, Edward, *Character: Acting and Being on the Pre-Modern Stage* (London: Macmillan, 1990)
Carson, Christie, and Farah Karim-Cooper (eds), *Shakespeare's Globe: A Theatrical Experiment* (Cambridge: Cambridge University Press, 2008)
Carter, Philip, *Men and the Emergence of Polite Society: Britain 1660–1800* (London: Longman, 2001)
Cartwright, Kent, 'The confusions of *Gallathea*: John Lyly as popular dramatist', *Comparative Drama* 32 (1998), 207–39
Carver, Robert H. F., *The Protean Ass: The Metamorphoses of Apuleius from Antiquity to the Renaissance* (Oxford: Oxford University Press, 2008)
Chakravorty, Swapan, *Society and Politics in the Plays of Thomas Middleton* (Oxford: Clarendon Press, 1996)
Chapman, George, *The Poems of George Chapman*, ed. Phyllis Brooks Bartlett (1941; New York: Russell & Russell, 1962)
Chartier, Roger, *The Order of Books: Readers, Authors, and Libraries in Europe Between the Fourteenth and Eighteenth Centuries*, tr. Lydia G. Cochrane (Stanford: Stanford University Press, 1994)
Cheney, Patrick, 'Perdita, Pastorella and the romance of literary form: Shakespeare's counter-Spenserian authorship', in J. B. Lethbridge (ed.), *Shakespeare and Spenser: Attractive Opposites* (Manchester: Manchester University Press, 2008)
Cheney, Patrick, *Shakespeare, National Poet-Playwright* (Cambridge: Cambridge University Press, 2004)
Child, Clarence Griffin, *John Lyly and Euphuism* (Leipzig: G. Böhme, 1894)
Cibber, Theophilus *The Lives of the Poets of Great Britain and Ireland*, 5 vols (London: R. Griffiths, 1753)
Clark, Sandra, *The Plays of Beaumont and Fletcher: Sexual Themes and Dramatic Representation* (London: Harvester Wheatsheaf, 1994)
Clery, E. J., *The Feminization Debate in Eighteenth-Century England: Literature, Commerce and Luxury* (Basingstoke: Palgrave Macmillan, 2004)
Cochrane, J. G., *Catalogue of the Library at Abbotsford* (Edinburgh: [n.pb.], 1838)
Cohen, Adam Max, *Technology and the Early Modern Self* (New York: Palgrave Macmillan, 2009)
Cohen, Michèle, *Fashioning Masculinity: National Identity and Language in the Eighteenth Century* (London: Routledge, 1996)
Cohen, Michèle, 'Manliness, effeminacy and the French: gender and the construction of national character in eighteenth-century England', in T. Hitchcock and M. Cohen (eds), *English Masculinities 1660–1800* (London: Longman, 1999)
Crane, William G., *Wit and Rhetoric in the Renaissance: The Formal Basis of Elizabethan Prose Style* (1937; Gloucester, MA: Peter Smith, 1964)
Croll, Morris William, *'Attic' and Baroque Prose Style: The Anti-Ciceronian Movement*, ed. J. Max Patrick and Robert O. Evans, with John M. Wallace (Princeton: Princeton University Press, 1966)
Coward, Noel, *The Vortex* (London: Methuen, 2002)
Dabbs, Thomas, *Reforming Marlowe: The Nineteenth-Century*

Canonization of a Renaissance Dramatist (London: Associated University Presses, 1991)

Daniel, Carter A., 'John Lyly's critical reputation to the mid-twentieth century', paper given at the John Lyly Symposium, University of Birmingham 24.03.07

Davis, Walter, *Idea and Act in Elizabethan Fiction* (Princeton: Princeton University Press, 1969)

Dent, R. W., *Proverbial Language in English Drama Exclusive of Shakespeare, 1495–1616: An Index* (London: University of California, 1984)

Dessen, Alan C., *Elizabethan Stage Conventions and Modern Interpreters* (Cambridge: Cambridge University Press, 1984)

Dickens, Charles, *The Letters of Charles Dickens II: 1840–1841*, gen. eds Madeline House, Graham Storey and Kathleen Tillotson (Oxford: Clarendon Press, 1969)

Dickens, Charles, *The Mystery of Edwin Drood* (London: Oxford University Press, 1966)

Dickens, Charles, 'Thomas Griffiths Wainewright (Janus Weathercock)', in Robert Shelton Mackenzie, *The Life of Charles Dickens* (Philadelphia: T. B. Peterson, [1870])

Dickenson, John, *Arisbas, Euphues amidst his slumbers* (London: Thomas Woodcocke, 1594)

Dilke, Charles Wentworth (ed.), *Old English Plays; Being a Selection from the Early Dramatic Writers: Vol. 1* (London: John Martin, 1814)

Dillon, Janette, *The Cambridge Introduction to Early English Theatre* (Cambridge: Cambridge University Press, 2006)

Dillon, Janette, *The Language of Space in Court Performance, 1400–1625* (Cambridge: Cambridge University Press, 2010)

DiPietro, Cary, *Shakespeare and Modernism* (Cambridge: Cambridge University Press, 2006)

Dobranski, Stephen B., *Readers and Authorship in Early Modern England* (Cambridge: Cambridge University Press, 2005)

Dobson, Michael, *The Making of the National Poet: Shakespeare, Adaptation, and Authority, 1660–1769* (Oxford: Clarendon Press, 1992)

Dodsley, Robert (ed.), *A Select Collection of Old English Plays* (London: Robert Dodsley, 1744)

Donaldson, Ian, *Jonson's Magic Houses: Essays in Interpretation* (Oxford: Clarendon Press, 1997)

Donaldson, Ian, '"Not of an age": Jonson, Shakespeare and the verdicts of posterity', in James Hirsh (ed.), *New Perspectives on Ben Jonson* (Cranbury, NJ: Associated University Presses, 1997)

Dover Wilson, John, *John Lyly* (Cambridge: Macmillan and Bowes, 1905)

Dugas, Don-John, *Marketing the Bard: Shakespeare in Performance and Print, 1660–1740* (Columbia: University of Missouri Press, 2006)

Dunn, Kevin, *Pretexts of Authority: The Rhetoric of Authorship in the Renaissance Preface* (Stanford: Stanford University Press, 1994)

Eger, Elizabeth, 'Fashioning a female canon: eighteenth-century women poets and the politics of the anthology', in Isobel Armstrong and Virginia Blain (eds), *Women's Poetry of the Enlightenment: The Making of a Canon, 1730–1820* (Basingstoke: Palgrave Macmillan, 1999)

Eggleston, Edward, *The End of the World: A Love Story* (London: Routledge, 1872)

Eisenstein, Elizabeth, *The Printing Press as an Agent of Change: Communications and Cultural Transformations in Early Modern Europe*, 2 vols (Cambridge: Cambridge University Press, 1979)

Eliot, George, *Felix Holt, The Radical*, ed. Lynda Mugglestone (London: Penguin, 1995)

Eliot, George, *Scenes of Clerical Life*, 2 vols, Works of George Eliot (London: Virtue, [n.d.])

Ellmann, Richard, *Oscar Wilde* (Harmondsworth: Penguin, 1988)

Erne, Lukas, *Shakespeare as Literary Dramatist* (Cambridge: Cambridge University Press, 2003)

Escolme, Bridget, *Talking to the Audience: Shakespeare, Performance, Self* (Abingdon: Routledge, 2005)

Farmer, Alan B., and Zachary Lesser, 'The popularity of playbooks revisited', *Shakespeare Quarterly* 56:1 (Spring 2005), 1–32

Farmer, Alan B., and Zachary Lesser, 'Structures of popularity in the early modern book trade', *Shakespeare Quarterly* 56:2 (Summer 2005), 206–13

Farmer, Alan B., and Zachary Lesser, 'Vile arts: the marketing of English printed drama, 1512–1660', *Research Opportunities in Renaissance Drama* 39 (2000), 77–165

Fenton, Geoffrey, *Certain Tragical Discourses of Bandello*, ed. W. E. Henley, 2 vols (1898; New York: AMS Press, 1967)

Feuillerat, Albert, *Lyly: Contribution à l'histoire de la Renaissance en Angleterre* (1910; New York: Russell & Russell, 1968)

Fielding, Henry, *Plays*, ed. Tom Lockwood, 3 vols (Oxford: Oxford University Press, 2004–11)

Fleming, Juliet, 'The ladies' man and the age of Elizabeth', in James Grantham Turner (ed.), *Sexuality & Gender in Early Modern Europe: Institutions, Texts, Images* (Cambridge: Cambridge University Press, 1993)

Foucault, Michel, 'What is an author?' (1969), tr. Josué V. Harari, originally published in Harari (ed.), *Textual Strategies: Perspectives in Post-Structuralist Criticism* (1980), rev. and rpt in *The Foucault Reader: An Introduction to Foucault's Thought*, ed. Paul Rabinow (1984; London: Penguin Books, 1986)

Fowler, Elizabeth, and Roland Greene (eds), *The Project of Prose in Early Modern Europe and the New World* (Cambridge: Cambridge University Press, 1997)

Fox, Adam, *Oral and Literate Culture in England 1500–1700* (Oxford: Oxford University Press, 2000)

Fox, Alistair, 'The complaint of poetry for the death of liberality: the decline of literary patronage in the 1590s', in John Guy (ed.), *The Reign of Elizabeth I: Court and Culture in the Last Decade* (Cambridge: Cambridge University Press, 1995)

Franklin, Colin, *Shakespeare Domesticated: The Eighteenth-Century Editions* (Aldershot: Scolar Press, 1991)

Fuchs, Barbara, *Romance* (New York: Routledge, 2004)

Fulford, Tim, *Romanticism and Masculinity: Gender, Politics and Poetics in the Writing of Burke, Coleridge, Cobbett, Wordsworth, De Quincey and Hazlitt* (Basingstoke: Macmillan, 1999)

Gager, Valerie L., *Shakespeare and Dickens: The Dynamics of Influence* (Cambridge: Cambridge University Press, 1996)

Gair, Reavley, *The Children of Paul's: The Story of a Theatre Company, 1553–1608* (Cambridge: Cambridge University Press, 1982)

Gallienne, Richard Le, *Retrospective Reviews: A Literary Log*, 2 vols (London: Bodley Head and Dodd Mead & Co., 1896)

Gants, David L., 'Creede, Thomas', *Oxford Dictonary of National Biography* (Oxford University Press, 2004)

Gascoigne, George, *A Hundreth Sundrie Flowres*, ed. G. W. Pigman III (Oxford: Clarendon Press, 2000)

Gaskell, Elizabeth, *Wives and Daughters* (Harmondsworth: Penguin, 1969)

Gieskes, Edward, *Representing the Professions: Administration, Law and Theater in Early Modern England* (Newark: University of Delaware Press, 2006)

Godzich, Wlad, and Jeffrey Kittay, *The Emergence of Prose: An Essay in Prosaics* (Minneapolis: University of Minnesota Press, 1987)

Goldberg, Jonathan, *Endlesse Worke: Spenser and the Structures of Discourse* (Baltimore: Johns Hopkins University Press, 1981)

Gohlke, Madelon, 'Reading "Euphues"', *Criticism* 19:2 (Spring 1977), 103–17

Gorak, Jan, *The Making of the Modern Canon: Genesis and Crisis of a Literary Idea* (London: Athlone, 1991)

Grady, Hugh, *The Modernist Shakespeare: Critical Texts in a Material World* (Oxford: Clarendon Press, 1991)

Grafton, Anthony, and Lisa Jardine, '"Studied for action": how Gabriel Harvey read his Livy', *Past and Present* 129 (1990), 30–78

Grazia, Margreta de, and Peter Stallybrass, 'The materiality of the Shakespearean text', *Shakespeare Quarterly* 44 (1993), 255–83

Green, Ian, *Print and Protestantism in Early Modern England* (Oxford: Oxford University Press, 2000)

Greene, Robert, *Alcida*[:] *Greene's Metamorphosis* (London: George Purslowe, 1617)

Greene, Robert, *A Critical Edition of Robert Greene's 'Ciceronis Amor: Tullies Love'*, ed. Charles Howard Lardson (Salzburg: Institut für Englische Sprache und Literatur, Universität Salzburg, 1974)

Greene, Robert, *Gwydonius, or The Card of Fancy*, ed. Carmine di Biase (Ottawa: Dovehouse Editions, 2001)

Greene, Robert, *The Life and Complete Works in Prose and Verse of Robert Greene*, ed. Alexander B. Grosart, 15 vols (1881–86; New York: Russell & Russell, 1964)

Greene, Robert, *Menaphon: Camilla's Alarm to Slumbering Euphues*, ed. Brenda Cantar (Ottawa: Dovehouse Editions, 1996)

Greene, Robert, *Rosalind: Euphues Golden Legacy*, ed. Donald Beecher (Ottawa: Dovehouse Editions, 1997)

Greening, Anna 'Tottel, Richard', *Oxford Dictionary of National Biography* (Oxford University Press, 2004)

Greg, W. W., *Pastoral Poetry and Pastoral Drama* (London: A. H. Bullen, 1906)

Guenther, Leah, '"To parley euphuism": fashioning English as a linguistic fad', *Renaissance Studies* 16:1 (March 2002), 24–35

Gurr, Andrew, 'Did Shakespeare own his own playbooks?', *Review of English Studies*, n.s., 60:244 (2009), 206–29

Gurr, Andrew, 'The great divide of 1594', in Brian Boyd (ed.), *Words that Count: Early Modern Authorship: Essays in Honor of MacDonald P. Jackson* (Newark: University of Delaware Press, 2004)

Gurr, Andrew, *The Shakespeare Company, 1594–1642* (Cambridge: Cambridge University Press, 2004)

Gurr, Andrew, *Shakespeare's Opposites: The Admiral's Company 1594–1625* (Cambridge: Cambridge University Press, 2009)

Hackel, Heidi Brayman, *Reading Material in Early Modern England: Print, Gender and Literacy* (Cambridge: Cambridge University Press, 2005)

Hackett, Helen, *Women and Romance Fiction in the English Renaissance* (Cambridge: Cambridge University Press, 2000)

Hadfield, Andrew, *Shakespeare, Spenser and the Matter of Britain* (Basingstoke: Palgrave Macmillan, 2004)

Halasz, Alexandra, *The Marketplace of Print: Pamphlets and the Public Sphere in Early Modern England* (Cambridge: Cambridge University Press, 1997)

Hallam, Henry, *Introduction to the Literature of Europe in the Fifteenth, Sixteenth, and Seventeenth Centuries*, 4 vols (London: John Murray, 1837–39)

Han, Younglim, *Romantic Shakespeare: From Stage to Page* (London: Associated University Presses, 2001)

Harris, Jonathan Gil, *Foreign Bodies and the Body Politic: Discourses of Social Pathology in Early Modern England* (Cambridge: Cambridge University Press, 1998)

Hart, Alfred, *Stolne and Surreptitious Copies: A Comparative Study of Shakespeare's Bad Quartos* (Melbourne: Melbourne University Press, 1942)

Harte, Bret, *The Luck of Roaring Camp* (New York: P. F. Collier, 1892)

Harvey, Gabriel, *The Works of Gabriel Harvey*, ed. Alexander B. Grosart, 3 vols (1884; New York: AMS Press, 1966)

Hausted, Peter, *Senile Odium*, ed. and tr. Laurens J. Mills (Bloomington: Indiana University Press, 1949)

Hawkes, Terence, *That Shakespeherian Rag: Essays on a Critical Process* (London: Methuen, 1986)

Hazlitt, William, *Lectures on the Dramatic Literature of the Age of Elizabeth; Delivered at the Surrey Institution*, 2nd edn (London: John Warren, 1821)

Heckscher, William, *Rembrandt's Anatomy of Dr Nicholaas Tulp* (New York: New York University Press, 1958)

Heinemann, Margot, *Puritanism & Theatre: Thomas Middleton and Opposition Drama under the Early Stuarts* (Cambridge: Cambridge University Press, 1982)

Helgerson, Richard, *Forms of Nationhood: The Elizabethan Writing of England* (Chicago: University of Chicago Press, 1992)

Hensher, Philip, 'An exercise in non-speak', *The Spectator*, 10 February 2001, consulted at www.spectator.co.uk (30.07.09)

Heywood, John, *The Plays of John Heywood*, eds Richard Axton and Peter Happé (Cambridge: D. S. Brewer, 1991)
Hill, Tracey, *Anthony Munday and Civic Culture: Theatre, History, and Power in Early Modern London 1580–1633* (Manchester: Manchester University Press, 2004)
Hirschfeld, Heather Anne, *Joint Enterprises: Collaborative Drama and the Institutionalization of the English Renaissance Theater* (Amherst: University of Massachusetts Press, 2004)
Hirst, Derek, 'Text, time and the pursuit of "British identities"', in David J. Baker and Willy Maley (eds), *British Identities and English Renaissance Literature* (Cambridge: Cambridge University Press, 2002)
Hodges, Devon L., *Renaissance Fictions of Anatomy* (Amherst: University of Massachusetts Press, 1985)
Honan, Park, *Shakespeare: A Life* (Oxford: Oxford University Press, 1998)
Hoskyns, John, *Directions for Speech and Style*, ed. H. H. Hudson (Princeton: Princeton University Press, 1935)
Howard-Hill, T. H., 'The evolution of the form of plays in English during the Renaissance', *Renaissance Quarterly* 43 (1990), 112–45
Howell, W. S., *Logic and Rhetoric in England 1500–1700* (1956; New York: Russell & Russell, 1961)
Hudson, Nicholas, *Writing and European Thought 1600–1830* (Cambridge: Cambridge University Press, 1994)
Hunter, G. K., *English Drama 1586–1642: The Age of Shakespeare* (Oxford: Clarendon Press, 1997)
Hunter, G. K., 'John Lyly', in A. C. Hamilton (gen. ed.), *The Spenser Encyclopedia* (London: Routledge, 1990)
Hunter, G. K., *John Lyly: The Humanist as Courtier* (London: Routledge and Kegan Paul, 1962)
Hunter, J. Paul, *Before Novels: The Cultural Contexts of Eighteenth-Century English Fiction* (New York: Norton, 1990)
Hutson, Lorna, *Thomas Nashe in Context* (Oxford: Clarendon Press, 1989)
Ingram, William, *The Business of Playing: The Beginning of Adult Professional Theater in Elizabethan London* (Ithaca: Cornell University Press, 1992)
Jagodzinski, Cecile M., *Privacy and Print: Reading and Writing in Seventeenth-Century England* (Charlottesville: University of Virginia Press, 1999)
Javitch, Daniel, *Poetry and Courtliness in Renaissance England* (Princeton: Princeton University Press, 1978)
Jefferies, Richard, *After London* (Oxford: Oxford University Press, 1980)
Jeffery, Violet M., *John Lyly and the Italian Renaissance* (1928; New York: Russell & Russell, 1969)
Johns, Adrian, *The Nature of the Book: Print and Knowledge in the Making* (Chicago: University of Chicago Press, 1998)
Johnson, Lionel, Obituary notice, *Fortnightly Review* 62 (1894)
Jones, Mike Rodman, *Radical Pastoral, 1381–1594: Appropriation and the Writing of Religious Controversy* (Aldershot: Ashgate, 2010)
Jonson, Ben, *Every Man Out of His Humour*, ed. Helen Ostovich (Manchester: Manchester University Press, 2001)
Jonson, Ben, 'To the memory of my beloved, The AUTHOR MR. WILLIAM

SHAKESPARE: And what he hath left us', in *The Works of William Shakespeare in Reduced Facsimile from the Famous First Folio Edition of 1623*, with an introduction by J. O. Halliwell-Phillipps (London: Chatto and Windus, 1876)

Jonson, Ben, Francis Beaumont and John Fletcher, *The Dramatic Works of Ben Jonson, and Beaumont and Fletcher: The First Printed from the Text, and with the Notes of Peter Whalley; the Latter, from the Text, and with the Notes of the Late George Colman*, 4 vols (London: John Stockdale, 1811)

Jowett, John, *Shakespeare and Text* (Oxford: Oxford University Press, 2007)

Judd, Sylvester, *Richard Edney and the Governor's Family* (Boston: Phillips and Sampson, 1850)

Justice, George L., *The Manufacturers of Literature: Writing and the Literary Marketplace in Eighteenth-Century England* (London: Associated University Presses, 2002)

Kastan, David Scott, *Shakespeare After Theory* (London: Routledge, 1999)

Kastan, David Scott, *Shakespeare and the Book* (Cambridge: Cambridge University Press, 2001)

Kay, W. David, 'The shaping of Ben Jonson's career: a reexamination of facts and problems', *MP* 67:3 (February 1970), 224–37

Kennedy, John Pendleton, *Swallow Barn*, ed. Lucina H. MacKethan (Baton Rouge: Louisiana State University Press, 1986)

Kesson, Andy, and Emma Smith, 'Towards a definition of print popularity', in Andy Kesson and Emma Smith (eds), *The Elizabethan Top Ten: Defining Print Popularity in Early Modern England* (Farnham: Ashgate, 2013)

King, W. N., 'John Lyly and Elizabethan rhetoric', *SP* 52:2 (April 1955), 149–61

Kingsley, Charles, *Westward Ho!* (Cambridge: Macmillan, 1855)

Kingsley-Smith, Jane, *Cupid in Early Modern Literature and Culture* (Cambridge: Cambridge University Press, 2010)

Kinney, Arthur F. (ed.), *The Cambridge Companion to English Literature, 1500–1600* (Cambridge: Cambridge University Press, 2000)

Kinney, Arthur F., *Humanist Poetics: Thought, Rhetoric and Fiction in Sixteenth-Century England* (Amherst: University of Massachusetts Press, 1986)

Kintgen, Eugene R., *Reading in Tudor England* (Pittsburgh: University of Pittsburgh Press, 1996)

Knight, Leah, *Of Books and Botany in Early Modern England: Sixteenth-Century Plants and Print Culture* (Farnham: Ashgate, 2009)

Knutson, Roslyn L., *Playing Companies and Commerce in Shakespeare's Time* (Cambridge: Cambridge University Press, 2001)

Lamb, Mary Ellen, and Valerie Wayne (eds), *Staging Early Modern Romance: Prose Fiction, Dramatic Romance and Shakespeare* (London: Routledge, 2009)

Landmann, F., 'Shakespeare and euphuism: *Euphues* an adaptation from Guevara', *New Shakespeare Society Transactions* 3 (1880–82), 241–76

Langbaine, Gerard, *An Account of the English Dramatick Poets* (1691; Menston, Yorkshire: Scolar Press, 1971)

Lanham, Richard A., *Analyzing Prose*, 2nd edn (1983; London: Continuum, 2003)

Lesser, Zachary, 'Playbooks', in Joad Raymond (ed.), *The Oxford History of Popular Print Culture, vol. 1: Cheap Print in Britain and Ireland to 1660* (Oxford: Oxford University Press, 2011)

Lesser, Zachary, *Renaissance Drama and the Politics of Publication: Readings in the English Book Trade* (Cambridge: Cambridge University Press, 2004)

Lesser, Zachary, 'Typographic nostalgia: popularity and the meanings of black letter', in Michael Denbo (ed.), *New Ways of Looking at Old Texts, IV: Papers of the Renaissance English Text Society 2002–2006* (Tempe: Arizona Center for Medieval and Renaissance Studies, in conjunction with Renaissance English Text Society, 2008)

Liddle, Rod, 'A big thank you to Guy Goma: the wrong man in the right place', *The Spectator*, 17 May 2006

Liebler, Naomi Conn (ed.), *Early Modern Prose Fiction: The Cultural Politics of Reading* (London: Routledge, 2007)

Lockwood, Tom, *Ben Jonson in the Romantic Age* (Oxford: Oxford University Press, 2005)

Lodge, Thomas, *A Margarite of America*, ed. Donald Beecher and Henry D. Janzen (Toronto: Centre for Reformation and Renaissance Studies, 2005)

Lodge, Thomas, *Rosalind: Euphues Golden Legacy*, ed. Donald Beecher (Ottawa: Dovehouse Editions, 1997)

Lodge, Thomas, *Wits Miserie, and the worlds madness* (London: Cuthbert Burby, 1596)

Loewenstein, Joseph, *The Author's Due: Printing and the Prehistory of Copyright* (Chicago: University of Chicago Press, 2002)

Loewenstein, Joseph, *Ben Jonson and Possessive Authorship* (Cambridge: Cambridge University Press, 2002)

Lowe, Eleanor, 'A critical edition of George Chapman's *The Comedy of Humours*, later printed as *An Humorous Day's Mirth*' (unpublished doctoral thesis, University of Birmingham, 2004)

Lyly, John, *'Campaspe' and 'Sappho and Phao'*, ed. G. K. Hunter and David Bevington (1991; Manchester: Manchester University Press, 1999)

Lyly, John, *The Complete Works of John Lyly*, ed. R. Warwick Bond, 3 vols (Oxford: Clarendon Press, 1902)

Lyl[y], John, *The Dramatic Works of John Lilly, (The Euphuist.), With Notes and Some Account of His Life and Writings*, ed. F. W. Fairholt, 2 vols (1858; London: Reeves & Turner, 1892)

Lyly, John, *Endymion*, ed. David Bevington (Manchester: Manchester University Press, 1996)

Lyly, John, *'Euphues: The Anatomy of Wit' and 'Euphues and His England'*, ed. Leah Scragg (Manchester: Manchester University Press, 2003)

Lyly, John, *'Euphues: The Anatomy of Wit' and 'Euphues and His England'*, ed. Morris William Croll and Harry Clemons (London: Routledge, 1916)

Lyly, John, *'Euphues. The Anatomy of Wit.' Editio princeps. 1579. 'Euphues and His England.' Editio princeps. 1580.*, ed. Edward Arber (1868; London: Alex Murry & Son, 1919)

Lyly, John, *'Galatea' and 'Midas'*, ed. G. K. Hunter and David Bevington (Manchester: Manchester University Press, 2000)

[Lyly, John], *Gallathea*, ed. Leah Scragg (Oxford: Oxford University Press, 1998)

Lyly, John, *Love's Metamorphosis*, ed. Leah Scragg (Manchester: Manchester University Press, 2008)

Lyly, John, *Mother Bombie*, ed. Leah Scragg (Manchester: Manchester University Press, 2010)

Lyly, John, *The Plays of John Lyly*, ed. Carter A. Daniel (London: Associated University Presses, 1988)

[Lyly, John], *Sapho and Phao*, ed. Leah Scragg (Oxford: Oxford University Press, 2002)

Lyly, John, *Selected Prose and Dramatic Work*, ed. Leah Scragg (Manchester: Carcanet Press, 1997)

Lyly, John, *Sixe court comedies* (London: by William Stansby for Edward Blount, 1632)

Lyly, John, *The Woman in the Moon*, ed. Leah Scragg (Manchester: Manchester University Press, 2006)

Mack, Peter, *Elizabethan Rhetoric: Theory and Practice* (Cambridge: Cambridge University Press, 2002)

Margolies, David, *Novel and Society in Elizabethan England* (London: Croom Helm, 1985)

Marlowe, Christopher, *Tamburlaine the Great*, ed. J. S. Cunningham (Manchester: Manchester University Press, 1981)

Marotti, Arthur F., *Manuscripts, Print and the English Renaissance Lyric* (Ithaca: Cornell University Press, 1995)

Marotti, Arthur F., and Michael D. Bristol (eds), *Print, Manuscript, Performance: The Changing Relations of the Media in Early Modern England* (Columbus: Ohio State University Press, 2000)

Marsden, Jean I., *The Re-Imagined Text: Shakespeare, Adaptation, & Eighteenth-Century Literary Theory* (Lexington: University Press of Kentucky, 1995)

Marshall, Gail, and Adrian Poole (eds), with a foreword by Stanley Wells, *Victorian Shakespeare, Vol. 1: Theatre, Drama and Performance* (Basingstoke: Palgrave Macmillan, 2003)

Maslen, Robert W., *Elizabethan Fictions: Espionage, Counter-Espionage and the Duplicity of Fiction in Early Elizabethan Prose Narratives* (Oxford: Clarendon Press, 1997)

Massai, Sonia, [review of Andrew Murphy, *Shakespeare in Print*], *Library* 7th ser. 6:2 (June 2005), 196–8

Massai, Sonia, *Shakespeare and the Rise of the Editor* (Cambridge: Cambridge University Press, 2007)

Masten, Jeffrey, *Textual Intercourse: Collaboration, Authorship and Sexualities in Renaissance Drama* (Cambridge: Cambridge University Press, 1997)

Maus, Katharine Eisaman, *Inwardness and Theater in the English Renaissance* (Chicago: University of Chicago Press, 1995)

McCarthy, Jeanne H., 'The Queen's "unfledged minions": an alternate account of the origins of Blackfriars and of the boy company phenomenon', in Paul Menzer (ed.), *Inside Shakespeare: Essays on the Blackfriars Stage* (Selinsgrove: Susquehanna University Press, 2006)

McDonald, Russ, 'Compar or parison: measure for measure', in Sylvia Adamson, Gavin Alexander and Katrin Ettenhuber (eds), *Renaissance Figures of Speech* (Cambridge: Cambridge University Press, 2007)

McGrath, Lynette, 'Gascoigne's moral satire: the didactic use of convention in *The adventures passed by Master F.J.*', *JEGP* 70 (1971), 432–50
McIntosh, Genista, 'Interlude II: Casting and marketing Jonson', in Richard Cave, Elizabeth Schafer and Brian Woolland (eds), *Ben Jonson and Theatre: Performance, Practice and Theory* (London: Routledge, 1999)
McKenzie, D. F., *Making Meaning: 'Printers of the Mind' and Other Essays*, eds Peter D. McDonald and Michael F. Suarez, S.J. (Amherst: University of Massachusetts Press, 2002)
McKerrow, Ronald B., *An Introduction to Bibliography for Literary Students* (Oxford: Clarendon Press, 1927)
McMillin, Scott, 'Middleton's theatres', in Gary Taylor and John Lavagnino (gen. eds), *The Collected Works of Thomas Middleton* (Oxford: Oxford University Press, 2007)
McMillin, Scott, and Sally-Beth MacLean, *The Queen's Men and Their Plays, 1583–1603* (Cambridge: Cambridge University Press, 1998)
Meek, Richard, Jane Rickard and Richard Wilson (eds), *Shakespeare's Book: Essays in Reading, Writing and Reception* (Manchester: Manchester University Press, 2008)
Melnikoff, Kirk, and Edward Gieskes (eds), *Writing Robert Greene: Essays on England's First Notorious Professional Writer* (Aldershot: Ashgate, 2008)
Mentz, Steve, *Romance for Sale in Early Modern England: The Rise of Prose Fiction* (Aldershot: Ashgate, 2006)
Menzer, Paul (ed.), *Inside Shakespeare: Essays on the Blackfriars Stage* (Selinsgrove: Susquehanna University Press, 2006)
Meredith, George, *Evan Harrington* (London: Constable, 1910)
Meres, Francis, *Palladis Tamia* (London: Cuthbert Burby, 1598)
Middleton, Thomas, '*The Nightingale and the Ant*' and '*Father Hubberd's Tales*', ed. Adrian Weiss, in Gary Taylor and John Lavagnino (gen. eds), *The Collected Works of Thomas Middleton* (Oxford: Oxford University Press, 2007)
Mieder, Wolfgang, *The Politics of Proverbs: From Traditional Wisdom to Proverbial Stereotypes* (Madison: University of Wisconsin Press, 1997)
Miller, Edwin Haviland, *The Professional Writer in Elizabethan England: A Study of Nondramatic Literature* (Cambridge, MA: Harvard University Press, 1959)
Mills, Perry, 'Directing Lyly', programme note for the King Edward VI School, Stratford-upon-Avon production of Lyly's *Endymion*, Shakespeare's Globe, 08.02.09
Montrose, Louis Adrian, '"Shaping fantasies": figurations of gender and power in Elizabethan culture', *Representations* 2 (1983), 61–94
Morgan, Edwin, *From Glasgow to Saturn* (Cheadle: Carcanet Press, 1973)
Morley, Henry, 'Euphuism', *Quarterly Review* 109 (April 1861), 350–83
Moss, Ann, *Printed Commonplace-Books and the Structuring of Renaissance Thought* (Oxford: Clarendon Press, 1996)
Mottram, Stewart, '"An empire of itself": Arthur as icon of an English empire, 1509–1547', in Elizabeth Archibald and David F. Johnson (eds), *Arthurian Literature 25* (Cambridge: D. S. Brewer, 2008)
Mowat, Barbara A., 'The theater and literary culture', in John D. Cox and David Scott Kastan (eds), *A New History of Early English Drama*, with a

foreword by Stephen J. Greenblatt (New York: Columbia University Press, 1997)

Mueller, Janel, *The Native Tongue and the Word: Developments in English Prose Style 1380–1580* (Chicago: University of Chicago Press, 1984)

Munday, Anthony, *Zelauto: The Fountaine of Fame*, ed. Jack Stillinger (Carbondale: Southern Illinois University Press, 1963)

Munro, Ian, 'Page wit and puppet-like wealth: orality and print in *Three Lords and Three Ladies of London*', in Helen Ostovich, Holger Schott Syme and Andrew Griffin (eds), *Locating the Queen's Men, 1583–1603: Material Practices and Conditions of Playing* (Farnham: Ashgate, 2009)

Munro, Lucy, 'Early modern drama and the repertory approach', *Research Opportunities in Renaissance Drama* 42 (2003), 1–33

Munro, Lucy, 'Read Not Dead: a review article', *Shakespeare Bulletin* 22.1 (Spring 2004), 23–40

Munro, Lucy, 'Reading printed comedy: Edward Sharpham's *The Fleer*', in Marta Straznicky (ed.), *The Book of the Play: Playwrights, Stationers and Readers in Early Modern England* (Amherst and Boston: University of Massachusetts Press, 2006)

Murphy, Andrew, *Shakespeare in Print: A History and Chronology of Shakespearean Publishing* (Cambridge: Cambridge University Press, 2003)

Murphy, Andrew (ed.), *A Concise Companion to Shakespeare and the Text* (Oxford: Blackwell, 2007)

Murphy, James J. (ed.), *Renaissance Eloquence: Studies in the Theory and Practice of Renaissance Rhetoric* (Berkeley: University of California Press, 1983)

Narveson, Kate, 'The *Ars longa* trope in a sublunary world', in Jeanne Shami (ed.), *Renaissance Tropologies: The Cultural Imagination of Early Modern England* (Pittsburg: Duquesne University Press, 2008)

Nashe, Thomas, *The Works of Thomas Nashe*, ed. Ronald B. McKerrow, rev. F. P. Wilson, 5 vols (Oxford: Basil Blackwell, 1958)

Newcomb, Lori Humphrey, *Reading Popular Romance in Early Modern England* (New York: Columbia University Press, 2002)

Ong, Walter J., *Orality & Literacy: The Technologizing of the Word* (London: Routledge, 1982)

Orgel, Stephen, *The Authentic Shakespeare and Other Problems of the Early Modern Stage* (London: Routledge, 2002)

Østermark-Johansen, Lene, 'The death of Euphues: Euphuism and decadence in late-Victorian literature', *English Literature in Transition (1880–1920)* 45:1 (2002), 4–25

Ostovich, Helen, Holger Schott Syme and Andrew Griffin (eds), *Locating the Queen's Men, 1583–1603: Material Practices and Conditions of Playing* (Farnham: Ashgate, 2009)

Painter, William, *The Palace of Pleasure*, ed. Joseph Jacobs, 3 vols (London: David Nutt, 1890)

Parnell, Paul E., 'Moral allegory in Lyly's *Love's Metamorphosis*', *Studies in Philology* 52:1 (January 1955), 1–16

Paster, Gail Kern, *Humoring the Body: Emotions and the Shakespearean Stage* (Chicago: University of Chicago Press, 2004)

Pater, Walter, *Marius the Epicurean: His Sensations and Ideas*, 2 vols (1885; London: Macmillan, 1927)

Pater, Walter, 'Style', *Fortnightly Review* 50 (December 1888), 728–43
Patterson, Annabel, *Censorship and Interpretation: The Conditions of Writing and Reading in Early Modern England* (Madison: University of Wisconsin Press, 1984)
Peacham, Henry, *The Garden of Eloquence (1593)* [2nd and enlarged edition of *The Garden of Eloquence* (1577)], with an introduction by William G. Crane (Gainesville, FL: Scholars' Facsimiles and Reprints, 1954)
Peele, George, *The Love of King David and Fair Bethsabe* (London, 1599)
Peters, Julie Stone, *Theatre of the Book, 1480–1880: Print, Text, and Performance in Europe* (Oxford: Oxford University Press, 2000)
Pettie, George, *A Petite Pallace of Pettie his Pleasure*, ed. Herbert Hartman (London: Oxford University Press, 1938)
Phelps, William Lyon, *The Advance of the Novel in English* (New York: Dodd and Mead, 1916)
Phillips, Edward, *Theatrum Poetarum* (London: Charles Smith, 1675)
Pincombe, Michael, *The Plays of John Lyly: Eros and Eliza* (Manchester: Manchester University Press, 1996)
Poole, Adrian, *Shakespeare and the Victorians* (London: Arden Shakespeare, 2004)
Pope, Alexander, 'Preface to Edition of Shakespeare', in D. Nichol Smith (ed.), *Eighteenth Century Essays on Shakespeare* (Glasgow: MacLehose and Sons, 1903)
Powell, Jocelyn, 'John Lyly and the language of play', in John Russell Brown and Bernard Harris (gen. eds), *Elizabethan Theatre 9* (London: Edward Arnold, 1966)
Prescott, Anne Lake, 'Making the Heptaméron English', in James M. Dutcher and Anne Lake Prescott (eds), *Renaissance Historicisms: Essays in Honor of Arthur F. Kinney* (Newark: University of Delaware Press, 2008)
Price, J. L., *Dutch Culture in the Golden Age* (London: Reaktion Books, 2011)
Prince, Kathryn, *Shakespeare in the Victorian Periodicals* (London: Routledge, 2008)
Purcell, Stephen, *Popular Shakespeare: Simulation and Subversion on the Modern Stage* (Basingstoke: Palgrave Macmillan, 2009)
Quiller-Couch, Sir Arthur (ed.), *The Oxford Book of English Prose* (Oxford: Clarendon Press, 1925)
Raven, James, *The Business of Books: Booksellers and the English Book Trade 1450–1850* (London: Yale University Press, 2007)
Raymond, Joad, *Pamphlets and Pamphleteering in Early Modern Britain* (Cambridge: Cambridge University Press, 2003)
Relihan, Constance C., *Cosmographical Glasses: Geographic Discourse, Gender and Elizabethan Fiction* (Kent, OH: Kent State University Press, 2004)
Relihan, Constance C., '"Dissordinate desire" and the construction of geographic otherness in the early modern novella', in Constance C. Relihan and Goran V. Stanivukovic (eds), *Prose Fiction and Early Modern Sexualities in England, 1570–1640* (Basingstoke: Palgrave Macmillan, 2004)
Relihan, Constance C., *Fashioning Authority: The Development of*

Elizabethan Novelistic Discourse (Kent, OH: Kent State University Press, 1994)

Relihan, Constance C. (ed.), *Framing Elizabethan Fictions: Contemporary Approaches to Early Modern Narrative Prose* (Kent, OH: Kent State University Press, 1996)

Rhodes, Neil, *The Power of Eloquence and English Renaissance Literature* (Hemel Hempstead: Harvester Wheatsheaf, 1992)

Rhodes, Neil, 'Shakespeare's popularity and the origins of the canon', in Andy Kesson and Emma Smith (eds), *The Elizabethan Top Ten: Defining Print Popularity in Early Modern England* (Farnham: Ashgate, 2013)

Richards, Jennifer, *Rhetoric and Courtliness in Early Modern Literature* (Cambridge: Cambridge University Press, 2003)

Richards, Jennifer (ed.), *Early Modern Civil Discourses* (Basingstoke: Palgrave Macmillan, 2003)

Richardson, Catherine, *Domestic Life and Domestic Tragedy in Early Modern England: The Material Life of the Household* (Manchester: Manchester University Press, 2006)

Richardson, Catherine, 'Properties of domestic life: the table in Heywood's *A Woman Killed With Kindness*', in Jonathan Gil Harris and Nastasha Korda (eds), *Staged Properties in Early Modern English Drama* (Cambridge: Cambridge University Press, 2002)

Riche, Barnabe, *The second tome of the trauailes and aduentures of Don Simonides* (London: Robert Walley, 1584)

Richetti, J. J., *Popular Fiction Before Richardson: Narrative Patterns 1700–39* (Oxford: Clarendon Press, 1969)

Rimmon-Kenan, Shlomith, *Narrative Fiction* (London: Methuen, 1983)

Ringler, William, '*Beware the Cat* and the beginnings of English fiction', *Novel* 12 (1979), 113–26

Ringler, William, 'The immediate source of Euphuism', *Publications of the Modern Language Association* 53:3 (1938), 678–86

Robertson, J.M., 'Concerning preciosity', *Yellow Book* 13 (April 1897)

Rodax, Yvonne, *The Real and the Ideal in the Novella* (Chapel Hill: University of North Carolina Press, 1968)

Rozmovits, Linda, *Shakespeare and the Politics of Culture in Late Victorian England* (London: Johns Hopkins University Press, 1998)

Rumbold, Kate, '"Alas, poor YORICK": quoting Shakespeare in the mid-eighteenth-century novel', *Borrowers and Lenders: The Journal of Shakespeare and Appropriation* 2:2 (Winter 2006), accessed at www.borrowers.uga.edu (03.08.09)

Runnals, Graham, 'The catalogue of the Tours bookseller and late medieval French drama', *Le moyen français* 11 (1982), 112–28

Rushton, William Lowes, *Shakespeare's Euphuism* (London: Longman's, Green & Co., 1871)

Ryrie, Alec, 'Cawood, John', *Oxford Dictionary of National Biography* (Oxford University Press, 2004)

Saccio, Peter, *The Court Comedies of John Lyly: A Study in Allegorical Dramaturgy* (Princeton: Princeton University Press, 1969)

Sacks, David Harris, 'London's dominion: the metropolis, the market economy, and the state', in Lena Cowen Orlin (ed.), *Material London, ca. 1600* (Philadelphia: University of Pennsylvania Press, 2000)

Saenger, Michael, *The Commodification of Textual Engagements in the English Renaissance* (Aldershot: Ashgate, 2006)

Saintsbury, George, 'Modern English prose', *Fortnightly Review* 25 (1876), 243–59

Saker, Austen, *Narbonus: The Laberynth of Libertie* (London: Richard Jones, 1580)

Salzman, Paul, *English Prose Fiction 1558–1700: A Critical History* (Oxford: Clarendon Press, 1985)

Salzman, Paul, 'Placing Tudor fiction', *Yearbook of English Studies* 38:1–2 (2008), 136–49

Sawday, Jonathan, *The Body Emblazoned: Dissection and the Human Body in Renaissance Culture* (London: Routledge, 1995)

Schelling, Felix E., *The Life and Writings of George Gascoigne With Three Poems Heretofore Not Reprinted* (1893; New York: Russell & Russell, 1967)

Schlauch, Margaret, *Antecedents of the English Novel 1400–1600* (London: Oxford University Press, 1963)

Scholes, Robert, *Semiotics and Interpretation* (New Haven: Yale University Press, 1982)

Scholz, Susanne, *Body Narratives: Writing the Nation and Fashioning the Subject in Early Modern England* (London: Macmillan, 2000)

Schoneveld, Cornelis W., *Intertraffic of the Mind: Studies in Seventeenth-Century Anglo-Dutch Translation With a Checklist of Books Translated from English into Dutch, 1600–1700* (Leiden: E. J. Brill and Leiden University Press, 1984)

Scott, Charlotte, *Shakespeare and the Idea of the Book* (Oxford: Oxford University Press, 2007)

Scott, Mary Augusta, *Elizabethan Translations from the Italian* (Cambridge, MA: Harvard University Press, 1916)

Scott, Walter, *The Monastery*, ed. Penny Fielding (Edinburgh: Edinburgh University Press, 2000)

Scragg, Leah, 'Edward Blount and the history of Lylian criticism', *Review of English Studies*, n.s. 46 (1995), 1–10

Scragg, Leah, 'John Lyly and the politics of language', *Essays in Criticism* 55:1 (2005), 17–38

Scragg, Leah, *The Metamorphosis of 'Gallathea': A Study in Creative Adaptation* (Washington, DC: University Press of America, 1982)

Scragg, Leah, 'Speaking pictures: style and spectacle in Lylian comedy', *English Studies* 86:4 (August 2005), 298–311

Scragg, Leah, 'The victim of fashion? Rereading the biography of John Lyly', *Medieval and Renaissance Drama in England* 19 (2006), 210–26

Selleck, Nancy, *The Interpersonal Idiom in Shakespeare, Donne, and Early Modern Culture* (Basingstoke: Palgrave Macmillan, 2008)

Shakespeare, William, *Complete Works*, ed. Jonathan Bate and Eric Rasmussen (Basingstoke: Macmillan, 2007)

Shakespeare, William, *The First Part of King Henry IV*, ed. Herbert Weil and Judith Weil (Cambridge: Cambridge University Press, 1997)

Shakespeare, William, *Henry IV Part 1*, ed. David Bevington (Oxford: Oxford University Press, 1987)

Shakespeare, William, *Poems: written by Wil. Shake-speare* (London: John

Benson, 1640)
Shakespeare, William, *The Winter's Tale*, ed. J. H. P. Pafford (New York: Routledge, 1963)
Shakespeare, William, *The tragicall historie of Hamlet* (London: Nicholas Ling and John Trundell, 1603)
Shapiro, James, *Contested Will: Who Wrote Shakespeare?* (London: Faber and Faber, 2010)
Shapiro, Michael, *Children of the Revels: The Boy Companies of Shakespeare's Time and Their Plays* (New York: Columbia University Press, 1977)
Sharpe, Kevin, *Reading Revolutions: The Politics of Reading in Early Modern England* (New Haven: Yale University Press, 2000)
Shaughnessy, Robert, *The Shakespeare Effect: A History of Twentieth-Century Performance* (Basingstoke: Palgrave, 2002)
Shawcross, John T., 'Signs of the times: Christopher Marlowe's decline in the seventeenth century', in Kenneth Friedenreich, Roma Gill and Constance B. Kuriyama (eds), *'A Poet & a filthy Play-maker': New Essays on Christopher Marlowe* (New York: AMS Press, 1988)
Sherman, William H., *John Dee: The Politics of Reading and Writing in the English Reniassance* (Amherst: University of Massachusetts Press, 1995)
Sherman, William H., *Used Books: Marking Readers in Renaissance England* (Philadelphia: University of Pennsylvania Press, 2008)
Shohet, Lauren, *Reading Masques: The English Masque and Public Culture in the Seventeenth Century* (Oxford: Oxford University Press, 2007)
Simms, William Gilmore, *The Scout; or, The Black Riders of Congaree* (1841; New York: Redfield, 1854)
Sinfield, Alan, *The Wilde Century: Effeminacy, Oscar Wilde and the Queer Moment* (London: Cassell, 1994)
Smith, Charles W., 'Structural and thematic unity in Gascoigne's *The Adventures of Master F.J.*', *Papers on Language and Literature* 2 (1966), 99–108
Smith, Emma, 'Shakespeare and early modern tragedy', in Emma Smith and Garrett A. Sullivan Jr (eds), *The Cambridge Companion to English Renaissance Tragedy* (Cambridge: Cambridge University Press, 2010)
Smith, Helen, and Louise Wilson (eds), *Renaissance Paratexts* (Cambridge: Cambridge University Press, 2011)
Spencer, Jane, *The Rise of the Woman Novelist: From Aphra Behn to Jane Austen* (Oxford: Blackwell, 1986)
Spivak, Gayatri Chakravorty, *Outside in the Teaching Machine* (London: Routledge, 1993)
Spufford, Margaret, *Small Books and Pleasant Histories: Popular Fiction and Its Readership in Seventeenth-Century England* (London: Methuen, 1981)
Squires, Claire, *Marketing Literature: The Making of Contemporary Writing in Britain* (Basingstoke: Palgrave Macmillan, 2007)
Stallybrass, Peter, and Roger Chartier, 'Reading and authorship: the circulation of Shakespeare 1590–1619', in Andrew Murphy (ed.), *A Concise Companion to Shakespeare and the Text* (Oxford: Blackwell, 2007)
Steadman, John M., *Redefining a Period Style: 'Renaissance', 'Mannerist' and 'Baroque' in Literature* (Pittsburgh: Duquesne University Press, 1990)

Steinberg, Theodore L., 'The anatomy of *Euphues*', *Studies in English Literature* 17 (1977), 27–38

Stern, Tiffany, *Documents of Performance in Early Modern England* (Cambridge: Cambridge University Press, 2009)

Stern, Tiffany, 'Taking part: actors and audience on the stage at Blackfriars', in Paul Menzer (ed.), *Inside Shakespeare: Essays on the Blackfriars Stage* (Selinsgrove: Susquehanna University Press, 2006)

Stern, Tiffany, 'Watching as reading: the audience and written text in the early modern playhouse', in Laurie Maguire (ed.), *How To Do Things With Shakespeare* (Oxford: Blackwell, 2007)

Straus, Ralph, *Robert Dodsley: Poet, Publisher & Playwright* (New York: Burt Franklin, 1910)

Stredder, James, *The North Face of Shakespeare: Activities for Teaching the Plays* (2004; Cambridge: Cambridge University Press, 2009)

Sturgess, Philip J. M., *Narrativity: Theory and Practice* (Oxford: Clarendon Press, 1992)

Sugg, Richard, *Murder After Death: Literature and Anatomy in Early Modern England* (London: Cornell University Press, 2007)

Sullivan, Garrett A., Jr, *The Drama of Landscape: Land, Property and Social Relations on the Early Modern Stage* (Stanford: Stanford University Press, 1998)

Swift, Carolyn Ruth, 'The allegory of wisdom in Lyly's *Endimion*', in Clifford Davidson, C. J. Gianakaris and John H. Stroupe (eds), *Drama in the Renaissance: Comparative and Critical Essays* (New York: AMS Press, 1986)

Symes, Carol, 'The appearance of early vernacular plays: forms, functions and the future of medieval theater', *Speculum* 77 (2002), 778–831

Symonds, John Addington, 'Euphuism', *Pall Mall Gazette* 8 (1868), 12

Symonds, John Addington, 'Notes on style', in *Essays Speculative and Suggestive*, 2 vols (London: Chapman & Hall, 1890)

Symonds, John Addington, *Shakespeare's Predecessors in the English Drama* (1884; New York: Cooper Square, 1967)

Taylor, Gary, 'Blount, Edward', *Oxford Dictionary of National Biography* (Oxford University Press, 2004)

Taylor, Gary, 'Making meaning marketing Shakespeare 1623', in Peter Holland and Stephen Orgel (eds), *From Performance to Print in Shakespeare's England* (Basingstoke: Palgrave Macmillan, 2006)

Taylor, Gary, *Reinventing Shakespeare: A Cultural History from the Restoration to the Present* (Oxford: Oxford University Press, 1989)

Thomas, James, *Script Analysis for Actors, Directors, and Designers*, 2nd edn (1992; Oxford: Focal Press, 1999)

Tooke, William, *A New and General Biographical Dictionary*, 15 vols (London: G. G. et al., 1798)

Tottell, Richard, *'Songes and Sonettes': The Elizabethan Version*, ed. Paul A. Marquis (Tempe, AZ: Arizona Center for Medieval and Renaissance Studies, in conjunction with Renaissance English Text Society, 2007)

Tribble, Evelyn B., *Margins and Marginality: The Printed Page in Early Modern England* (Charlottesville: University Press of Virginia, 1993)

Trollope, Anthony, *Doctor Thorne* (London: J. M. Dent, 1908)

Tulloch, Graham, *The Language of Walter Scott: A Study of His Scottish and Period Language* (London: André Deutsch, 1980)

Turley, Richard Marggraf, *The Politics of Language in Romantic Literature* (Basingstoke: Palgrave Macmillan, 2002)

Twain, Mark, *Life on the Mississippi* (New York: Collier, 1917)

Twyning, John, *London Dispossessed: Literature and Social Space in the Early Modern City* (London: Macmillan, 1998)

Vickers, Brian, *The Artistry of Shakespeare's Prose* (London: Methuen, 1968)

Vickers, Brian, *In Defence of Rhetoric* (Oxford: Clarendon Press, 1988; corrected edn, 1989)

Vickers, Brian, *Shakespeare, Co-author: A Historical Study of Five Collaborative Plays* (Oxford: Oxford University Press, 2002)

Vickers, Brian, and Nancy S. Struever, *Rhetoric and the Pursuit of Truth: Language Change in the Seventeenth and Eighteenth Centuries* (Los Angeles: William Andrews Clark Memorial Library, University of California, 1985)

Voss, Paul J., 'Books for sale: advertising and patronage in late Elizabethan England', *Sixteenth Century Journal* 29 (1998), 733–56

Walker, Greg, *Plays of Persuasion: Drama and Politics at the Court of Henry VIII* (Cambridge: Cambridge University Press, 1991)

Walker, Greg, *The Politics of Performance in Early Renaissance Drama* (Cambridge: Cambridge University Press, 1998)

Walker, Greg, *Writing under Tyranny: English Literature and the Henrician Reformation* (Oxford: Oxford University Press, 2005)

Wall, Wendy, *The Imprint of Gender: Authorship and Publication in the English Renaissance* (Ithaca, NY: Cornell University Press, 1993)

Wallace, James, '"That scull had a tongue in it, and could sing once": staging Shakespeare's contempories', in Christie Carson and Farah Karim-Cooper (eds), *Shakespeare's Globe: A Theatrical Experiment* (Cambridge: Cambridge University Press, 2008)

Warley, Christopher, *Sonnet Sequences and Social Distinction in Renaissance England* (Cambridge: Cambridge University Press, 2005)

Watson, Thomas, *The Hekatompathia; or, Passionate Centurie of Love (1582)*, ed. S. K. Heninger, Jr (Gainesville, FL: Scholars' Facsimiles & Reprints, 1964)

Watt, Ian, *The Rise of the Novel: Studies in Defoe, Richardson, and Fielding* (1957; London: Pimlico, 2000)

Watt, Tessa, *Cheap Print and Popular Piety, 1550–1640* (Cambridge: Cambridge University Press, 1991)

Webbe, William, *A Discourse of English Poetrie* (London: Robert Wallet, 1586)

Webber, Joan, *Contrary Music: The Prose Style of John Donne* (Madison: University of Wisconsin Press, 1963)

Weimann, Robert, *Author's Pen and Actor's Voice: Playing and Writing in Shakespeare's Theatre*, ed. Helen Higbee and William West (Cambridge: Cambridge University Press, 2000)

Weimann, Robert, *Shakespeare and the Popular Tradition in the Theater: Studies in the Social Dimension of Dramatic Form and Tradition*, ed. Robert Schwartz (London: Johns Hopkins University Press, 1978)

Wells, Stanley, *Shakespeare and Co.: Christopher Marlowe, Thomas*

Dekker, Ben Jonson, Thomas Middleton, John Fletcher and the Other Players in His Story (London: Allen Lane, 2006)
Wells, Stanley, 'To read a play: the problem of editorial intervention', in Hanna Scolnicov and Peter Holland (eds), *Reading Plays: Interpretation and Reception* (Cambridge: Cambridge University Press, 1991)
West, Anthony James, 'The life of the First Folio in the seventeenth and eighteenth centuries', in Andrew Murphy (ed.), *A Concise Companion to Shakespeare and the Text* (Oxford: Blackwell, 2007)
West, William N., *Theatres and Encyclopedias in Early Modern Europe* (Cambridge: Cambridge University Press, 2002)
Weymouth, Richard F., 'On euphuism', *Philological Society Transactions 1870–72*, Part III, 1–17
Whalley, Peter, *An Inquiry into the Learning of Shakespeare* (London: T. Waller, 1748)
White, Paul Whitfield, 'Playing companies and the drama of the 1580s: a new direction for Elizabethan theatre history?', *Shakespeare Studies* 28 (2000), 265–84
Whitworth, Charles, 'Reviews', *Cahiers Élizabéthains* 66 (2004), 77–80
Wickham, Glynne, *Early English Stages 1300 to 1660*, 2 vols (London: Routledge and Kegan Paul, 1959–72)
Wiggins, Martin, *Shakespeare and the Drama of His Time* (Oxford: Oxford University Press, 2000)
Wiggins, Martin, 'When did Marlowe write *Dido, Queen of Carthage*?', *Review of English Studies* 59:241 (September 2008), 521–41
Wilson, Katharine, *Fictions of Authorship in Late Elizabethan Narratives: Euphues in Arcadia* (Oxford: Oxford University Press, 2006)
Wilson, Katherine, 'Transplanting Lillies: Greene, tyrants and tragical comedies', in Kirk Melnikoff and Edward Gieskes (eds), *Writing Robert Greene: Essays on England's First Notorious Professional Writer* (Aldershot: Ashgate, 2008)
wind-up-bird, 'i'd much rather have a caravan in the hills than a mansion in the slums', posted 06.08.2005, www.metwee.blogspot.com (accessed 12.06.07)
Winstanley, William, *The Lives of the most Famous English Poets, or the Honour of Parnassus* (1687), ed. William Riley Parker (Gainesville, FL: Scholars' Facsimiles & Reprints, 1963)
Wood, Frederick T., *Current English Usage* (London: MacMillan, 1962)
Woolf, Virginia, 'Donne after three centuries' (1932) in Andrew McNeillie (ed.), *The Common Reader Vol. 2* (London: Vintage, 2003)
Woolf, Virginia, *The Voyage Out* (1915; London: Vintage, 2004)
Woudhuysen, H. R., *Sir Philip Sidney and the Circulation of Manuscripts 1558–1640* (Oxford: Clarendon Press, 1996)
Yamada, Akihiro, *Thomas Creede: Printer to Shakespeare and His Contemporaries* (Tokyo: Meisei University Press, 1994)
Zedler, Johann Heinrich, *Grosses Vollständiges Universal Lexicon*, 68 vols (Leipzig: Johann Heinrich Zedler, 1738)
Zwicker, Steven N., 'Habits of reading and early modern literary culture', in David Loewenstein and Janel Mueller (eds), *The Cambridge History of Early Modern English Literature* (Cambridge: Cambridge University Press, 2002)Andy Kesson, *John Lyly and early modern authorship*

INDEX

Lightning Source UK Ltd.
Milton Keynes UK
UKOW02f2128250316

270911UK00001B/10/P

9 781784 99369